MBA
IN A BOOK

MBA
IN A BOOK

XANDER CANSELL

ARCTURUS

ARCTURUS

This edition published in 2023 by Arcturus Publishing Limited
26/27 Bickels Yard, 151–153 Bermondsey Street,
London SE1 3HA

ISBN: 978-1-83857-448-2
AD008017UK

Printed in China

CONTENTS

INTRODUCTION

Business surrounds and supports our lives, influences our culture and shapes our environment. Almost everything in the modern world now includes some element of commerce, so it is more vital than ever that we understand what drives *good* business, and crucially what 'good' means in the modern business world.

The MBA curriculum is designed to provide students with a comprehensive understanding of business and its broader context. Although business is ever-changing, there are always going to be key skills and principles which underpin the basic functions, forecasts, and philosophies of the commercial world.

The MBA is aimed at developing ability across all these areas – to produce detail oriented, versatile and strategic thinkers who can thrive in a modern business world.

This is a world in which businesses must be sustainable in both senses, not just aimed at profit, but also intent on having a positive impact on society. This book explores some of these ideas.

Many of the skillsets from an MBA are applicable in a wide range of situations and industries. Critical and analytical thought, effective leadership and teamwork, creativity, and the capacity to communicate clearly are useful almost everywhere.

This book is designed to give you an overview of the skills covered by an MBA – to introduce you to the concepts and principles with which to analyze, describe and create businesses.

Although the topics which are a standard part of MBA courses around the world are covered in this book, the limitations of space mean that there is always more to say on any subject (and a few things that didn't make the final edit). If something you'd like to explore or learn isn't written about here, seek it out elsewhere – there is an abundance of resources available, some of which you can find in the further reading section. Curiosity is the best qualification for success.

Modern businesses need to be flexible and able to move swiftly to embrace change. Over the past few years many have used new technology to allow them to connect virtually with staff working from home, clients and partners, without the need for travel.

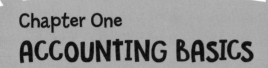

*The value of money now • Net present value •
The balance sheet • T-accounts • The general journal and
the general ledger • Other financial statements
• Revenues and expenses • Assets*

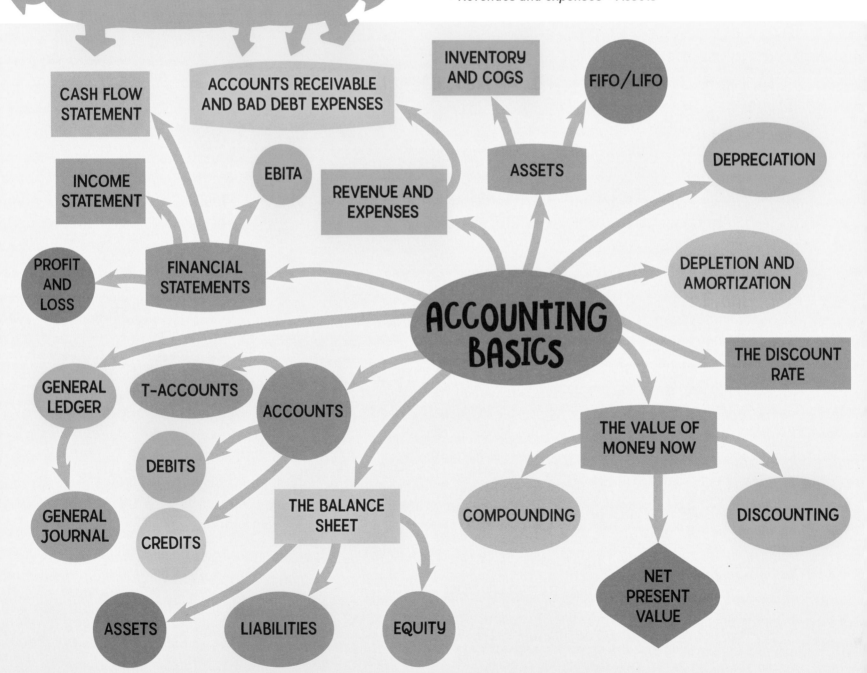

CASH FLOW STATEMENT

ACCOUNTS RECEIVABLE AND BAD DEBT EXPENSES

INVENTORY AND COGS

FIFO/LIFO

INCOME STATEMENT

EBITA

REVENUE AND EXPENSES

ASSETS

DEPRECIATION

PROFIT AND LOSS

FINANCIAL STATEMENTS

DEPLETION AND AMORTIZATION

ACCOUNTING BASICS

THE DISCOUNT RATE

GENERAL LEDGER

T-ACCOUNTS

ACCOUNTS

GENERAL JOURNAL

DEBITS

CREDITS

THE BALANCE SHEET

THE VALUE OF MONEY NOW

COMPOUNDING

DISCOUNTING

ASSETS

LIABILITIES

EQUITY

NET PRESENT VALUE

The basic principles of accounting form a key part of the language of business, allowing us to talk about the story of a company. This can be expressed in the different financial statements and through information from their regular accounts.

Keeping financial records

Accounting is the process of making, and keeping an accurate record of, the financial transactions of a business. It can track not just the amounts, but also how money comes into a business, what is done with that money, where and how it leaves a business and how much is left over as profit.

To be able to understand this information and read the story of a company, you will need to understand the fundamental concepts of profit and loss, debits and credits, and value to accurately describe the position of a business – where it has been and where it is likely to go in the future. Before we look at the story of a company through its financial statements, there are some fundamental concepts that need explaining.

THE VALUE OF MONEY NOW

The *time value of money* (TVM) is the idea that money you have now is worth more than the same amount of money in the future because of its potential to earn – for instance, interest in a savings account or as an investment – between now and then. Money you have now is worth more to you now than the same quantity of money paid to you in the future. This is also known as present discounted value.

Earning potential of money

Money grows through investing (in this context, this can mean either investing in stocks or shares, interest from a savings account or another method of earning money based on the initial amount).

The formula for working out the time value of money (how much a future payment is worth now, or how much a payment now will be worth in the future) looks at the amount of money, the future value, the time period involved and the amount it can earn.

A fortunate example

As an example, let's imagine you are lucky enough to have the choice of being given £100,000 now or £100,000 in two years' time. The two amounts look equal, but £100,000 today has more value (and utility) because of opportunity costs* associated with the two years that you don't have access to the money – the things you can't do.

The formula to work out the actual value of these two amounts is comprised of these parts:
- FV = future value of money
- PV = present value of money
- i = interest rate

---

*Utility – an economics term that means 'the total satisfaction received from consuming a good or service'. This is explored further in Chapter 3: Macroeconomics.

- n = number of compounding periods per year
- t = number of years

And the formula itself is:

$$**FV = PV[1 + (i/n]^{(nt)}**$$

There can be some other slight changes to the formula when dealing with things like annuities, but the general formula is as above.

If we assume that £100,000 is invested for one year at 10% interest compounded annually, then the future value of that money is:

$$FV = £100,000 \times [1 + (10\% / 1)] \wedge (1 \times 1) = £110,000$$

We can also rearrange the formula to find the present value of a future amount. For example, the present-day amount compounded annually at 7% interest that would be worth £5,000 a year from now is:

$$PV = £5,000 / [1 + (7\% / 1)] \wedge (1 \times 1) = £4,673$$

Compounding interest

The number of times compounding happens (how often interest is earned) has an impact on the value. Using the first example of £100,000, this is how is impacts the total value:

- Quarterly compounding: FV = £10,000 x [1 + (10% / 4)] ^ (4 x 1) = £110,380
- Monthly compounding: FV = £10,000 x [1 + (10% / 12)] ^ (12 x 1) = £110,470
- Daily compounding: FV = £10,000 x [1 + (10% / 365)] ^ (365 x 1) = £110,520

COMPOUNDING ▶ *Moving money forward through time.*
DISCOUNTING ▶ *Moving money backward through time.*

NET PRESENT VALUE

Net present value (NPV) is a concept that allows for the time value of money. You can use it to compare similar investment options. It relies on a discount rate that comes from how much you need to invest – the *cost of capital*. A project with a negative NPV is not usually a good idea.

A positive NPV suggests that the projected earnings generated by a given investment – in present value – exceeds the present value of expected costs (these are also given in 'present money'). It is usually assumed that an investment that has a positive NPV will be profitable.

The NPV calculation is asking the question 'What is the total money I will make if I go ahead with this specific investment, when accounting for the time value of money?'

The formula for NPV is:

$$*NPV = \Sigma_{t=1}^{n} \frac{Rt}{(1+i)^t} *$$

A slightly simpler method of thinking about this concept is:

$$NPV = TVECF - TVIC$$

where:

TVECF = today's value of the expected cash flows
TVIC = today's value of invested cash

A useful example

A theoretical company can invest in a Really Useful Machine that will cost £1,000,000 and is expected to generate £25,000 a month in revenue for five years. The company has the money available to buy the machine but could otherwise invest it in stocks and shares for an expected return of 8% per year. The company feel that buying the machine or investing in the stock market are similar risks.

Step 1: the initial investment

Because the machine is paid for straightaway, this is the first cash flow to be calculated. No time has passed so the outflow of £1,000,000 doesn't need discounting.

- *Identify the number of periods (t):* The machine is expected to create monthly cash flow and continue to work for five years. This means that there will be 60 cash flows and 60 periods to be accounted for in the calculation.
- *Identify the discount rate (i):* The other investment option is anticipated to pay 8% per year. But because the machine results in monthly cash flows, the annual discount rate needs

THE DISCOUNT RATE

A *discount rate* is the rate of return (the net gain or loss of an investment over a particular period) used to discount future cash flows back to their present value. This can be the required rate of return for an investor (the minimum percentage amount they would expect to earn on their capital), a company's *weighted average cost of capital* (see Chapter 6) or the *hurdle rate*, also known as the *minimum acceptable rate of return* for an investor.

Also, a company can determine the discount rate using the expected return of alternative projects with a risk level that is similar (or the cost of a loan to finance the project). For example, they might avoid a project with an expected return of 11% per year if it costs 13% to finance the project or if an appropriate alternative project is expected to return 16% per year.

to be turned into a monthly (or periodic) rate. Using the formula below, you can see that the periodic rate is 0.64%.

$$Periodic\space Rate = ((1 + 0.08) ^\frac1{12}) - 1 = 0.64\%$$

Step 2: future cash flows

The cash flows are earned at the end of the month, with the first payment a month after the machine was bought. This payment happens in the future, so you need to account for the time value of money. You can see the first five payments here:

Period	Cash Flow	NPV
Month 1	£25,000	◑ = £24,841.02
Month 2	£25,000	◑ = £24,683.05
Month 3	£25,000	◑ = £24,526.08
Month 4	£25,000	◑ = £24,370.11
Month 5	£25,000	◑ = £24,215.13

Working out present value The total calculation of the present value is the same as the present value of all 60 of the future cash flows added together, minus the initial investment. In this example we are ignoring any salvage value for the machine at the end of this period (whether it could be sold on to another company, for instance). This is the formula:

$$NPV = -£1,000,000 + \sum_{t=1}^{60} \frac{25,000}{(1 + 0.0064)^{60}} \Bigg|^{60}$$

That formula can be simplified to the following calculation:

$$NPV = -£1,000,000 + £1,242,322.82 = £242,322.82$$

So here the NPV is positive – the company should buy the machine. If the NPV of this calculation had been negative, because the discount rate was higher or the net cash flows were lower, the company should have avoided the investment.

The downsides: working out profitability with NPV relies a great deal on estimates and assumptions, so there can be quite a lot of room for mistakes. Estimated elements can include things like cost of investment, the discount rate and the projected returns.

The balance sheet

The *balance sheet* is one of the most important financial statements, which helps tell the story of a business. It shows a company's total assets and how these assets are paid for, either through debt or equity. It can also sometimes be called a statement of net worth or a statement of financial position.

Importance of the balance sheet

A balance sheet uses the important accounting equation:

$$\text{Assets} = \text{Liabilities} + \text{Equity}$$

The balance sheet only displays a snapshot of the finances of a company at a single moment in time, so to get a sense of trends, you need to compare it to balance sheets from previous periods.

However, balance sheets by themselves are still useful to investors. There are certain ratios that you can establish from a balance sheet that assess the financial health of an organization, such as the debt-to-equity ratio, or the *quick ratio* (also known as the *acid-test ratio*).

Quick ratio

This is the general layout of a balance sheet. Assets are put on the left and liabilities and equity are put on the right.

A balanced example

If a business takes out a five-year, £20,000 bank loan, their assets (in terms of the balance sheet, specifically their cash account because they now have this money in cash, available to spend) will increase by £20,000.

At the same time, its liabilities (in this case, the long-term debt account) will also increase by £20,000, balancing the two sides of the equation.

The accounting equation

Similarly, if a business were to receive £50,000 from investors, their assets will increase by that amount, as will their shareholder equity. What's key here is that the balance sheet always keeps the two sides of the equation balanced.

T-accounts

T-accounts are used to record increases and decreases to the individual accounts found on a balance sheet. They are called T-accounts because of their shape.

The entry on the left side of a T-account is called a debit, the entry on the right is called a credit.

TOTAL ASSETS   TOTAL LIABILITIES AND EQUITY

THE ACCOUNTING EQUATION – LIABILITIES AND EQUITY

This is the fundamental basis of the *double-entry accounting system*. If you sell a chocolate bar for a dollar, you need to account for both the chocolate bar and the dollar.

The *accounting equation* shows on a balance sheet that the sum of the assets of a business are the same as the sum of the liabilities of the business and the shareholders' equity.

Here are some definitions of the terms you can find on a balance sheet. These are the basic elements:

- *Assets:* Items of value the company owns. For instance, equipment, cash.
- *Liabilities:* Money the company owes to others. For instance, loans, mortgage on property.
- *Equity:* The portion of assets the company owns outright with no debt.
  - Equity = Assets - Liabilities
- *Revenue/income:* Money the company is earning.
- *Expenses:* Money the company is spending. For instance, rent, advertising.

Below is an example balance sheet for an imaginary company. As you can see, the two sides have two equal totals at the bottom of each column.

It should be easy to understand why this formula works. A business needs to pay for all the things it owns (assets) by either borrowing the money (taking on liabilities) or taking it from investment (issuing shareholder equity or using existing money kept from previous profits to effectively invest in themselves).

$$\underline{Assets = Liabilities + Equity}$$

ASSETS

Current assets		
Cash	$	625
Accounts receivable		175
Inventory		325
Prepaid expenses		5
Total current assets		1,130
Noncurrent assets		
Property, plant and equipment		1,250
(less accum, depreciation)		(330)
Total noncurrent assets		920
TOTAL ASSETS		$2,050

LIABILITIES

Current liabilities		
Accounts payable	$	200
Bank loan payable		25
Estimate tax liability		10
Total current liabilities		235
Long-term liabilitiies		
Bank loan payable		840
Total long-term liabilities		840
EQUITY		
Total paid-In capital		300
Retained earnings		675
Total equity		975
TOTAL LIABILITIES AND EQUITY		$2,050

Example balance sheet

---

*The balance sheet follows the accounting equation above, with assets on one side, and liabilities plus equity on the other, balancing each other out:

In T-accounts, a debit represents an increase in an asset, but a decrease in a liability or equity. Equally, a credit represents a decrease in an asset but an increase in a liability or equity (see example below).

Asset accounts normally have a debit balance and liability, and equity accounts usually have a credit balance. This is because each of these accounts usually have positive balances.

Whenever one of these T-accounts is debited, another will be credited, so that the balance sheet remains balanced after every transaction.

The general journal and the general ledger

Although the balance sheet is a crucial statement of a company's accounts, it is not the first place where transactions are usually recorded, and it doesn't include every individual business transaction. The general journal is the first point of record for all the transactions in an accounting system. The journal is a record of the accounting transactions for a business. These are recorded in chronological order and demonstrate how each account is credited or debited for each transaction.

Along with helping to create the income statement and the balance sheet, the journal means that transactions down to the day level can be compared as needed (whether or not you sold more gadgets on a Wednesday or a Thursday, for instance).

Each transaction has a date, credits are recorded on the right, debits on the left and the debited account is listed first.

DEBITS AND CREDITS

Debits and credits mean specific things in accounting. Unlike in general use, when using the words in relation to accounting, debit means adding to an account, and credit means taking away from an account.

Debits always have matching credits. Every time you credit one account, you must debit another to match. This is called double-entry bookkeeping.

Debits always go on the left, credits to the right.

ACCOUNTS

In this context, an 'account' is a record of business transactions that tracks the activity of a specific asset, liability, expense, revenue or equity.

- *Asset accounts* normally have a debit balance and are presented first on the balance sheet.
- *Liability accounts* normally have a credit balance and come after the assets on the balance sheet.
- *Equity accounts* represent the stake in the business held by the owners.
- *Revenue accounts* track the income that the business generates. They have a credit balance and increase total equity (they are a kind of temporary equity account).
- *Expense accounts* show the resources used to generate income for the business. They have a debit balance and reduce total equity.

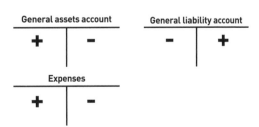
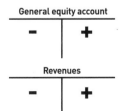

Example of T-accounts

1.

Inventory	1,000	
Accounts payable		1,000

1. If you bought £1,000 worth of inventory for your business on credit, this is how the entry would appear in the journal:

2.

April	29	Inventory	1,000	1,000
		Accounts payable		1,000
	30	**Cash**	800	
		Revenues		800
	30	**Expenses**	500	
		Inventory		500

2. Left is an example of how a sale might then be recorded. £500 paid in by a customer (debit the Cash account, credit Revenues) for an item that cost £300 (debit Expenses, credit Inventory):

3. The general ledger keeps track of all the account balances, which help to build the balance sheet. It is composed of a series of T-accounts (see box). At the end of each accounting period (usually monthly), all the entries from the general journal are categorized and totalled so they can be added to the general ledger.

3.

CASH		ACCOUNTS PAYABLE		REVENUES	
750	500		500	1,750	750
200	*Total*	*Total credits*	1,000		200
800	*debits*		1,500		800
1,750	500			1,750	1,750
1,250	*Account balance*				0

INVENTORY		RETAINED EARNINGS		EXPENSES	
500	50		1,075	50	675
500	125			125	
1,000	500			500	
2,000	675			675	675
1,325				0	

4. The final balances of the permanent accounts appear on the balance sheet like this below left:

Below, the temporary accounts (Revenue, Expenses) are closed to zero after they've had their balances moved to the income statement (see page 17).
This is a layout of how this accounting process works.

4.

Assets		Liabilities and equity	
Cash	£ 1,250	Accounts Payable	£1,500
Inventory	1,325	Retained Earnings	1,075
Total assets	**£ 2,575**	**Total Liabilities & equity**	**£2,575**

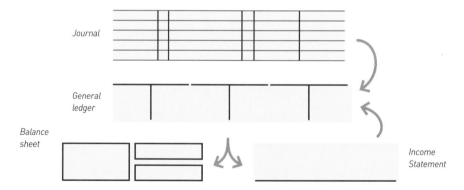

Other general purpose financial statements

Other financial statements

Financial statements such as the balance sheet are reports prepared and issued by a business to give investors and creditors extra information about the performance and financial standing of the business. Along with the balance sheet, there are three other kinds of general-purpose financial statement: the income statement, the cash flow statement and statement of stockholders' equity.

GROSS PROFIT ▶ *Subtract cost of goods sold (COGS) from revenue*
OPERATING PROFIT ▶ *The net income coming from a company's primary business operations.*

An *income statement*, sometimes known as a *profit and loss statement*, is a financial statement that shows revenue (income), expenses and the resulting profit and losses of a business over a specific time frame.

The net income of a business is calculated by deducting total expenses from total income. This statement is prepared first, as the net profit (or loss) must be determined and then used in the statement of owner's equity so other financial statements can be written. In an income statement, revenues are presented before expenses.

The cash flow statement

A cash flow statement reflects how changes in the balance sheet accounts have an impact on the cash account during an accounting period. Cash flow statements reconcile the beginning and ending cash and cash equivalent account balances.

Cash flow usually refers to the ability of a business to collect and maintain enough cash to pay their forthcoming bills.

The cash flow statement format is normally separated into three sections: 1) operating activities, 2) investing activities and 3) financing activities:

1. Cash flows from operating activities include all activities that are on the income statement under expenses or operating income. They are calculated by adjusting the net income by the changes in the liability and current asset accounts.
2. Cash flows from investing activities demonstrate cash inflows and outflows from the sales and purchases of long-term assets. This is effectively the business investing in itself.
3. Cash flows from financing include cash transactions that have an impact on the long-term liabilities and equity accounts.

Basically, the cash flow statement converts net income into the change in the Cash account over that accounting period.

EBITDA

Earnings before interest, taxes, depreciation and amortization (EBITDA) is a financial metric that measures the operating profitability of a business.

An EBITDA calculation shows the amount of cash flow that is generated by a business from its operations. Investors often use this calculation to analyze a company without having to look at the financing costs, tax burden and accounting treatments of the business.

Because EBITDA is not a ratio, it isn't generally used to directly compare businesses of different sizes.

The components of a cash flow statement.

An important rule to remember is that if an asset account increases, this is subtracted from the cash flow statement but if a liability account increases then that is added to the cash flow statement. Asset accounts require the opposite action to an increase or decrease, whereas if liability accounts increase or decrease, they do the same on the cash flow statement.

Here is an example cash flow statement:

Net income	176	Capital expenditures	(60)
Depreciation expense	40	Cash flows from investing activities	(60)
Increase in accounts receivable	(20)	Debt repayment	(15)
Decrease in inventory	5	Dividends paid	(70)
Increase in accounts payable	15	Cash flows from financing activities	(85)
Decrease in salaries payable	(10)	Change in cash	61
Cash flows from operating expenditures	206	Cash at beginning of period	140
		Cash at end of period	**201**

The statement of stockholders' equity

Recording shareholder's equity

The *statement of stockholders' equity* is a financial statement that records the changes in equity from the beginning to the end of an accounting period. It shows the equity accounts that affect the equity balance: common stock, net income, paid in capital, and dividends.

First, the equity as it stands at the beginning of the period is reported, followed by any new investments from shareholders and the net income for the year. Next, all dividends and net losses are deducted from the equity balance, which provides the ending equity balance for the accounting period.

Revenues and expenses

Expenses and matching concept

The *matching concept* says that an expense should be recognized and recorded when that expense can be matched with the revenues which that expenses helped to generate. So, expenses aren't necessarily recorded when they are paid out by the business, but expenses should be recorded as the revenues that relate to them are recorded.

Revenue recognition

The revenue recognition principle.

This is the idea that revenue should be recognized and recorded when it is realized (or realizable) and when it is earned. Another way of putting it is a business shouldn't wait until revenue is received to record it in their books. When the business has earned the revenue, the revenue should be recorded.

EXAMPLE 1 – Joe's Jukeboxes, Ltd. sells a jukebox to a pub on 31 January for £3,000. But the jukebox was not paid for until 15 March and it was not delivered to the pub until 31 March. According to the revenue recognition principle, Joe's would not record the sale in January. Even though the sale was realizable (in that the sale for £3,000 was initiated) it was not earned until March when the jukebox was delivered.

EXAMPLE 2 – Felix's Funky Clothes, Ltd. sells clothing from its retail shops. A customer purchases a T-shirt on 12 May and pays for it on a credit card. Felix's processes the credit card but does not receive any actual cash until June. Credit card purchases are treated the same as cash (this kind of purchase is called a 'claim to cash') so this revenue should be recorded in May when it was realized and earned.

Accounts receivable and bad debt expenses

Accounts receivable is the amount of money that people or companies currently owe to a business for any goods or services that were bought on credit. Accounts receivable has a debit balance because it is an asset account.

Accounts receivable are normally expected to be converted into cash within a year, so they are recorded in the current assets portion of the balance sheet at the end of each accounting period.

Often, accounts receivable are reported along with an allowance for doubtful accounts. The allowance for doubtful accounts has a negative balance and this decreases the outstanding accounts receivable balance. This is a contra asset because it reduces the balance in accounts receivable.

Whereas accounts receivable is an asset (money owed to the business), accounts payable is liability because it represents money owed by the business to others. Both are about purchasing goods or services 'on credit'.

A *bad debt expense* is a cost connected to removing a balance from a receivable when a customer cannot pay or refuses to pay, and it is no longer reasonably possible to collect the money.

Assets

Inventory and COGS

Cost of goods sold (COGS) – sometimes called the *cost of sales* – is the total price of all inventory sold to customers during a specific period. This isn't the price in the shop that a customer pays for the product but is the price that it cost the retailer to acquire (or the manufacturer to produce).

The cost of goods sold equation is the beginning inventory plus purchases made during that period minus the ending inventory:

> **THE GOING CONCERN CONCEPT**
> The *going concern concept* is the idea that we should assume that businesses will continue to exist. This means that we assume that the business isn't going to declare bankruptcy or be dissolved (unless there is some evidence showing this). Therefore, when making financial statements, and spreading expenses or costs over multiple years, we should presume that there will always be another accounting period in the future.

The income received for this jukebox is not recorded until delivery, two months after the initial order.

Beginning inventory + Purchases − Ending = Cost of goods sold

As a result of the way in which inventory is valued (FIFO, LIFO, see below) the cost of this inventory sold to customers during a given time period can change.

FIFO and LIFO

First in, first out (FIFO) is a method of accounting in which assets (i.e. a product) that are acquired or produced first are sold, used up or disposed of first. This is useful in an inflationary market (where costs are higher as time goes on) because this method of accounting results in a higher net income.

The way this works is that as a unit is sold as finished inventory, the associated costs for that unit must be recognized as an expense. These costs could be purchase costs of the unit, purchase of materials to create the unit or for the use of labour. FIFO assigns these costs based on which unit was entered into the inventory first.

For example, if 50 units were bought for £10 and then later (perhaps because of price rises in the market) 50 of the same units were bought for £15, the FIFO method would assign the first item sold a cost of £10. After the first 50 units were sold, the next units would be assigned a cost of £15.

FIFO is widely used globally and is the most accurate method of assigning expected cost flow with the actual flow of assets – so it presents a truer picture of inventory costs. It also reduces the impacts of inflation.

Last in, first out (LIFO) is the opposite of this process, assigning the cost of the last item added to the inventory first. This can sometimes be useful if there are rising prices, as it better matches expenses to the most recent costs as well as offering a tax advantage. If the product the company sells is perishable, it is unlikely they can use LIFO as they would want to sell their oldest inventory first to avoid losses.

Lastly, *average costs* can also be used. This takes the weighted average of all the units in an inventory and uses that average cost to work out the value of ending inventory and COGS.

Depreciation

Depreciation is the concept of spreading the expense of a long-term asset over its useful life, so that the cost of an asset is more accurately matched to the period over which it offers a benefit. This is particularly useful when a business is purchasing expensive assets such as equipment or property.

Straight line depreciation

Straight line depreciation is the simplest version of depreciation. It accounts for an equal depreciation expense each year over the useful working life of the asset:

$$\text{Depreciation expense} = (\text{Fair value} - \text{Residual value}) / \text{Useful life of asset}$$

For example, Business X buys an office building for £50,000,000, to be used over 25 years, with a residual value of £25,000,000. The annual depreciation expense is £1,000,000.

Units of production and accelerated depreciation methods

There are other ways of accounting for assets that depreciate at different rates. *Accelerated depreciation* can be used when an asset depreciates faster in the first few years (vehicles are an example of this). A multiplying factor is added to the equation to accomplish this. It results in expenses that are higher at the beginning and decrease over time.

Accelerated depreciation

The *units of production method* divides the value of the asset (the fair value minus residual value) by the 'useful life in units' – the number of products a piece of equipment is expected to make, for instance. It records higher expenses when production is highest, which corresponds with how much the equipment is being used. This is obviously most useful for machines that manufacture or produce physical things.

HUATENG MA: TENCENT

Huateng 'Pony' Ma is a Chinese business magnate, investor, and philanthropist. He is the co-founder, chairman, and CEO of the Chinese tech giant Tencent Holdings Limited. Ma is one of the richest men in China, with a net worth of over $50 billion as of 2020.

Ma co-founded Tencent in 1998, and it is now one of the world's largest internet companies, with a market capitalization of over $500 billion. Its flagship products include the social networking platform WeChat and the mobile messaging app QQ. Tencent also has a majority stake in the Chinese e-commerce giant JD.com, and invested heavily in the ride-hailing app Uber.

Under Ma's leadership, Tencent has achieved profitable growth in all three of its core businesses – internet services, online games, and social networking. Tencent is also one of the most innovative companies in China, with a strong track record of launching successful new products and services.

The company has been successful in part due to its strategic investments and partnerships with other companies. For example, Tencent was an early investor in the Chinese e-commerce company Alibaba, and the two companies have since formed a close partnership. Tencent has also invested in a number of successful startups, such as the video-sharing app TikTok.

Ma has said that he wants Tencent to be 'an AI company' and has investments in a number of AI startups. Ma is also a philanthropist, and has donated billions of dollars to various causes, including education and healthcare.

Chapter Two
MICROECONOMICS

Supply and demand • Incentives and behaviours • Costs and benefits • Law of diminishing marginal utility • Consumer surplus and producer surplus • Price elasticity of demand • Price elasticity of supply • Costs of production • Asymmetric information • The theory of markets • Production possibilities frontier • Marginal utility and budget lines • International trade at the local level • Markets and externalities • Monopolies, oligopolies and monopolistic competition

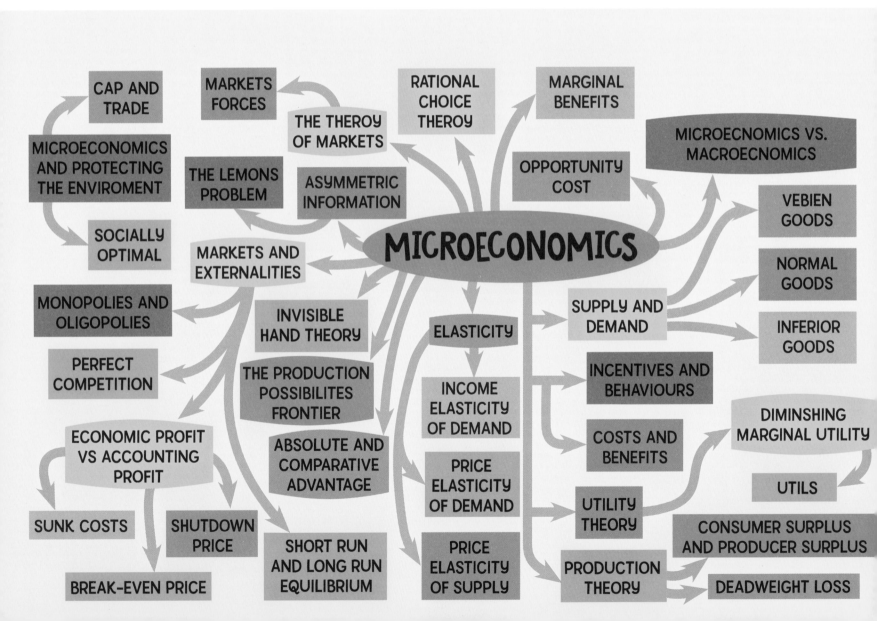

MICROECONOMICS

CAP AND TRADE

MARKETS FORCES

RATIONAL CHOICE THEROY

MARGINAL BENEFITS

MICROECONOMICS AND PROTECTING THE ENVIRMENT

THE THEROY OF MARKETS

MICROECNOMICS VS. MACROECNOMICS

THE LEMONS PROBLEM

ASYMMETRIC INFORMATION

OPPORTUNITY COST

SOCIALLY OPTIMAL

MARKETS AND EXTERNALITIES

VEBIEN GOODS

NORMAL GOODS

MONOPOLIES AND OLIGOPOLIES

INVISIBLE HAND THEORY

ELASTICITY

SUPPLY AND DEMAND

INFERIOR GOODS

PERFECT COMPETITION

THE PRODUCTION POSSIBILITES FRONTIER

INCOME ELASTICITY OF DEMAND

INCENTIVES AND BEHAVIOURS

DIMINSHING MARGINAL UTILITY

ECONOMIC PROFIT VS ACCOUNTING PROFIT

ABSOLUTE AND COMPARATIVE ADVANTAGE

PRICE ELASTICITY OF DEMAND

COSTS AND BENEFITS

UTILS

SUNK COSTS

SHUTDOWN PRICE

SHORT RUN AND LONG RUN EQUILIBRIUM

PRICE ELASTICITY OF SUPPLY

UTILITY THEORY

CONSUMER SURPLUS AND PRODUCER SURPLUS

BREAK-EVEN PRICE

PRODUCTION THEORY

DEADWEIGHT LOSS

Economics is the study of how people make decisions about what to buy, what to sell and what to produce in a world that has limited economic resources. When we say 'people' in this context we could mean individuals, but also groups or companies. It is concerned with decisions that involve money, but also trade-offs that involve how we use resources, what quantities of goods or services should be produced, how markets work and how to optimize all these decisions and compromises. *Economic resources*

There are two main categories of economic resources that form the building blocks of an economy:

1. *Human resources*: People who work and the people who manage them.
2. *Non-human resources*: Things like land, minerals, oil, technology, etc.

Economists are particularly interested in the decisions that need to be taken where there is a trade-off – a situation where the choosing of one thing means giving up another thing. This is where the important concept of scarcity comes in. If resources are not scarce there is no need for any trade-offs. If everything were abundantly available and anyone could have anything that they wanted, then there would be no need to talk about allocating resources.

Microeconomics is the study of how people (or companies, or groups) make decisions about using limited resources, which can include things like buying, selling and producing them (as well as other economic actions).

For instance, if you were to offer the last sweet in the packet to your friend, you would be making a microeconomic decision – you would be deciding how to use a limited resource, the last sweet. To help understand this further, there is the concept of opportunity cost.

OPPORTUNITY COST

Opportunity cost is not what you pay for a thing, but what you give up for a thing. It is the loss of potential value or benefits of the next best alternative when one thing is chosen over another. An example could be if you choose to spend your time and money going to the cinema; you cannot spend that same time at home reading a magazine, and you cannot use that money for something else. If your next best option were reading a magazine, then your opportunity cost is the money spent, plus the pleasure you gave up by not reading it. When economists talk about cost, they usually mean opportunity cost.

Microeconomics looks at individual decisions such as these, but it is also concerned with the collective behaviour of these individuals, groups and companies (they tend to call these *economic units*).

To make the analysis of these economic units possible (rather than try to account for all the chaotic possible aspects of human behaviour in the real world) economists make two key assumptions about behaviour (this is called *rational choice theory*):

1. They are rational. They will always select the best choice available for themselves.
2. They seek to maximize the benefits they can gain from their opportunities.

This second assumption comes from the fact that microeconomists have found that people are normally motivated to optimize even small, everyday decisions (i.e. buying the cheaper of two options), which they describe as the *idea of marginal benefits*.

MARGINAL BENEFITS

Marginal benefits are what are gained from consuming the next unit of a particular good.

Marginal benefit (MB): The immediate positive impact of a particular decision to consume the next unit.

Marginal cost (MC): The immediate negative impact of a particular decision to consume the next unit.

When MB > MC, it is rational to select that option. When MC > MB, it is rational to reject that option.

RATIONAL CHOICE THEORY

Rational choice theory has two principles:

1. Economic actors – people making economic decisions – seek to maximize their satisfaction when making decisions.
2. When making a rational decision, they believe that the benefits of the decision will outweigh the costs.

Some of the other fundamental concepts of microeconomics it is useful to have a basic understanding of are:

- supply and demand
- incentives and behaviours
- costs and benefits
- utility theory
- production theory

Supply and demand

Supply is the total amount of a good or services available at a particular time for consumers to purchase, at a particular price. *Demand* represents the desire of consumers to purchase these goods or services.

The *supply curve* goes up and to the right on a graph – as the price of a product or service increases, the company making the product is incentivized to produce more of the product.

The *demand* curve is the other way around – as the price increases, demand for the product decreases (down and to the right).

There is therefore a point where the two curves intersect, which is known as the equilibrium. This is where supply matches demand and the optimum price for the product has been achieved.

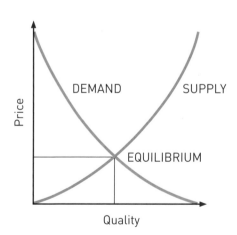

Supply and demand curves

If there is a change in demand or supply (or both), the point of equilibrium can change or shift. An increase in demand would shift the equilibrium point to the right on the graph, resulting in higher prices and a higher supply. A decrease in demand would shift the equilibrium point to the left and have the opposite impact. The equivalent shifts are true for increases or decreases in supply.

As an example, assuming a hypothetical perfect market (meaning all consumers and producers instantaneously know everything

MICROECONOMICS VS. MACROECONOMICS

Microeconomics looks at how and why different goods or services have different values, at individual consumer behaviour and supply and demand in single markets, as well as how individuals best co-ordinate or co-operate with one another. It uses various types of models based on logic and observed behaviour and tests these models against real-world observations.

Microeconomics deals with production and prices in single markets and the interactions between different markets; the study of economy-wide attributes and metrics is what macroeconomics examines.

Macroeconomics is the study of the economy in a much broader sense. It looks to take a general perspective, rather than the view of an individual at the consumer level. It examines things such as gross domestic product (GDP), inflation, employment and unemployment, monetary policy, and concepts such as aggregate demand and international trade.

Many of the fundamental principles of microeconomics are used in macroeconomics. But there is far more debate about the principles of macroeconomics than those of microeconomics, with various schools of thought offering very different explanations or solutions for economic problems.

about all market prices, their own utility and their own costs) if someone is growing potatoes and selling them at a local farmers' market as the only supplier of potatoes, then supply would be relatively low, and the relevant demand would be relatively high – meaning the price would likely be higher. If a second potato merchant began to attend the same farmers' market, then supply would be higher, and therefore the relevant demand per-potato-merchant (i.e. the number of potato purchasers) would be lower, and the price would be lower.

EXCEPTIONS TO THE LAW OF DEMAND

Veblen goods are things where the demand increases as the price increases (often things like status symbols and luxury items such as designer jewellery, luxury cars or yachts). Similarly, the demand for *Giffen* goods (which are often common necessities or essential items such as wheat, rice or toilet paper) rises when the price rises and falls when the price falls.

Income elasticity of demand (IED) is a measure of how a change in income affects the amount a consumer purchases of a good.

Necessity goods are goods with inelastic demand that have price elasticity of demand (PED) < 1. These goods are considered essential by consumers and are usually going to be bought regardless of a change in the price or a change in income (milk, petrol, etc.).

Normal goods see an increase in income leading a consumer to purchase more. They have positive IED values.

Inferior goods see an increase in income lead a consumer to purchase fewer. They have negative IED values.

Economic actions

Incentives and behaviours

When talking about *incentives* and *behaviours*, we mean reasons that you might want to do (or not do) a thing. This thing could be buying or selling something, but economic actions could also include using your time to do one thing rather than another, giving something away, etc.

Costs and benefits

When we talk about *costs* and *benefits*, we mean both in terms of monetary value, but also other elements of utility for the consumer (this is value that they might get in another manner – the cachet of having a designer brand for instance, or the time it takes to do something).

Utility

Defining utility

The definition of *utility* in economics comes from the concept of *usefulness* or *satisfaction*. An economic good or service gives utility to the extent to which it's useful for satisfying a consumer's want or need. It refers to the total satisfaction received, which can include almost anything from the pleasure of using a particular brand, to the desire for a certain object, to the necessity of consuming food to survive.

Just too much food: a demonstration of the law of diminishing marginal utility.

Alfred Marshall, in *Principles of Economics* (1920) says: 'Utility is taken to be correlative to Desire or Want ... in those cases with which economics is chiefly concerned the measure is found in the price which a person is willing to pay for the fulfilment or satisfaction of his desire.'

Economic theories that are based on rational choice assume that a consumer will try to maximize their utility. The economic utility of a good or service directly influences the demand, and thus the price, of that good or service.

Law of diminishing marginal utility

Utility, when it is used in an economic sense, refers to the usefulness or enjoyment a particular consumer can get from a good or service. But economic utility can reduce as the supply of a good or service increases. The utility gained by consuming an additional unit of a good or service is called *marginal utility*, and the way in which this decreases as you consume more of something is called the *law of diminishing marginal utility*.

For instance, if you are hungry, a first plate of food gives you a lot of utility (it satisfies your hunger, and you enjoy it), but a second plate of food, or a third or fourth plate of food immediately afterwards will give you less and less utility as you become increasingly less hungry and more and more full.

UTILS ▶ *A util is a theoretical measure of the satisfaction a consumer gets from consuming a good. It means economists can measure total utility, or the total utils, a consumer gets from consuming a quantity of a good and can then use this to make comparisons more easily.*

Consumer surplus and producer surplus

Producers have a minimum price they are prepared to charge to make a profit. If the market price is higher than the minimum amount they are prepared to charge and still make a profit, then they have a *producer surplus*.

On the other hand, if consumers are prepared to pay more than the current market price for a product, then there is a *consumer surplus*.

Producer surplus is the difference between the market price and the minimum amount a business must charge to make a profit. Consumer surplus is the amount above the market price that a consumer is willing to pay.

You can calculate the amounts of consumer surplus and the producer surplus by figuring out the area of the triangle formed, as in the graph right.

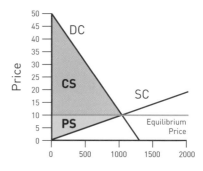

Calculating consumer and producer surplus.

Deadweight loss

Deadweight loss (DWL) is the loss of economic surplus – consumer surplus plus producer surplus – due to some kind of market intervention, such as a legal price minimum or maximum.

Price floor is a minimum price at which a good can be legally sold (if it is high enough, this could lead to DWL).

Price ceiling is a legal maximum on the price, which leads to DWL.

Quota is a legal limit on the quantity of a good that can be made available to consumers, which can lead to DWL.

Deadweight loss is impacted by elasticity: the more elastic a supply is, the larger the possible deadweight loss.

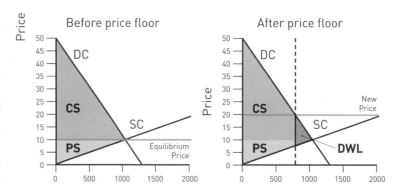

27

Some products have a far greater degree of demand and price elasticity than others.

Elasticity

Elastic is a term used in economics to describe a change in the behaviour of buyers and sellers in response to a change in price for a good or service. Its opposite term is inelasticity.

In other words, *demand elasticity* or inelasticity for a product is determined by how much the demand for the product changes as the price increases or decreases.

An elastic product is something that consumers buy a different amount of when the price changes. An inelastic product is one that consumers continue to buy at the same rate even after a change in price.

The *elasticity* of a product or service sometimes changes according to the number of close substitutes available, the relative cost and the amount of time since a price change happened.

Price elasticity of demand

Price elasticity of demand (PED) is a measurement of the change in quantity demanded of a product in relation to a change in the price. It is expressed as a ratio of the percentage change.

Most consumers for most goods or services are sensitive to the price of a product or service, and it is assumed that more people will buy the product or service if it's cheaper and fewer will buy it if it's more expensive. Price elasticity shows more accurately how responsive consumer demand is for a particular product based on its price.

Economists use this to assess how supply and demand can change when the price of a product changes:

How price affects demand

Price elasticity of demand = % change in quantity demanded / % change in price

There are a few things to note:

- As a general rule, if the amount of goods demanded or purchased changes more than the price changes, the product is considered to be elastic. For example, the price of the product goes up by 10%, but demand falls by 20%.
- If the change in quantity purchased matches the price change (i.e. 20% / 20% = 1), such a product is described as having unit – or unitary – price elasticity.
- If the amount purchased changes less than the price (i.e. –10% demanded for a +20% change in price) then the product is called inelastic.

The price elasticity of demand for perfectly elastic, or perfectly inelastic, goods can be represented on a graph, as left.

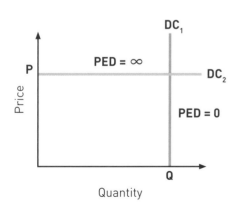

PERFECTLY INELASTIC ▶ *Goods with PED = 0. At any price, the quantity you demand does not change (see DC$_1$ on the facing page).*

PERFECTLY ELASTIC: ▶ *Goods with PED = ∞. Any change in price will cause an infinite change in the quantity demanded (see DC$_2$).*

Price elasticity of supply

Similar to price elasticity of demand, *price elasticity of supply* is a measure of the responsiveness to the supply of a good or service after a change in price. Economic theory suggests that the supply of a good will increase when the price of it rises. And the supply of a good will decrease when the price of it falls.

Generally, businesses aim to keep the price elasticity of supply high so they can react should the price of their products shift. They will try to capture more profit if prices rise, or reduce production if prices fall.

The calculation for the price elasticity of supply is:

Price elasticity of supply = % change in supply / % change in price

The importance of price elasticity in supply

Costs of production

If the cost of an element of production – labour, raw materials, equipment – decreases, the quantity that producers are willing and able to supply at a particular price increases.

Producers with lower costs will usually be able to supply more of a product at a particular price than those with higher costs. Thus, any reduction in producers' costs should increase the supply.

Alternatively, if production costs go up, the quantity supplied at a particular price will decrease. These higher costs mean that producers will have to produce less to be able to sell a product at a particular price.

Substitute goods

In simple terms, a *substitute* is a good (or service) that can be used in place of another. Coke instead of Pepsi, an iPhone instead of an Android phone. Consumers need to view it as essentially the same, or similar enough to another product to be able to replace it for their purposes.

A production line like this has many parts making up the total cost of production.

As the price of a particular product goes up, the demand for a substitute tends to increase. The opposite is also true: as the price of a product decreases, the demand for substitutes tends to reduce. Said another way, A and B are substitutes if demand for A increases when the price of B increases, or if there is positive *cross-elasticity of demand* (the responsiveness in the quantity demanded of one particular product when the price of another product is altered).

There are perfect and imperfect substitutes – so although one dollar bill is a perfect substitute for another dollar bill, an apple is not a perfect substitute for an orange if what the consumer really wants is an orange. So, although it is possible to substitute one for the other, consumers may stick with the original, even if the price has increased if they perceive the degree of difference to be high enough.

Substitution is possible but not necessarily the outcome of a rise in price or reduction in supply.

FURTHER IMPORTANT PRINCIPLES IN MICROECONOMICS
Asymmetric information

Asymmetric information is when one person or group involved in an economic transaction knows more than the other person or group. This typically happens when the seller of a good or service has more knowledge about the product than the buyer; however, the reverse dynamic is also possible. Almost every economic transaction involves some kind of information asymmetry.

Potential impacts of asymmetric information include:

Impacts of asymmetric information

- *Adverse selection*: When a seller has more information than a buyer, or vice versa, and this imbalance in information can be exploited. An example of this might be in the used car market where sellers tend to know more than the buyers about the possible downsides of a particular car. This is a point when asymmetric information causes market failure.
- *Market failure*: A market outcome based on incorrect information or with undesirable results.
- *Moral hazard*: When someone takes more risks knowing that someone else bears the impact of those risks. For instance, if a homeowner has insurance, they may be less inclined to take care not to damage the property, despite their contract with the insurer assuming that they will avoid situations that cause damage.
- *Principal-agent problem*: Agents (for instance, employees) can't always be trusted to act in the best interest of their *principals* (for instance, employers).

Ways to combat asymmetric information:

- *Screening* is when the uninformed party draws out information from the more informed party.
- *Signalling* is revealing private information to the uninformed party.

THE 'LEMONS' PROBLEM

There is a famous research paper, 'The Market for "Lemons": Quality Uncertainty and the Market Mechanism', written in 1970 by George A. Akerlof, an economics professor at the University of California, Berkeley in the 1960s.

In the second-hand car industry, defective or poor-quality used cars are commonly referred to as 'lemons'. In this market, the seller usually has more information regarding the value of a given car than the buyer.

The seller of used cars in this scenario has an incentive to present a low-quality car (a 'lemon') as being higher quality than it is because they can then make a bigger profit.

However, the buyer is aware of this and knows they can't accurately determine the quality of the car, so will only pay the average price (above the true price of a 'lemon', but below the price of a high-quality car).

Since nobody will pay the price of a quality car (because it could be a 'lemon'), dealers who sell quality cars will lose business. The market becomes more attractive to those selling 'lemons', but this means that buyers will realize it is harder to get a good used car. Akerlof argued that this would create a feedback loop that resulted in the market becoming saturated with 'lemons' but no quality cars, and ultimately no one willing to buy used cars.

The theory of markets

A market, in the context of economics, is the place where buyers and sellers interact (either physically or digitally) and engage in exchanging goods or services.

Market forces are how markets function. They drive the behaviours responsible for the exchange of goods and services in a free market, for instance, the tendency of consumers to buy more of a product when its price is low, or the impact of a governmental policy on consumer behaviour, such as subsidies for electric cars.

How markets function

Factors of production are the basic building blocks of businesses, including raw materials, investment capital and labour. They make up the factor market, which is where businesses come to buy what they need to operate and produce goods and services. The product market is where these businesses sell their goods and services to customers.

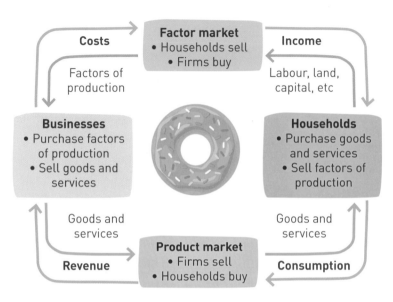

The circular flow model of market forces.

Using an imaginary doughnut shop as an example, in the product market, consumers exchange money for their doughnuts and in the factor market an employee of the doughnut shop exchanges their labour for a pay cheque.

All these market forces work together to make transactions possible. On the left is the circular flow model of market forces. You can see that money (in green) flows in the opposite direction from goods and services (red) and factors of production (blue).

Because some people will be prepared to pay more for a specific product, and some people less, the potential price for a particular product is likely to have a range of possibilities. If they charge too much, they could end up with a surplus of products, but if they charge too little, they may have a shortage.

A business must take into account the value that all consumers might get from their product, and this will be how the market price is set. The demand curve can show this range of potential prices and help businesses set their market price at an equilibrium.

Because some people will be prepared to pay more for a specific product, and some people less, the potential price for a particular product is likely to have a range of possibilities. If they charge too much, they could end up with a surplus of products, but if they charge too little, they may have a shortage.

A business must take into account the *value* that all consumers might get from their product, and this will be how the market price is set. The demand curve can show this range of potential prices and help businesses set their market price at an equilibrium.

The production possibilities frontier

The *production possibilities frontier* (PPF) is a curve that represents a trade-off – all the possibilities that exist between choosing only choice X or only choice Y, as shown on the graph opposite.

The slope of this curve between two particular points is equal to the *opportunity cost* for choosing X instead of Y.

Constant opportunity cost: If the opportunity cost between two choices is constant, then the PPF will be a straight line.

Any point on this curve is known as *Pareto efficient* – it is impossible to increase one side of things without decreasing the other.

Marginal utility and budget lines

Let's say that you need to buy six bottles of beer in a shop, all the beer in the shop costs the same per bottle and you have exactly enough money to buy six bottles. You could buy five Belgian Lagers and one English Ale, but if you want to buy one more Belgian Lager, you must buy one less English Ale.

This can be expressed as an *indifference curve*. This is the combination of two goods that give the same level of utility. The further away the indifference curve moves from zero, the greater the utility, often measured in utils (see page 27).

What is important here is *diminishing marginal utility* – the more of one thing you have, the more you might be prepared to give up. You can use the two figures on the top graph on page 34 to calculate the ratio of a trade-off. If you give up 3 of your lagers, you can have 2 more ales, so the ratio is 3 divided by 2 (which equals 1.5). This is the *marginal rate of substitution*, which equals the slope of the indifference curve between the two points.

If you were able to buy more of each good, you could move the whole indifference curve to the right. You would be increasing your total utility. But the real world usually has limitations, including the amount available to spend on goods or services.

The budget constraint is this limit that is placed on choices. The most utility that is possible is where the indifference curve (IC) and the budget constraint (BC) meet – the point where you are spending the money you have and getting the most possible utility for that money (page 34 (centre).

However, if the price of one of the goods were to change, then the total amount you would be able to buy would increase (your budget constraint would change) and so would the indifference curve. If the price of the English Ale in our example were to decrease to £3 then the indifference curve and the budget constraint would both move to the right because you now have more total utility – you can buy more for your money. If the price were to increase, the opposite would happen, and both would move to the left (page 34 (below).

When prices drop like this, it causes consumers to feel richer, and buy accordingly even though their actual income hasn't changed. This is known as the *income effect*.

INVISIBLE HAND THEORY

This is a famous metaphor from economist Adam Smith about the forces that move the free market economy. It is driven by the notion that self-interest motivates both buyers and sellers.

The idea is that when consumers can freely choose what they want to buy and sellers are free to choose how and what they want to sell, this self-interest will mean they set good prices and provide the right goods to the market. This also means the equilibrium reached avoids oversupply or shortages.

Adam Smith argued that intervention from government is not needed to achieve this because this 'invisible hand' will guide things towards the best interests of society, overall.

However, some critics point out that this often doesn't account for external costs that don't directly affect the consumer or producer – such as long-term pollution or overfishing – impacts on society that are not accounted for in the final cost of goods.

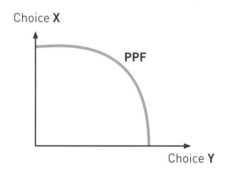

The production possibilities frontier.

INDIFFERENCE CURVE

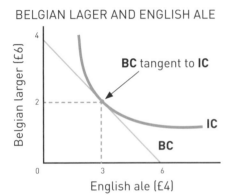

BELGIAN LAGER AND ENGLISH ALE

BELGIAN LAGER AND ENGLISH ALE

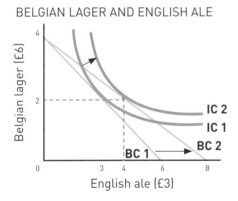

Conversely, if prices increase then it can make consumers feel poorer.

In addition, once the price for ale drops, not only can consumers buy more, but consumers tend to *want* to buy more. Because it is cheaper, it is now the more attractive choice. This is known as the *substitution effect*.

INTERNATIONAL TRADE AT THE LOCAL LEVEL
Absolute and comparative advantage

When we look at the microeconomic elements of free trade, the important decisions that need making are around who is best placed to produce certain goods and services, and how you decide. There are three key principles here:

1. *Absolute advantage*: This is the ability of an individual to produce more of a good or service than their competitors. If you are a chicken farmer, you can produce more eggs than the bicycle factory down the road – you have an absolute advantage in terms of producing eggs.
2. *Comparative advantage*: This represents the ability of an individual to produce a good or service at a lower opportunity cost than their competitors.
3. *Specialization*: Prioritizing production of a good or service made with comparative advantage.

As an example, imagine you own a small bicycle factory that can make either 6 bicycles or 12 unicycles in a month. If you have to give up making 6 bicycles to produce 12 unicycles, then your opportunity cost per unicycle is 0.5 bicycles. You must give up making half a bicycle for every unicycle you make (or vice versa, 2 unicycles to make 1 bicycle).

Your rival factory would have to give up making 4 bicycles to make 4 unicycles, so they must give up 1 bicycle to make 1 unicycle.

If we compare these figures, we can see that your rival has the comparative advantage in producing bicycles (they only have to give up 1 unicycle to make a bicycle, whereas you have to give up making 2 unicycles). You have the comparative advantage in making unicycles, as you only need give up making half a bicycle for each unicycle you make (see graphic opposite).

If you and your rival were in a free trade situation, for instance between two countries, then it would make sense for one of you to focus on making the type of good that you are best at, which you can then trade for the alternative kind of good, both maximizing your production. This would be *specialization*.

MARKETS AND EXTERNALITIES
The perfectly competitive market
This is a theoretical market structure, used for economic thought experiments, to prove principles of economic theory or as a base to compare other markets to.

This kind of structure has several key characteristics, including:

- All the companies sell an identical product (a commodity or homogeneous product).
- All of those selling are price takers (they can't affect the market price of their products).
- Market share doesn't have an impact on prices.
- Buyers have completely perfect information about the product for sale and the prices charged by each seller.
- Capital resources and labour are perfectly mobile, and transport is always efficient, reliable and cheap.
- Companies are able to enter or exit the market without any costs.
- A large number of buyers and sellers exist. These sellers are small firms, not large corporations capable of controlling prices through supply adjustments.
- There is little or no government intervention.

In this theoretical market situation, prices completely reflect supply and demand. Over time, companies will earn just enough profit to stay in business and no more. If they do start to earn excess profits, other companies would enter the market and drive profits down over time. The companies involved always tend towards break even.

MONOPOLIES, OLIGOPOLIES AND MONOPOLISTIC COMPETITION
In a *monopoly*, there is only one seller of a particular product. This monopoly seller determines the price and quantity made, and there are barriers to entering the market. These barriers could include high set-up costs, better technological skills or network externalities.

Natural monopoly: This is a situation where consumers benefit from a monopoly existing, such as with public utilities (water, gas or electricity). These then usually have strong government regulation to prevent them from overly exploiting their monopoly status.

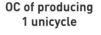

OC of producing 1 bicycle	OC of producing 1 unicycle

Rival: 1 unicycle | 1 bicycle

YOU: 2 unicycle | 0.5 bicycle

Comparing the opportunity costs of producing different products.

Monopolistic competition

ECONOMIC PROFIT VS. ACCOUNTING PROFIT

These traders at a farmers' market have a number of price considerations when looking at their overall profitability.

When we talk about profit in these circumstances, we mean economic profit, which is different from accounting profit. Accounting profit is the net income of a company, whereas economic profit also includes implicit or opportunity costs – any cost that results from using an asset instead of renting, selling or lending it.

Economic profit, which includes opportunity costs, is usually lower than accounting profit, which is concerned with dollars-in vs. dollars-out. It is possible to have a positive accounting profit and zero or negative economic profit.

The other elements of a perfectly competitive market include:

- *Break-even price:* When the market price is exactly equal to the minimum average total cost (ATC). At this price, a producer makes zero profit. Any time market price > break-even price, a producer will turn a profit.
- *Shutdown price:* When the minimum average variable cost (AVC) ≥ market price. At this price, a producer should stop producing.
- *Shutdown point:* When minimum AVC = market price.
- *Sunk costs:* Unrecoverable costs. These costs should not be factored into a decision as to whether to continue producing. In the short run, fixed costs are sunk.
- *Total revenue (TR):* Price per unit multiplied by quantity sold.
- *Constant marginal cost:* The cost of producing the next unit of a good is always the same.

Finding the break-even point for a given product involves working out what the marginal cost and the average total cost is and finding where they intersect.

There are not any examples of perfect competition in the real world, though some circumstances can get close to certain elements – produce at farmers' markets, rival supermarkets stocking the same products, etc.

The opposite of perfect competition is imperfect competition, which exists when a market doesn't completely adhere to one or more of the abstract tenets of perfect competition.

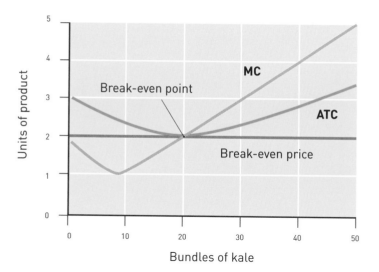

SHORT-RUN AND LONG-RUN EQUILIBRIUM

In the short run, fixed costs are sunk costs (you have to pay for things like next month's rent). But in the long run, they are variable costs – you could always go and rent a different property, meaning that this cost could change. These costs will affect the point of equilibrium. *Equilibrium* is where the market demands will be equal to market supply, which helps determine the price that the market will bear.

In the short run, equilibrium will be affected by demand, but in the long run it is affected by both demand and supply.

In a perfectly competitive market, the market has reached long-run equilibrium when the market price is exactly equal to break-even price, the supply curve is perfectly elastic, and firms make zero *economic profit*.

MARGINAL COST (MC) ▶ *The cost of producing one additional unit of a product.*

AVERAGE TOTAL COST (ATC) ▶ *Total cost to produce a certain number of units of a product divided by the number of units produced.*

AVERAGE VARIABLE COST (AVC) ▶ *Variable cost divided by the quantity being produced.*

Rival goods

Non-rival goods

Excludable goods

Oligopoly: This is when a small number of select companies dominate a particular market and can arrange prices and production quantities between themselves (collude) to maximize individual profits.

Cartel: This is a collection of producers with a formal agreement to collude. An example of this would be OPEC – a group that tries to manage the supply of oil in the world market to prevent massive fluctuations.

Monopolistic competition: This is when a specific group of producers compete with similar – but distinct – products. Because of this sufficient product differentiation, each is free to charge their own price for a good or service.

Types of goods

In the world of microeconomics there are four major types of goods – private, common, club and public. These goods then can be categorized in various combinations:

- *Rival goods:* These are individual goods that can be consumed by only one person at a time – an ice cream, a T-shirt, timber.
- *Non-rival goods:* These can be consumed by more than one person at once – a TV show, a concert.
- *Excludable goods:* People who don't pay can be excluded from using them – clothes, motorbikes, golf clubs.
- *Non-excludable goods:* People can't be stopped from using these goods once they're made available – public spaces like parks, lighthouses.

There are two significant problems that can occur with common and public goods:

1. The *free-rider problem* happens when people who enjoy public goods don't contribute to the costs of running them. If nobody donates to the museum when they visit, it may not have enough funding to stay open in the future.
2. The *tragedy of the commons* happens if the invisible hand of the market doesn't prevent individual exploitation of common goods. This is often demonstrated with the example of a public field – a commons – where everyone can graze their sheep for free. Let us say that this field has a capacity of five sheep before it starts to degrade, and there are five farmers. As long as all the farmers only graze one sheep on the commons, it remains sustainable. But each farmer has an economic incentive to graze as many of their sheep as they can. So, if one or more farmers graze two sheep on the commons, it degrades for everyone, and as farmers continue to add more sheep (as they are incentivized to do), this ultimately leads to the land being unusable for them all despite them being motivated by logical economic incentives. Private goods are market goods; they're subject to market forces such as the laws of supply and demand.

Non-excludable goods

Externalities and their solutions

In economics, an *externality* is when a private transaction impacts a third party who is otherwise not involved. For instance, if you paid a DJ to play an all-night set in the garden of your terraced house for your birthday, your neighbours might be affected by this.

Usually, externalities are negative, but sometimes externalities can be positive. If you pay to improve your front garden, for instance, the community also benefits from having a nicer front garden to look at, although they weren't involved in the transaction. These kinds of impacts are known as *external benefits*.

Another example of these kinds of impacts is *network externality*. This means that if the vast majority of consumers already use a product, everyone else also needs to use it to be able to join them. An example of this would be social networks such as Facebook. It becomes more and more useful as more people use it.

	Excludable	Non-excludable
Rival	**Private goods** Housing, cars, clothes 	**Common goods** Timber, fisheries 
Non-rival	**Club goods** Cable TV, country clubs 	**Public goods** Public radio, lighthouses 

The relationships between consumers and different types of goods.

Solutions to externalities

There can be both public and private solutions to externalities.

Public solutions involve the use of laws or regulations to influence the behaviour of private parties. There are two main types:

1. *Command and control*, whereby a government passes regulations that mandate behaviour intended to correct the externality, such as banning the dumping of chemicals in a river.
2. *Market-based solutions*, where a government creates incentives or penalties to correct the externality, such as taxes that encourage companies to produce less of a given product, or quotas that limit production.

However, public solutions are sometimes ineffective. For example, if a government makes it illegal to dump in the river, the companies and their customers might suffer because the products will be made in a more inefficient way. However, if the government allows too much to be dumped in the river, they would have failed to solve the negative externality.

Therefore, an alternative is to create systems of incentives or disincentives that work alongside the market to solve the negative externality. When this is in the form of taxes, they are designed to be set at the same value as the negative externality and to provide an incentive for the allocation of resources in a way that is more socially optimal. Using the example above of environmental pollution – the private cost of pollution to a polluter is less than its social cost. If there is a tax

Incentives and disincentives

placed on this pollution, it increases the polluter's private cost. As a result of this, the polluter has an incentive to create less pollution.

There are also entirely *private solutions* – the use of private negotiation between parties to reach a socially optimal resolution. In a perfectly efficient competitive market, the optimum outcomes can be achieved this way. Thus, there are specific conditions that need to be met to achieve this.

The Coase Theorum   This is known as the *Coase Theorem*, which says that private negotiations can work if:

- any property rights are clearly defined
- all transaction costs – the costs incurred during the negotiation process – are low

Because in the real world this perfectly efficient competitive environment is unlikely, one way of looking at this is not as a template for how disagreements should be resolved, but to explain why so many seemingly inefficient outcomes to economic disputes are found in the real world.

BILL GATES: MICROSOFT

While he was studying at Harvard, Bill Gates became interested in computer science, and after his second year, he dropped out to pursue this full-time at Microsoft Corporation, a company he and his childhood friend Paul Allen had founded just four years earlier in New Mexico, USA.

At Microsoft, Gates oversaw the company's product strategy, and was the driving force behind many of its most successful products, including MS-DOS, Microsoft Windows, Microsoft Office, and Internet Explorer. He also played a key role in developing the company's business strategy, which involved licensing Microsoft's software to other computer manufacturers.

Under Gates' leadership, Microsoft became the world's largest software company, and Gates became one of the richest men in the world. In addition to his work at Microsoft, Gates is also a prominent philanthropist, and has donated billions of dollars to charitable causes through the Bill & Melinda Gates Foundation.

Gates' business successes can be attributed to a number of factors, including his technical expertise, his understanding of the needs of customers and businesses, his focus on product development, and his ability to develop and execute effective business strategies.

His understanding of customer and business needs meant that Gates was always focused on developing products that met the needs of customers and businesses.

In terms of Gates' technical expertise, it is worth noting that he is a computer programming prodigy, and was writing code for computers before he even owned one. This gave him a deep understanding of how computers work, which was invaluable in his role at Microsoft.

MICROECONOMICS AND PROTECTING THE ENVIRONMENT

The global challenge of the climate crisis is a negative externality and a free-rider problem. One way to deal with the free-rider problem would be for countries to negotiate optimized pollution quotas.

Would a carbon tax encourage companies to limit pollution?

To do this, they would need to look at the marginal abatement cost and the marginal damage so they can then set a carbon tax that would encourage companies to only emit CO_2 at a socially optimal level.

SOCIALLY OPTIMAL ▶ *Here, we mean not what is best according to society in general, but what is best in economic terms. It is the optimal distribution of resources, accounting for all benefits to society and external costs, as well as the internal costs and benefits.*

Marginal abatement cost (MAC): The cost of reducing each additional metric ton of CO_2 – note that the X-axis on the right shows time running from right to left.

Marginal damage (MD): The relationship between the quantity of CO_2 emissions and the damage caused by these emissions – measured in dollars.

If you add the marginal damage (MD) curve to the graph, you can determine the optimal production point, where MAC = MD.

Therefore, a carbon tax, equal to the cost at Q, could be used to encourage producers to emit CO_2 at the *socially optimal* level.

An alternative to a carbon tax is something called *cap and trade*. This is where a government issues permits for each unit of pollution (for instance, ton of CO_2), up to the overall total optimal amount. Companies can then buy and sell these permits as needed, meaning that there is a market for them, and the distribution should be economically efficient.

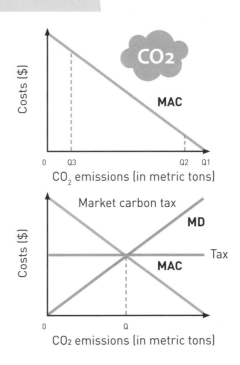

Chapter Three
MACROECONOMICS

Economic indicators • Gross domestic product • Consumer Price Index • Markets, unemployment and inflation • Unions and the market • The business cycle • US fiscal and monetary policy • International trade • Modern perspectives • Business and sustainability vs. CSR

THOMAS PIKETTY AND INCOME AND WEALTH INEQUALITTY

DOUGHNUT ECONOMICS

THE CONSUMER PRICE INDEX

MODERN ECONOMIC PERSPECTIVES

GROSS DOMESTIC PRODUCT

TRADE RESTRICTIONS

INTERNATIONAL TRADE

MACROECONOMICS

ECONOMIC INDICATORS

FLOATING AND FIXED EXCHANGE RATES

GOVERNMENT BUDGETS AND FISCAL POLICIES

MARKETS, UNEMPLOYMENT AND INFLATION

UNEMPLOYMENT FIGURES

MONETARY POLICY AND THE MARKET

THE BUSINESS CYCLE

BUILDING AGGREGATE DEMAND

PRICE OF CRUDE OIL

THE AD-AS MODEL

WEALTH EFFECT

CENTRAL BANKS

RECESSIONS AND DEPRESSIONS

DEFINING SRAS AND LRAS

INTEREST RATE EFFECT

RESERVE REQUIREMENT

DISCOUNT RATE

THE BOOM AND BUST CYCLE

FOREIGN PRICE EFFECT

Macroeconomics is concerned with national and global economies as well as the particular role of governments and central banks.

The types of questions that macroeconomists try to answer are:

- What causes the business cycle to fluctuate?
- How do prices end up being set?
- What is the rate of inflation and what affects it?
- What causes economic growth, or recession?
- What indicators successfully predict or measure these changes?
- What are the key outputs in an economy?
- What determines productivity?

They also study the role of governments in these areas and examine how policies have changed or will change these various economic circumstances.

HOW DO YOU MEASURE THE ECONOMY?

Any market economy is not static: the value of national income goes up when the economy is growing and decreases when the economy is shrinking. The way in which these fluctuations in the economy are measured and assessed is through a series of standardized economic indicators.

Economic indicators

Economic indicators are data about the national or global economy that are used to judge the overall health of the economy.

These data tend to come from government sources, nonprofits or academic institutions. They include:

- the Consumer Price Index (CPI)
- gross domestic product (GDP)
- unemployment figures
- the price of crude oil

There are *leading indicators*, which tend to come before trends; lagging indicators, which confirm trends that have already started; or coincident indicators, showing what is happening now.

The cost of a barrel of crude oil is a key economic indicator.

The Consumer Price Index is based on the relative cost of a number of grocery items which vary from year to year.

Gross domestic product

Gross domestic product, or GDP, represents the total value of all the goods and services produced within a nation's borders within a particular period. It is usually calculated on an annual basis. It gives an economic 'snapshot' of a country.

Calculating GDP

Usually, the goods and services that are measured include all public consumption (the things that are bought by households), government spending on goods and services, and investments by businesses – this includes things like capital expenditures. Exports are added to the value and imports are subtracted from it.

You can also calculate GDP from:

- the total value of goods and services produced (known as *output*)
- everyone's income

GDP can be calculated in two ways:

1. *Nominal basis:* The market value of goods and services produced in an economy, unadjusted for inflation.
2. *Real basis:* This is nominal GDP, adjusted for inflation to reflect changes in real output.

Calculating on a real basis makes comparing GDP from year to year (and to different years) more useful because it can provide comparisons for both the quantity and value of goods and services.

A simple formula for calculating GDP is:

$$GDP = C + I + G + NX$$

Where GDP = Consumption + Investment + Government + Net Exports (exports minus imports).

For 2019, the GDP of the USA was composed of 70% personal consumption, 18% business investment, 17% government spending, and negative 5% net exports.

WHAT IS NOT MEASURED BY GDP?

Things that are not measured by GDP include volunteering, caring for an older relative or similar activities. Because no money changes hands, this output is not included in the GDP calculation. It also doesn't represent inequality across a population. A higher GDP, or growth, could mean everyone is better off, or it could mean that just the people in the richest section of society are increasing their income.

Changes in the size of population can also impact the figures. If GDP rose by 3% but the population grew by 5% then the average income per person would have fallen, despite the GDP calculation suggesting it was growing.

There are also other factors that can raise GDP that have associated undesirable costs. War tends to raise GDP because lots of money gets spent by governments, as can environmental destruction such as deforestation, because it can produce lots of goods (timber) for sale.

There are other available measures that look to assess happiness or well-being. For instance, the Happy Planet Index (created by the New Economic Foundation) looks at how well a country is doing at achieving 'long, happy and sustainable lives'.

The Consumer Price Index

The *Consumer Price Index* (CPI) is a measure of living costs based on changes in retail prices for a 'basket' of representative goods. This basket is reviewed every year and items are added or removed to better reflect typical consumption.

CPI is the most widely used metric for measuring inflation as it tracks the change in consumer prices over time. Different countries use slightly different goods and services in each basket, but they tend to contain everyday products such as food, clothing, furniture and a range of expenses and services.

Markets, unemployment and inflation

The rate of *unemployment* (the amount of people who want to work but are not able to) is a useful way to measure how much a supply of labour is being underutilized. It is an indicator of how efficient (or inefficient) a particular economy is at providing work to its total workforce and how the labour market is performing.

You can calculate the *unemployment rate* by taking the number of people unemployed and dividing it by the total number of people employed, plus the number of people unemployed – the entire labour force, or economically active population. This will give you a percentage figure that is the rate of unemployment.

$$UR = \text{Persons unemployed} / \text{Persons employed} + \text{Persons unemployed}$$

Unemployment rates can have an impact on prices because – in theory – the more people who are unemployed, the more people there are per job, and the competition for these jobs leads to a higher cost of labour. If very few people are unemployed then there is less competition for each job, so the cost of labour goes up. If the cost of

THE VIMES BOOTS INDEX

In the UK in 2022, the writer and campaigner Jack Monroe launched the Vimes Boots Index to more accurately track the costs of inflation to those on lower incomes – for instance by tracking the cost of basic or value supermarket-brand food items, rather than the wide-ranging basket of goods, some of which are not representative of day-to-day living expenses, used by the traditional CPI model.

A queue of men seeking employment during the 1930s Depression era.

labour goes up, the cost of goods can increase, which combined with other economic factors can lead to inflation (and vice versa).

INFLATION ▶ *The purchasing power of the currency goes down and the price of goods and labour goes up. It rewards buying things now, as things will be more expensive tomorrow.*

DEFLATION ▶ *The purchasing power of the currency goes up and the price of goods and labour goes down. It 'punishes' buying things now (and rewards hoarding currency), as things will be cheaper in the future.*

Union members taking strike action to encourage a pay settlement.

Unions and the market

As these are market forces (the rate of unemployment affects the cost of labour to employees), there is an incentive for negotiation between employees and businesses to achieve the best price for the labour involved. A negotiation between a single employee and their employer is uneven in terms of power (the employee may struggle to find work if the unemployment rate is high, but businesses can probably replace the employee with ease), best available alternatives (rehiring for that job vs. finding a new one), and the employer has more information. Therefore, the single employee may not achieve the optimum price for their labour. This is where unions can be useful.

Unions represent groups of workers and can enter negotiations with businesses and other parties on the behalf of their union members. They have more power than a single employee because, for instance, hiring to replace many employees is difficult for a business and a union can bargain for the entire group of affiliated employees. They can act to restrict labour supply or increase labour demand.

The overall objectives of unions usually include making sure their members are paid fair wages, receive fair benefits and have improved working conditions. They sometimes provide other services to their members, such as legal advice or representation. Members pay union dues to cover the costs of running the union.

Collective bargaining is when a union enters negotiations on behalf of all their members with an employer, with the aim of increasing the wages of their members or improving working conditions.

If an agreement cannot be reached, or the employer refuses to negotiate, union members may take industrial action. This is when employees go on strike or take other forms of action, like refusing to do overtime (this is called 'action short of a strike').

Unions are usually legal in democratic nations, but there are rules about how they operate. In the UK, a union can only call for industrial action if a majority of its involved members support it in a properly organized vote – called a 'ballot'. You cannot be dismissed for taking industrial action if it is properly called; if it is a trade dispute between workers and their employer; and if there has been proper notice for the employer.

Legalities of union activity

Unions can also represent their workers by lobbying governments for specific regulations or changes to the law, often in return for promoting a particular political party to their members around elections or by providing funding. Data from the U.S. Bureau of Labor Statistics shows that usually, union members have higher wages and salaries than non-union members.

In the last few decades, the deregulation of industry, increased competition, new forms of labour such as gig-work, and labour mobility have made it more difficult for traditional unions to operate. However, some economists compare unions to cartels and suggest that changes to productivity and having a competitive labour market are more important market forces behind wage adjustments.

> **THE PRICE OF CRUDE OIL**
>
> Some countries, such as the USA, keep large reserves of crude oil for future use. The quantity of these oil reserves is used as an indicator for investors – changes in the stock levels of the reserve reflects trends in the rate of production and consumption in the broader economy. If more oil remains in the ground – in reserve – it suggests less is being produced and consumed, because oil is most commonly used to make petroleum, which is used as fuel, but also to provide electricity, for heating and as an ingredient in plastics and other goods.

THE BUSINESS CYCLE
What is the business cycle?

The business cycle is a description of the periods of economic growth (and decline) over time. It is a useful tool for examining the economy and the performance of businesses. It can also be known as the economic cycle.

These alternating periods of growth and decline are known as *boom* and *bust*. The Federal Reserve Bank of Richmond (also known as 'the Fed') says that these phases are inevitable, but

Boom and bust

RECESSIONS AND DEPRESSIONS

A *recession* is a period of declining economic performance across the whole of an economy that continues for a number of months. Recessions are often defined by two consecutive quarters of economic decline, measured by GDP in conjunction with other more regular indicators, such as an increase in unemployment. A *depression* is a deep and long-lasting recession that could last for many years.

Three particular things come together to impact the business cycle: forces of supply and demand, the availability of capital, and expectations for the future. How these forces combine results in each phase of the cycle.

When an economy is in a boom phase, consumer demand is strong and has the most impact. Consumer confidence about the future is high, so they buy more, they believe they can get better jobs and they are confident that property prices and the value of investments will rise.

Because of this increase in demand, companies try to increase supply by hiring new workers and because capital is available cheaply, companies and consumers can both borrow at low rates, which also stimulates demand.

If demand begins to outpace supply, then the economy is said to be 'overheating'. If there is too much money trying to buy too few goods, prices go up and you get inflation. This leads investors to try to outperform the market, and they are incentivized to increase their investment risks to achieve higher gains.

recessions have become less frequent. The economy in the USA has only been in recession 5% of the time since 1983, about ten times less frequently than the hundred years before 1945.

When the economy is in a bust phase, expectations about the future are low, which has the biggest impact. Investors and consumers are nervous, and stock market crashes or corrections can exacerbate this. Investors sell shares and buy less risky investments, such as government bonds, gold and reserve currencies. Because of the reduction in demand, companies reduce the size of their workforce, and as these consumers lose their jobs, they have less money for necessities. This causes a cycle of decline and eventually a recession.

This bust phase will stop when the forces of supply have lowered their prices enough to stimulate demand to start rising.

The phases of a business cycle follow a wave-like pattern over time.

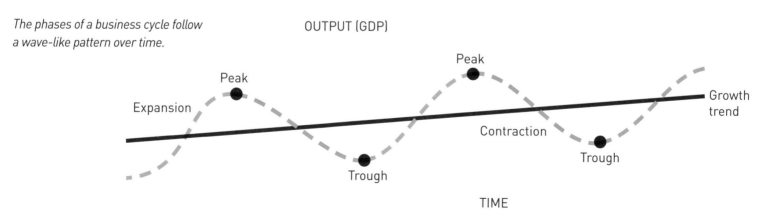

THE BOOM-AND-BUST CYCLE IN THE USA

Cycle	Duration	Significant Events
Bust	Aug 1929–Mar 1933	Stock market crash and higher taxes, dust bowl in Mid-west.
Boom	Apr 1933–Apr 1937	New Deal passed by FDR.
Bust	May 1937–Jun 1938	FDR attempted to balance budget.
Boom	Jul 1938–Jan 1945	Mobilization for World War II.
Bust	Feb 1945–Oct 1945	Demobilization for peacetime.
Boom	Nov 1945–Oct 1948	Employment Act and Marshall Plan.
Bust	Nov 1948–Oct 1949	Postwar adjustment.
Boom	Nov 1949–Jun 1953	Korean War.
Bust	Jul 1953–May 1954	Demobilization for peacetime.
Boom	Jun 1954–Jul 1957	Fed reduced rate to 1.0%.
Bust	Aug 1957–Apr 1958	Fed raised rate to 3.0%.
Boom	May 1958–Mar 1960	Fed lowered rate to 0.63%.
Bust	Apr 1960–Feb 1961	Fed raised rate to 4.0%.
Boom	Mar 1961–Nov 1969	Stimulus spending from JFK. Fed lowered rate to 1.17%.
Bust	Dec 1969–Nov 1970	Fed raised rate to 9.19%.
Boom	Dec 1970–Oct 1973	Fed lowered rate to 3.5%.
Bust	Nov 1973–Mar 1975	Wage-price controls. Gold standard ends. Oil embargo. Stagflation.
Boom	Apr 1975–Dec 1979	Fed lowered rate to 4.75%.
Bust	Jan 1980–Jul 1980	Fed raised rate to 20% to try to end inflation.
Boom	Aug 1980–Jun 1981	Fed lowered rates.
Bust	Jul 1981–Nov 1982	1980 recession resumed.
Boom	Dec 1982–Jun 1990	Reagan lowered the tax rate and increased defence budget.
Bust	Jul 1990–Mar 1991	Result of the 1989 Savings and Loan Crisis.
Boom	Apr 1991–Feb 2001	Dotcom bubble arrives at the end of this.
Bust	Mar 2001–Nov 2001	2001 recession due to dotcom bubble bursting, high interest rates.
Boom	Dec 2001–Nov 2007	Derivatives instruments created large housing bubble.
Bust	Dec 2007–Jun 2009	Subprime mortgage crisis.
Boom	Jul 2009–Jan 2020	American Recovery and Reinvestment Act (ARRA) and QE.
Bust	Feb 2020–Now	COVID-19 pandemic.

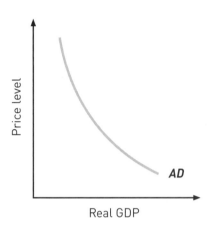

An aggregate demand curve.

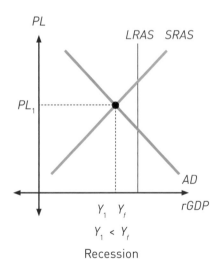

The AD-AS model.

THE COMPONENT PARTS OF THE BUSINESS CYCLE
Building aggregate demand

Aggregate demand (AD) is used to refer to the total spending in an economy on domestic goods and services. AD is used by economists to refer to total planned expenditure. It includes consumption expenditure, investment expenditure, government expenditure and net export expenditure (exports minus imports). This demand is affected by various factors, one of which is the *aggregate price level* (a measure of the average level of prices of goods and services in an economy). Therefore, the AD curve shows the total spending on domestic goods and services at each price level.

The AD–AS model

The *AD–AS model* is used to analyze economies. It illustrates an economy's *income determination* (the level of national income where purchasing and production plans are at equilibrium) and changes in the price level (which allows us to determine this). It can show the phases of the business cycle and how events lead to changes in GDP and inflation – two of the key indicators.

The example below left shows a recession, with $Y1$ representing current output and Yf representing full employment output. Observe that $Y1$ is less than Yf during a recession.

Defining SRAS and LRAS

Short-run aggregate supply (SRAS) is a term that refers to the relationship between the price level and real GDP when they are at an equilibrium. *Long-run aggregate supply* (LRAS) is theoretical but refers to what an economy can produce when using 100% of its factors of production – and is therefore at full employment.

When drawing SRAS on the graph it is normal to assume that productivity and the costs of production as well as the state of technology stays constant in the short run.

In the long run, prices and wages are very flexible, so all resources can be fully employed and real GDP will come to equal potential, irrespective of price level. Therefore, the LRAS will become a vertical line on the graph, independent of price level – as in the graph opposite. This is the full employment level of GDP.

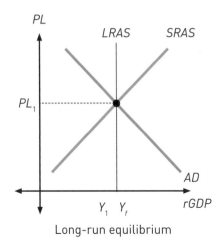

Long-run equilibrium

The full employment level of GDP.

US FISCAL AND MONETARY POLICY

When we talk about *monetary* or *fiscal policy*, we are talking about the ways in which the economic activity of a nation can be influenced – what can central banks and governments do to avoid recessions or reduce inflation, for instance?

Monetary policy is mostly to do with the management of interest rates and the total supply of money in circulation. These activities are usually taken by central banks, such as the US Federal Reserve or the Bank of England.

Fiscal policy is the overall term for the taxation and spending activities of a government. This could include lowering taxes, increasing welfare payments, spending on infrastructure or other activities that might impact the overall economy.

WEALTH EFFECT, INTEREST RATE EFFECT AND FOREIGN PRICE EFFECT

Wealth effect: The idea that if households become richer because of a rise in value of their assets, for instance their house or shares they might own, they increase their spending (for example on luxury goods, (below) and stimulate the wider economy.

Interest rate effect: This is where a change in interest rates set by the central bank leads to an increase (or decrease) in aggregate demand. Interest rates have an inverse relationship to aggregate demand, so when interest rates go up, demand is low and the other way around.

Exchange rate effect: When the price level changes in one country, leading to other countries buying more of that country's goods (because they are cheaper). This increases net exports (and real GDP). This can also be known as the foreign purchases effect.

Fiscal multipliers

A *fiscal multiplier* is a measure of the effects of an increase in government spending on national economic output, or GDP. If investment increases or there is an increase in government spending then consumers' income also increases, and they will then spend more.

Marginal propensity to consume

It is based on the idea of a marginal propensity to consume (MPC). This measures the increase in the amount a consumer spends (rather than saves), as a result of an increase in consumer income. In this instance, a 'consumer' could be an individual, a household or society.

As a simplified example, if an individual were to receive a bonus on top of their salary of $400, spent $300 on a new bicycle and saved $100, their MPC would be 0.75.

Economists use calculations based on household income and spending to predict MPC by income level. Generally, households with lower incomes have a higher MPC, as they may have fewer of their immediate needs and desires already sufficiently satisfied than a higher-income household.

However, because fiscal policy is generally not enacted through direct payments to consumers, an MPC can also depend on the way in which fiscal spending happens. Different fiscal policies can have very different fiscal multipliers.

Government budgets and fiscal policies

Government sources of finance

In the USA, the federal budget is the government's estimate of revenue and spending for each fiscal year – other national governments produce similar budgets. The budget sets out what the government will be spending money on – what the main fiscal policies might be over that year. This money can come from direct taxation, the sale of government bonds (a form of borrowing), loans or other securities.

The Federal Reserve is the monetary policy authority. It can impact the cost of money and the cost of credit to help achieve a healthy economy. It has three main goals – maximizing employment, stabilizing prices and monitoring interest rates.

Monetary policy and the market

How markets impact policy

Monetary policy is what central banks can do to influence the supply of money and credit in the economy. What happens to this supply affects the cost of credit (this is what we mean when economists say interest rates are rising or falling). These changes can impact the wider economy in positive and negative ways.

By implementing effective monetary policy, central banks try to keep prices stable (avoiding high inflation), aiming towards long-term economic growth and maximizing the employment rate.

Specific things that central banks can do

As an example of the kinds of things central banks can do, there are three main instruments with which the US Federal Reserve influences the economy. They are *open market operations*, the *discount rate* and *reserve requirements*.

Open market operations

This is the trading of government securities – money loaned to the government to help fund day-to-day activities, particular infrastructure or military projects. They guarantee the full repayment of the principal invested at maturity and often pay periodic interest payments as well. It is the most flexible and therefore the most commonly used monetary policy instrument.

The Fed offers these government-issued securities for sale to various primary dealers on an open market, and they also buy them back from these primary dealers. These activities change the price paid for these as the demand goes up and down (the more the Fed buys, the less is available so the more the price goes up, but the lower their yield).

When the Fed buys these securities, it is increasing the money in the market (putting money into the economy from the Federal Reserve). This in turn decreases the cost of borrowing – the interest rate – as more money is available.

If the Fed sells these securities, this can be a signal that the interest rate will go up – with less money supply in the economy, it is more expensive to borrow it. This might happen to stop too much money being in the market (liquidity), which can result in inflation.

The discount rate

The discount rate is the interest rate at which banks and other qualified institutions are charged to borrow money from the Federal Reserve. This decreases the cost of money and is another way of increasing the supply of money in the economy.

Reserve requirements

Reserve requirements are the amount of money that banks must keep either in their vaults or on deposit at a Federal Reserve Bank as a proportion of their liabilities. Increasing these requirements reduces the money supply in the economy.

The monetary policies of central banks allow them to influence the supply, demand and cost of money, which can impact national economies. They are directly responsible for interest rates and the overall cost of money, which affects the financial lives of everyone.

Keynesianism and monetarism

John Maynard Keynes proposed that most of the negative effects of the Great Depression in the USA could have been avoided if the government had enacted fiscal policies that increased spending. This was the beginning of a new era of economic thought that demonstrated that governments should actively manage economies.

Graphing the money market.
(i) MD = Money demand
MS = Money supply
(ii) Money supply increases at MS_3 when the central bank buys securities, interest rate falls at i_3 due to more supply
(ii) Money supply decreases at MS_2 when the central bank sells securities, interest rate rises at i_2 due to less supply.

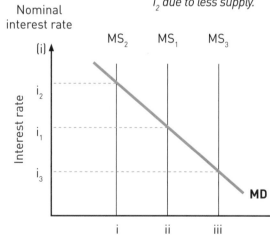

John Maynard Keynes (1883–1946), who set out the principles of Keynesian economics.

This is because as the sales of a company reduce, this in turn reduces income and thus demand. This can lead to a long-term *recessionary cycle*. Keynesian economics suggests that governments can generate the demand needed to escape this cycle by increasing their spending on goods and services.

The alternative approach is called *monetarism*, where controlled increases in the money supply are used to combat recessions. Monetarists would say that apart from this, governments should avoid getting involved in free markets, or the rest of the economy.

In essence, the difference between the two is that monetarism involves the control of money in the economy, whilst Keynesianism involves government expenditure.

INFLATION CAUSED BY GOVERNMENT POLICY

Inflation is a description for an increase in prices, sustained over a period. It means that the same amount of currency buys less than before – or the same amount of goods costs more – therefore the purchasing power of consumers decreases.

Inflation normally happens slowly over time, but certain economic conditions can increase it too quickly. For instance, if there is too much readily available money or credit in the economic system this can result in inflation increasing too quickly.

INTERNATIONAL TRADE
Trade restrictions

National governments commonly use three tools to restrict trade: tariffs (which are a kind of tax, and the most used), quotas and regulations.

Tariffs: These are taxes on goods imported from abroad. The effect is to artificially increase the price of these imported products when they come into the domestic market. This means that domestic products should be more attractive to consumers due to price. They represent income for the government, and they reduce competitive pressure on domestic producers. However, they do reduce consumer choice.

Quotas: This is about setting a limit on the quantity of goods coming into the domestic market to reduce supply. If domestic producers are unable to increase output to compensate, this can create shortages (as there is more demand than supply). This can cause the price of domestic goods to rise.

Floating and fixed exchange rate systems

Regulations: Both imports and exports can have licence requirements imposed, introducing restrictions to trade for those without a licence and reducing supply. There are also minimum standards (such as for health or environmental safety) that can be imposed on products that are being traded, which can also reduce supply.

Four of the key currencies involved in the exchange rate system.

When one currency is traded for another, the rate at which one is bought and sold compared to the other is known as the exchange rate. It is the value of one currency in another.

A *fixed exchange rate* is a nominal rate set by an authority (such as a central bank) and pegged *Fixed exchange rate* to another currency (or a collection of them, known as a basket). A floating exchange rate is set in foreign exchange markets depending on supply and demand and it changes up and down constantly.

If a central bank decides to fix the exchange rate at US$1 per local currency unit, they will have to keep enough reserves of foreign currency to be able to supply the market at that rate.

In a floating model, when demand is low, the value of a currency will reduce. This makes *A floating model* foreign, imported goods more expensive and increases demand for domestic goods and services, which in turn creates more jobs and this can correct the market.

In a fixed system, market pressures can still create changes in the rate. For instance, a central bank may revalue the rate if an underground market for currency develops. This is to bring the two rates in line with each other, thereby stopping the need for the illegal market.

MODERN PERSPECTIVES
Thomas Piketty and income and wealth inequality

Piketty's basic idea in his 2019 book *Capital and Ideology* is a moral one: that inequality is illegitimate, and thus needs constructed ideologies in order to be justified and moderated. He suggests that a 90% rate of inheritance tax would be one part of the solution to this inequality.

The Doughnut Economy

Created by economist Kate Raworth, Doughnut Economics envisions a different economic system focused on sustainability, society and the environment rather than endless GDP growth.

It is designed around two metaphorical concentric rings – the first a social foundation of minimum societal standards and the second an ecological ceiling to prevent economic activity from overwhelming the life-supporting systems of the planet. The idea is that between these two boundaries is a space that is socially just as well as ecologically safe.

It aims for regenerative economies that thrive and incorporates systems-thinking to recognize that societies and economies and the living world are interdependent systems.

For businesses, this means adopting regeneration and distributive practices as key components of their strategy and operations as well as aligning the design of the business through their purpose, networks, governance, ownership and finance.

The Doughnut Economy model.

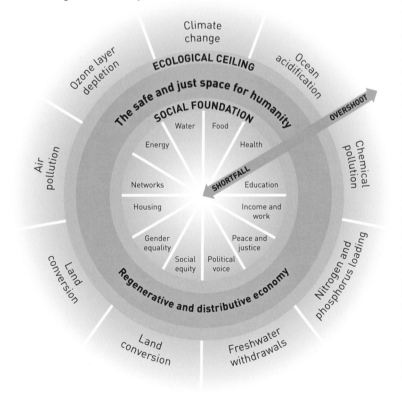

CHRISTINE LAGARDE: IMF
Christine Lagarde is a French lawyer and politician who has been the Managing Director of the International Monetary Fund (IMF) since 2011. Lagarde was the first woman to become finance minister of a G8 economy and is the first woman to head the IMF.

In her early career, Lagarde worked for several international law firms in Paris and New York, specializing in labour, antitrust, and mergers and acquisitions law. In 2005, she became the Minister of Economy, Finances, and Industry under French Prime Minister Dominique de Villepin.

Because of her ministerial position, she was a key figure in the French government's response to the global financial crisis of 2008 and proposed a $45 billion government stimulus package to help boost the French economy and a $160 billion loan from the IMF to stabilise the global financial system.

In 2011, Lagarde was nominated by the French government to succeed Dominique Strauss-Kahn as managing director of the IMF. She was elected to the position by the IMF's Board of Governors and took office on 5 July 2011. As chairman of the G20 in that year she set in motion a wide-ranging work agenda on the reform of the international monetary system.

Lagarde has been credited with helping to stabilize the global economy during her tenure as managing director of the IMF. In October 2016, Lagarde was re-elected by the IMF's Board of Governors to a second five-year term as managing director, beginning on 5 July 2017.

SUSTAINABILITY AND BUSINESS IN SOCIETY

Corporate social responsibility (CSR) is a wide-ranging idea that has many ways of being expressed. At its core are business practices and policies that try to have a positive impact on the world, in addition to maximizing profits. These could be anything from minimizing the environmental impacts of a business, to enabling employees to volunteer or donating directly to charity.

CSR can form a key part of the public relations strategy of a business, with the focus on improving the image of a brand, but both CSR and *corporate sustainability* aim to make companies ethically profitable.

However, there is some argument that CSR activities have tended to look to the past, adding up what has been done (amount of donations, volunteering days, etc.) and is mainly about reputation or compliance. Whereas corporate sustainability looks forward in a business – creating sustainable strategies to help secure the future, whether in opening new markets, creating more resilient and eco-friendly supply chains, or improving operations.

Another key difference is that CSR is often managed by communication teams, whereas sustainability is a key part of the operations and marketing structures and targets the whole value chain – from stakeholders to consumers.

There is evidence to suggest that companies that are 'high sustainability' firms outperform the competition over time (both in the stock market and in accounting terms).

Examples of corporate sustainability strategies

1. *Innovation and technology:* The ability to change the products and services created by a business to reduce waste production.
2. *Collaboration:* Facilitating knowledge sharing in networks of partner companies to help with innovation.
3. *Process improvement*: Continuous improvement is needed to reduce waste. Informing employees of plans is key, so the integration of new or improved processes is successful.
4. *Sustainability reporting:* Reporting of business performance in relation to goals. These goals are sometimes part of the corporate mission.
5. *Greening the supply chain:* Sustainable procurement is important if the impact of a business on the environment is larger than the products that they consume. The B Corporation certification model encourages companies to focus on this.

GREENWASHING

In certain circumstances, some less reputable companies might look to boost their image by appearing to be environmentally friendly, but not actually acting to reduce their environmental impact. This is a PR process known as *greenwashing*.

If a company is greenwashing, they might be making token gestures that show a small effort but ignore more important environmental issues – a courier asking customers to bundle their deliveries to reduce pollution, but not replacing their fleet with electric vehicles or bicycles.

They could be vague about their efforts, suggesting things without evidence or avoiding talking about how their activities might be checked.

They might use certain buzzwords such as 'non-toxic', 'all natural', or 'eco conscious' without explanation or definition. These don't mean anything by themselves. Or they may make claims that are redundant – for instance advertising that a packet of spinach is 'vegan' (when it is already obvious that it is).

The use of environmental imagery such as leaves or forests on obviously harmful products, such as petrol or oil, could be another example of greenwashing.

Some consider carbon offsetting to be a form of greenwashing, as it doesn't reduce the initial amount of carbon being released into the environment.

B Corps

One relatively new scheme is the *B Corporation Certification*, which encourages socially responsible governance and business practices by enforcing specific criteria. These then permit a company to advertise themselves as a 'B Corp'.

Becoming a B Corp involves completing an impact assessment that examines transparency about operating procedures, social and environmental performance, and legal accountability.

In the USA, Articles of Association need to be amended to ensure that the impacts of business decisions on all stakeholders are considered – this includes not just customers and shareholders, but also wider society and the environment. Equivalent legal changes exist for B-Corp certification in other countries.

Brought to you by the community of

Certified

B

Corporations®

A Certified B-Corp logo.

There is a process of regular recertification, and the criteria are dynamic, meaning that they can adapt to what is appropriate in the current business and environmental situation.

The organization that certifies B Corps is called B Lab, and they also provide a community, guidance and support to B Corps.

LEED certification

Businesses that have large amounts of real estate or own significant office space may aim to improve their environmental credentials and decrease the impact of their buildings while improving the efficiency, health and well-being of the occupants.

The most widely used certification scheme is LEED (Leadership in Energy and Environmental Design), which gives buildings a green rating. It provides a framework that allows businesses to measure sustainability achievements in the design, construction, operation and energy performance of many kinds of buildings.

Ensuring that buildings are LEED certified also provides businesses with economic advantages as rental rates tend to be higher, and vacancy rates are lower than non-green-rated properties. Certification can also help investors meet ESG goals (see below) because it encourages the implementation of management practices that focus on longer-term sustainable outcomes.

ESG investing

Environmental, social and governance (ESG) investing is the idea of identifying these non-financial factors as part of the analysis of investment opportunities – these areas can be considered a key part of the material risks and growth possibilities.

Although there isn't one specific list of ESG criteria, they are usually interlinked, combining aspects of environmental, social and governance matters.

Here are some of the areas of company behaviour or attitudes that potential ESG investments might want to examine:

Environmental issues (conserving the natural world)	Social issues (considering people and relationships)	Governance (the standards used to run the company)
Climate crisis and carbon emissions	Human rights and labour standards	Audit committee structure
Water or air pollution	Data protection	Make-up of the board
Biodiversity and deforestation	Diversity and gender	Bribery and corruption
Energy efficiency	Employee mental health	Political lobbying and donations
Waste management	Relations in the community	Executive compensation
Water scarcity	Customer satisfaction	Whistleblower schemes

Not all these components can be measured with a monetary value, and there is no specific standardized approach for ESG metrics so different weight might be given to different behaviours by different investors.

Chapter Four
OPERATIONS

Operations management • Theories of operational management • Forecasting • Supply chain management • What is a project? • Managing risks • What is agile? • Tracking progress

THEORY OF CONSTRAINTS

BUSINESS PROCESS REDESIGN

SIX SIGMA

LEARN ENTERPRISE STYLE OPERATIONS

SEASONALITY AND CYCLES

DAYS' INVENTORY OUTSTANDING

THEORIES OF OPERATIONAL MANAGEMENT

FORECASTING

INVENTORY MANAGEMENT

SUPPLY CHAIN MANAGEMENT

INVENTORY COSTS AND BENEFITS

OPERATIONS

OPERATIONS MANAGEMENT

EXPONENTIAL SMOOTHING

GANTT CHART

VISUAL MANAGEMENT TOOLS

THE PROCESS FLOW DIAGRAM

ACTIVITY ON NODE DIAGRAM

DEPENDENCY OR DESIGN STRUCTURE MATRIX

PROCESS STRUCTURES

QUEUE SYSTEM DESIGN

BOTTLENECKS WAIT TIMES PROCESS CAPACITY

JOB SHOPS   BATCH SHOPS
ASSEMBLY LINES
CONTINUOUS FLOW   FLOW LINES

Operations is the work of efficiently managing the way in which a business creates goods or services. Often, it is the behind-the-scenes work of managing the ongoing systems and processes that facilitate the outputs of your business.

Examples of this could be the documentation of specific work procedures, such as regular cleaning routines or the layout of a workspace to improve the speed of service. It can also refer to the small (or large) elements of work necessary to achieve a particular project.

OPERATIONS MANAGEMENT

Operations management provides frameworks and tools to analyze, maintain and optimize key decisions around operational processes. It looks at the planning, optimization of resources and inputs, and the organization and supervision of how products and services are designed and delivered.

The process flow diagram

The *process flow diagram* is a type of flowchart that shows the relationships between the main components at an industrial plant or factory. It is commonly used in chemical engineering and process engineering and is also sometimes called a *schematic flow diagram* or *system flow diagram*. It can help document, model or improve a process.

It uses symbols and notes to show how a process works and what is happening at each stage and usually consists of:

- *Flow units:* Inputs being transformed into outputs (such as raw materials).
- *Buffers:* Holding areas for flow units in between activities.
- *Activities:* Steps for transforming flow units into outputs.

Once you have a process model, the key terms and concepts involved in the analysis are:

- *Inventory* (sometimes called *work-in-progress*): The total number of flow units in a system. It doesn't include any inputs yet to be processed or outputs that have finished the process. In certain circumstances, customers can be referred to as inventory units.
- *Flow time:* The time taken for a flow unit to go through an entire process (e.g. the time it takes a truck to drive from Rome to Berlin).
- *Flow rate:* The number of flow units that complete the flow process within a given time frame (e.g. the number of trucks that have driven from Rome to Berlin in the past day).

A process flow diagram: the arrows indicate the direction of flow.

61

- *Demand-constrained:* When the flow rate is limited by customer demand for the output.
- *Supply-constrained:* When the flow rate is too slow relative to the rate of customer demand.
- *Queue:* The line of inventory units (e.g. customers, coffees, etc.) waiting for the next activity in the process flow.

Bottlenecks, wait times and process capacity

When a process is not optimized, the flow of units can get held up at certain activities, causing delays to all the following flow units.

A *bottleneck* is one way of referring to the slowest activity in the whole process flow. *Service time*, or *processing time*, is the time taken by an activity to process one flow unit (i.e. the time taken to make an order for a customer). *Wait time* is the time waiting in between each activity or step in the process and process capacity is the maximum number of flow units that can go through a given process or activity in a set time.

The capacity of a process is always defined by the weakest link – the slowest activity. Total *process capacity* always equals the process capacity of the bottleneck. If only 20 people can get through the bottleneck in 40 minutes, then only 20 people can clear all the steps in a process.

The red box below shows the bottleneck in fittings for snowboarding equipment.

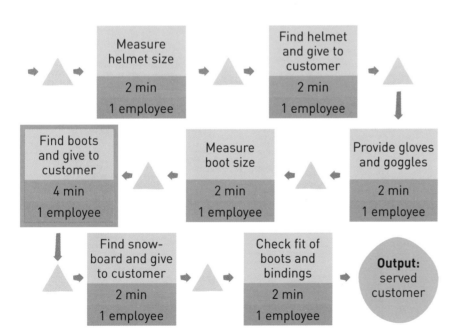

In the example at left, with customers as flow units, the activity that takes four minutes leads to a bottleneck – because the previous activity takes half as long, as more customers enter the flow, a queue will build up at that stage in the process.

Customers are going through the process of being fitted for snowboarding equipment. The bottleneck is highlighted in red.

Because the 'find boots' step takes four minutes but the previous step takes two minutes, each customer who is added to the queue will add two minutes to the wait time before the 'find boots' step.

You can see this in the row highlighted in orange in the table opposite:

To reduce wait times, and remove this bottleneck, you can add labour (increase employees to two) to decrease the processing time at the 'find boots' activity.

	Jo	Ed	Rashid
Measure helmet size	2	2	2
Wait time in queue	0	0	0
Find helmet	2	2	2
Wait time in queue	0	0	0
Measure boot size	2	2	2
Wait time in queue	0	2	4
Find boots	4	4	4
Wait time in queue	0	0	0
Find snowboard	2	2	2
Total flow time	**12**	**14**	**16**

Queue system design

Sometimes bottlenecks are a result of the design of the queuing system. For instance, if there are multiple queues to choose from then there are often unequal line lengths, which can lead to longer wait times.

Queuing theory looks at the whole system of queuing, including the customer arrival rate, the number of staff serving, the number of customers, the capacity of the waiting area, average service completion time, and queuing discipline. *Queuing discipline* refers to the rules of the queue, i.e. first-in-first-out, prioritized or serve-in-random-order.

Queuing discipline

Creating one single queue and then sending the customer at the front to the next available cashier reduces average wait times, minimizes the idle time for workers and increases the process capacity.

This single-line, multi-channel queueing system is much better at handling variability of inter-arrival times (the time between one customer arriving and the next). Whole Foods is an example of a company that has used this system successfully in high-volume locations.

Little's Law is a calculation that lets us solve for important variables, such as the average wait in a queue or the number of customers in the queue based on two other inputs:

Little's Law

$$L = \lambda W$$

Where L is the average number of units (this can be customers) in a queue, λ is the arrival rate of these units and W is the time a customer (or other kind of unit) spends in the system.

It can also be rearranged to determine wait time in a customer queue. This is another way of writing it out:

$$\frac{(Line\ length(L_q)}{Arrival\ rate(\lambda)} = Wait\ time(W_q)$$

How long will each customer have to wait for service?

Sakasegawa's Formula

Seasonal variations

Queueing at the cafe

For example, if you're queuing at a coffee shop, you can use Little's Law to estimate how long it would take to get your coffee.

Assume that there are 15 people in the queue, one barista making drinks, and two people are served per minute. Using the formula on page 63 shows that you would expect to wait 7.5 minutes for your coffee:

$$\frac{15 \text{ people in line}}{A2 \text{ people served per minute}} = 7.5 \text{ minutes of waiting}$$

It is also used in manufacturing to predict lead times based on production rates and the quantity of work-in-progress. The formula then is rearranged (and relabelled) to:

$$WIP = Throughput \times Lead\ time$$

The other important calculation of note here is (a simplified version of) Sakasegawa's Formula. You can use this formula to work out how long the average queue will be for a given process even when there are multiple queues (channels) involved. It also takes into account the utilization of the 'servers' – how much of their potential capacity is being used. This can sometimes be used as a proxy for productivity.
The formula is:

$$Line\ length = \frac{Utilization\ \sqrt{2(Number\ of\ channels + 1)}}{1 - Utilization}$$

Variability

When accounting for *seasonal variations* in customer numbers the changes are usually more predictable (more customers for coats in winter; more customers in a restaurant at lunchtime). But variability due to small fluctuations such as a delayed train, or day-to-day changes, means although you might on average get a stable number of customers in a day, the inter-arrival times can be very different. Businesses can usually mitigate the variability of inter-arrival times by making customers set appointments or make reservations.

Both Little's Law and Sakasegawa's Formula can account for this variability with minor adjustments.

Process structures: job shops to assembly line flows

In operations management, there are different categories of process structure, based on how the business needs to function. There are processes that relate to cost structure; standardization needs; output volume; and production flexibility. Each of these different process structures will suit certain kinds of business operation.

The process structures below are ordered from lowest fixed cost to highest fixed cost.

Job shops: Produce limited batches of many different products. Usually, each set of products is customized, and each product can require different steps and processing times. Examples of job shops include a printer that produces printed material, customized for each particular customer, or a developer who creates customized websites for their clients.

A batch shop such as a bakery can produce a wide variety of products.

Batch shops: Batch shops can produce different products in larger groups, but usually all the products they make have the same process flow. A business producing T-shirts of different sizes and colours or a bakery preparing different kinds of cakes are examples of batch shops. These processes make one type of T-shirt or cake in a batch and then set up to change to a different type of batch.

Flow lines or worker-paced assembly: This consists of independent stations that produce the same or very similar parts. Each part follows the same set of processes. The output on a flow line is determined by the slowest operation – the bottleneck. This is similar to an assembly line but the parts move at the pace of the slowest worker, rather than at a constant rate dictated by the line speed.

Flow lines

Assembly lines or machine-paced assembly: This process has individual parts moving at a controlled rate through a well-defined process. The assembly line moves each component part to the resources (worker or machine), and each of these must complete its task before the line can continue. This system needs a balanced line, meaning that each worker (or machine) completes its task in an amount of time that is similar. This line will move at the speed of the operation that is slowest.

Assembly lines

Continuous flow: This is producing items continuously, usually in an extremely automated process. Examples can include chemical plants, power plants and oil refineries. A continuous flow process can need to run 24 hours a day because starting or ending the process can be complicated.

Continuous flow

You can see how these process structures compare on the matrix overleaf (chart at top left):

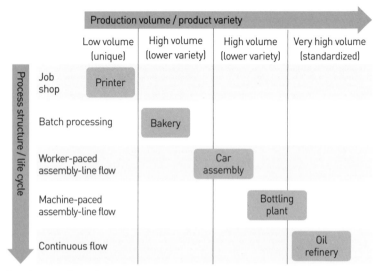

Continuous flow chart

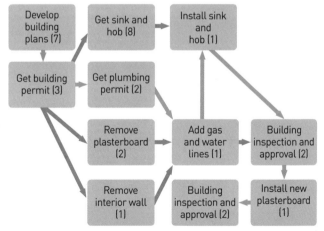

Design structure matrix

Activity-on-node diagram

Examples of other visual tools for managing projects

Dependency or design structure matrix (centre left)

A *design structure matrix* is a table that shows a list of tasks in the order they are performed (top to bottom and left to right). An X indicates that the downstream activity in a row requires the upstream task (at the top of the column) to be completed first.

Activity-on-node diagram (below left)

An *activity-on-node diagram* is used to show which tasks must be completed before other activities can start. This can be referred to as 'finish-to-start' precedence. The numbers refer to the time frame, in this example, days.

Gantt chart (below)

A *Gantt chart* uses a series of horizontal lines to visually demonstrate a project schedule. Modern versions often show the amount of work done vs. the planned time taken for that work as well as dependency relationships (work that requires other work to be completed first).

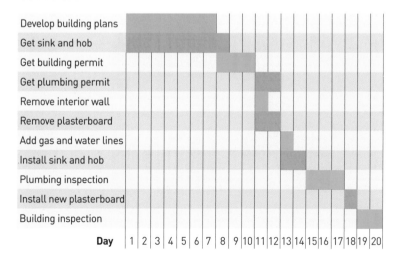

Gantt chart

Inventory costs and benefits

Managing warehouses and inventory levels to minimize costs but still successfully meet customer demand is an important aspect of operations, most particularly for manufacturing and other commercial companies.

As the amount of inventory available is increased, there are benefits and costs to the business:

Benefits:
- Products are available to consumers.
- Customer service level is higher as a result.

Costs:
- It requires more physical space to store.
- Working capital is tied up in stock.
- There is a risk of obsolescence if stock is held too long.

Checking inventory in a warehouse.

To try to balance these there are various systems that can be used to monitor inventory and make sure it is at the optimal level. There are certain measurements that are necessary to do this.

Inventory management

Successful *inventory management* means identifying which items (and how many) need ordering or creating at any given time. Inventory is tracked from purchase to sale, while identifying and responding to sales patterns and trends to ensure there is always enough stock for customer demand, and enough to warn of a shortage (and fix it) before inventory runs out.

To do this, you need to understand stock levels and stock location (where in the warehouse). Inventory management software can follow and track the flow of products from the supplier through a production process and on to the consumer. Inside a warehouse at a more detailed level, it can track the receipt of stock, picking, packing and shipping.

This kind of tracking and management of inventory allows a company to keep the appropriate levels of stock on hand, reducing the risk of stockouts or incorrect records.

DAYS INVENTORY OUTSTANDING

Days inventory outstanding (DIO) measures the days required for one *rotation of inventory* – the average number of days that a company holds their inventory for before selling it.

To calculate DIO, you divide average inventory by the cost of goods sold, multiplied by 365.

To improve DIO, there are various basic techniques:

- offering discounts on items that are spending a long time in inventory
- reducing the types of product available (reducing raw materials needed and speeding up the flow of inventory back into the system)
- reducing lead times for suppliers to reduce the need to hold stock as a safety buffer
- forecasting demand for inventory as accurately as possible

In the USA, all public companies must track inventory to comply with SEC rules and the Sarbanes-Oxley Act of 2002. Management processes must be documented to prove that they have complied.

These are some of the most common methods, techniques and processes used to manage inventory:

Types of inventory management

- *ABC analysis:* Identifying the most and least popular items in an inventory.
- *Batch tracking:* Grouping similar products to track expiration dates and find defective items.
- *Bulk shipments:* Usually unpacked materials that are loaded directly on to transport. This means buying, storing and shipping inventory in large amounts.
- *Consignment:* A business doesn't pay the supplier until a given product is sold. The supplier still has ownership of the inventory until it is sold.
- *Cross-docking:* Unloading products directly from a supplier's vehicle to a delivery vehicle. This massively reduces the need for warehousing.
- *Demand forecasting:* A form of predictive analytics that tries to predict customer demand.
- *Dropshipping:* A manufacturer or supplier ships products directly from its warehouse to the customer.
- *Economic order quantity* (EOQ): A management technique to determine exactly how much inventory to order to reduce warehousing and increase efficiency.
- *FIFO* and *LIFO:* First in, first out (FIFO) means the oldest stock is sold first. Last in, first out (LIFO) assumes that prices always rise, so the most recently-bought inventory is sold first.

This level of empty shelves in a store may be a sign that inventory management is not as good as it should be.

- *Just in time* (JIT) inventory: Receiving goods only as needed for production, to reduce inventory costs. This method requires accurate demand forecasting.
- *Lean manufacturing:* A methodology focused on reducing or removing waste or anything that provides no value to the customer from the manufacturing system.
- *Reorder point formula:* A formula to identify the minimum amount of stock reached before reordering.
- *Perpetual inventory management:* This involves recording stock sales and usage in real time through an automated process.
- *Safety stock:* Ensuring extra stock is always set aside in case the items become difficult to replenish.

THEORIES OF OPERATIONAL MANAGEMENT
Business process redesign

Business process redesign is the radical re-engineering of business processes to achieve dramatic improvements in critical elements, such as quality, output, cost, service and speed. It aims for specific goals such as cutting costs, increasing return on investment, or reducing process redundancies on a large scale.

Many kinds of business process, such as the workflows in sales, production or financial management can be redesigned to meet the goals. Sometimes, redesigning a particular process can influence other processes within a business.

Business process redesign

The process can be different from one business to another, but the steps listed below are a summary of how it can work:

1. Gather data about and map the current state of business processes. Understand how the process is performing currently.
2. Analyze and identify errors, gaps and delays that are holding the process up, in detail.
3. Search for possible improvements and validate them. Check that the steps are necessary. For instance, if there are steps that are only about informing someone, consider replacing them with an automated notification.
4. Design a new, future-state process map to solve the problems that have been identified. This might be an entirely new process. Create *key performance indicators* (KPIs) for each step.
5. Put in place these changes, inform on-board stakeholders, be aware of dependencies and monitor KPIs.

Six Sigma

Six Sigma is a methodology for improving operations management – primarily for engineering and manufacturing businesses, though it can be adopted for other businesses. It refers to quality control tools used to eliminate defects and improve processes and was created by Motorola in the 1980s.

Improving operations management

Six Sigma is a data-led process that reviews mistakes and defects and emphasizes time improvements, while also reducing manufacturing defects to no more than 3.4 per million units (or events).

One of the most important methodologies of Six Sigma is DMAIC (define, measure, analyze, improve and control). This is also the method that creates the steps for each project:

- *Define* the requirements for the customer or the key goals to be achieved.
- *Measure* what happens currently and what measurement would meet the goals as defined.
- *Analyze* underlying causes of the problem, to ascertain changes needed to meet the goals.
- *Improve* processes so that they achieve the goals.
- *Control* these processes so that in the future the goal is always achieved.

There are many tools used in the Six Sigma process, some of which are borrowed from other methodologies. For instance, the work-breakdown structure can be used as a project management tool; lean methodology from JIT manufacturing; various flowchart styles from engineering or data processing; the spaghetti diagram from manufacturing (this shows how things move back and forth from one place or department to the other – if this diagram looks like a pile of cooked spaghetti then there are efficiencies that can probably be made); or the 5S system from Japanese continuous improvement (known as kaizen).

Toyota and Motorola made key strides in getting rid of waste from their production processes.

Lean enterprise-style operations

Lean enterprise describes a practice of eliminating or reducing inefficiencies in a production process. The basic principles were created by Toyota's Toyota Production System and Motorola – they both emphasized removing wasteful elements of the production process.

There are eight basic areas in which lean enterprise looks to eliminate waste: defects, overproduction, waiting, non-utilized talent, transportation, inventory, motion, extra-processing. There is a Japanese term, *muda*, for these areas, which translates to 'waste'.

Lean enterprise principles

In *Lean Thinking: Banish Waste and Create Wealth in Your Corporation*, by economists James P. Womack and Daniel T. Jones, lean enterprise has the following five key tenets:

1. *Value:* How customers value a certain product as it relates to their wants or needs.
2. *Value stream:* A breakdown of the complete life cycle of a product or service, from where raw materials are acquired, to manufacturing, sale and delivery of inventory, and consumption of items by customers.
3. *Flow:* If any part of the value stream is inefficient, this is wasteful and doesn't create customer value.

4. *Pull:* No products or services should be produced until there is obvious demand (or actual orders) from end customers.
5. *Perfection:* To succeed, lean enterprise must become part of company culture – every member of staff has a role in putting in place and perfecting the lean process.

Theory of Constraints

The *Theory of Constraints* (TOC) is a methodology used to identify the most important constraint or limiting factor that is stopping a goal being achieved and then systematically working on improving this constraint until it ceases to be the limiting factor (often called a bottleneck in manufacturing) in the process. It was created by Dr Eliyahu Goldratt, and introduced in his 1984 novel *The Goal*.

The core idea is that all processes will have one specific constraint that needs improving to improve the total process. In addition, time spent optimizing elements of the process that are not constraints will not give significant benefits; only a sustained focus on improving the constraint itself will help achieve the goal (in most cases, this is ultimately achieving more profit). Once this constraint no longer limits the throughput of the process, the focus moves to the next constraint. Part of the power of the TOC comes from this strong focus on a single goal and a specific problem.

Theory of Constraints

There is a specific set of tools used in the Theory of Constraints to achieve that goal, which include:

- *The Five Focusing Steps:* Used to identify and eliminate constraints.
- *The Thinking Processes:* These are tools for analyzing and solving problems.
- *Throughput Accounting:* This is used to measure performance and guide management decisions.

FORECASTING

Forecasting demand is one of the key ways in which you can attempt to predict demand for products or services. There are a few methods for this.

Forecasting demand

Extrapolating from historical data is a time-series data method. It uses quantitative data on past outcomes to predict future ones. This can be from a short period (yesterday's sales data) or a longer period (last summer's sales data). It usually requires data from different points in time spread across regular intervals.

This method doesn't include the factors that might have caused a specific set of data – for instance, a cold winter might have caused high levels of sales of scarves – but extrapolation methods are neutral about such causes.

The simplest way of doing this is to use the last outcome as the forecast. For instance, if a cafe sold 100 coffees yesterday, they might expect to sell 100 coffees today. This is just a single observation and is referred to as the *naive method*.

In most other methods, multiple datapoints are needed and a formula is used to project the next value in a forecast.

In longer-term forecast trends, seasonality and cycles may begin to play a part in forecasting – a regular decrease or increase in values over time, repeatedly seeing higher sales in a particular season or patterns of consumer behaviour related to the business cycle.

Exponential smoothing is a method for calculating forecasts that gives greater weight to recent observations, reflects all observations, and adjusts for forecast errors. It includes a smoothing constant used to calibrate the effect of the error measure.

Exponential smoothing

The full formula for exponential smoothing is:

$$F_t = F_{t-1} + (A_{t-1} - F_{t-1}) \times \alpha$$

Where F = forecast, t = time period, A = actual outcome, and α = smoothing constant. You multiply the error measure by the smoothing constant and add the result to the last forecast from the last period.

The best value for the smoothing constant can be identified through trial and error, by testing the results for different values and comparing them.

There are a number of other methods for forecasting, and the increase in machine learning models that help to analyze business insights means there are many available.

You can compare forecasting methods to help choose the right one by using one of a series of measures:

- *Mean absolute error:* This determines the absolute errors in the relevant forecasts with equal weight.
- *Root mean squared error:* This gives greater weight to larger forecast errors.
- *Mean absolute percentage error:* This allows forecasts for two different products to be compared.

When you have no historical data, for instance with a new product, you can't extrapolate. Causal models can help here, as they use inferences about causes and effects as well as time-series data. For instance, you could use time-series data for a similar existing product to predict demand for a new product.

If there is no relevant time-series data, then you could conduct customer surveys to determine intent to purchase, or you could conduct expert panels to determine your best forecast for a new product.

SUPPLY CHAIN MANAGEMENT

In any supply chain, there are usually a series of sellers – from raw materials sold to a factory to a retailer selling to a consumer.

As demand increases, each seller might begin to order more units to supply demand. If the retailer orders more, the wholesaler might then order more, and this continues back up the chain. This is called the *bullwhip effect*, because at each step the number of orders over consumer demand increases – like an uncoiling whip. There are various reasons why this effect can be triggered – promotions, overreactive ordering, bulk ordering or forward buying.

Factory	←	Parts manufacturer	←	Raw materials suppliers
↓				
Wholesaler	→	Retailer	→	Consumer

Bullwhip effect

One approach to mitigate this is to increase the information available in the supply chain. If a retailer lets the wholesaler know that they are running a promotion this month, and that is why they have ordered more units, this might prevent the wholesaler over-ordering for the following month. By sharing both sales data and marketing and sales plans with suppliers up the chain, bullwhip effects can be avoided.

The risk of carrying too much or too little supply or inventory is likely different for each part of the supply chain and sometimes this can lead to a difference in the ideal quantity of supply that would maximize profit across the supply chain. There are ways of mitigating these differing incentives for the various players in a supply chain, for instance by creating a *buyback contract*, whereby the supplier agrees to buy back the units that the retailer is unable to sell. This may increase the order quantities from the retailer.

Buyback contract

SHERYL SANDBERG: FACEBOOK/META

The chief operating officer (COO) of Facebook (and then Meta), in June 2012, Sandberg was elected to Facebook's board of directors by the existing board members, becoming the first woman to serve on its board.

Her career began as an economist at the World Bank, and then at management consulting firm McKinsey & Company, she advised clients on strategy and operations. In 2001, she joined Google as vice president of global online sales and operations, growing the advertising and publishing businesses, launching programmes such as AdSense and AdWords, and Google's philanthropy initiatives, such as Google.org.

In 2007, she joined Facebook as its COO. At Facebook, Sandberg oversaw the company's business operations, including sales, marketing, business development, human resources, public policy, and communications. She has played a key role in helping Facebook grow to a global company with over two billion users.

Sandberg is also the founder of Leanin.org, a nonprofit organization that works to empower women in the workplace. She is the author of *Lean In: Women, Work, and the Will to Lead* (2013) and *Option B: Facing Adversity, Building Resilience, and Finding Joy* (2017).

WHAT IS A PROJECT?

Initiating the project.

Working out key schedule dates.

A *project* can be summarized simply as a series of tasks that must be completed to reach a desired outcome. You could also consider it as a set of inputs and outputs that are needed to achieve a particular goal.

Starting project initiation and completing project initiation

Project initiation is another way of talking about 'starting off' a project. There are a series of key steps to take to begin a project in the most effective way. They will differ from project to project or depending on the style of project management being used, but the core elements are usually similar.

First, you need to outline why the project is necessary and define how it will succeed. You should also research the reasons for the project and examine if it is likely to succeed.

Whatever the specific style of project management, you will need to create a form of project charter – an agreement on how the project is structured and executed. You will also need to create or assign your team – selecting the right sets of people and skills to successfully complete the project. This whole set of processes is then reviewed and updated as needed throughout the project.

After initiating a project, you will be able to outline the plans and schedules associated with the project, look at risk management and communication plans, establish status and tracking metrics, create KPIs and build forecasts, as appropriate.

Planning and the project schedule

A *project schedule* is a timetable that shows the start and end date of all the tasks that make up the project. In includes the relationship of these tasks to each other and who (or what resources) are responsible for delivering the tasks.

The project schedule:
• outlines time required for the tasks
• establishes milestones to be achieved to complete the project on time
• allocates available resources to the tasks
• can be represented in different ways to suit various stakeholders

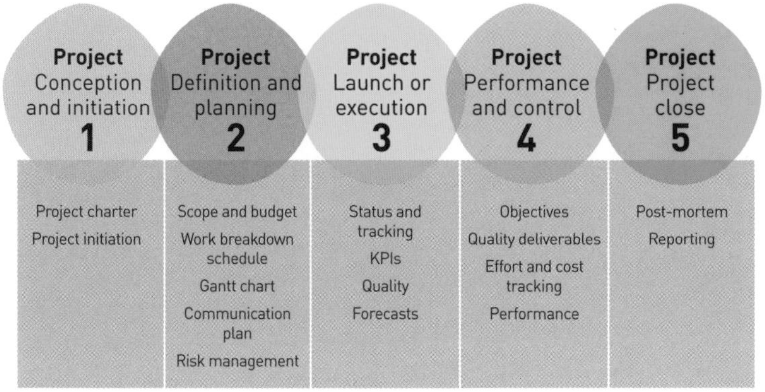
Project
Conception and initiation
1
Project
Definition and planning
2
Project
Launch or execution
3
Project
Performance and control
4
Project
Project close
5
Project charter
Project initiation
Scope and budget
Work breakdown schedule
Gantt chart
Communication plan
Risk management
Status and tracking
KPIs
Quality
Forecasts
Objectives
Quality deliverables
Effort and cost tracking
Performance
Post-mortem
Reporting

There are a number of benefits to a clearly communicated project plan:

- Projects with plans are more likely to be a success.
- It provides a clear roadmap to all participants and stakeholders from the start of the project.
- It manages the expectations of stakeholders.
- It allows the team to monitor and communicate progress.
- It creates 'buy-in' and accountability for deadlines and tasks.
- It demonstrates which tasks rely on others.
- It helps to highlight potential project issues.

Estimating task duration and deadlines

Task duration is the difference between the planned completion date and the planned start date. To estimate task duration, you can use the following kinds of approach:

1. Decide on the aim of the task with your team.
2. *Analogous estimating:* Look to the past for examples of similar tasks.
3. *Predictive estimating:* Look to the future for examples of similar tasks.

THE GANTT CHART

In the 1910s, Henry Gantt (right), an American engineer and social scientist, invented the Gantt chart. This is a kind of bar chart that visually represents the schedule of a project and the time taken for each task and enables planning, co-ordinating, and tracking specific tasks related to a single project.

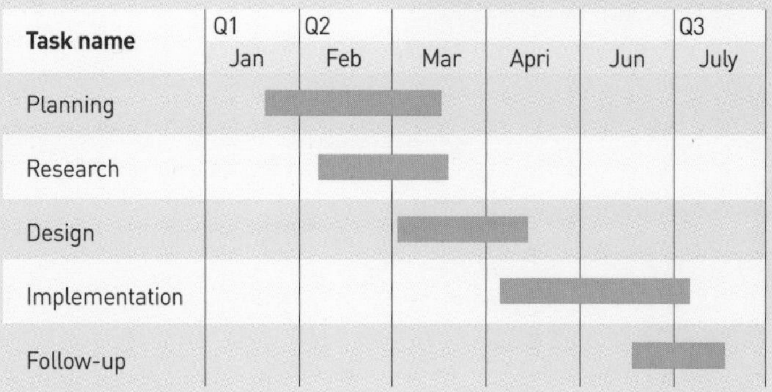
Task name
Q1
Jan
Q2
Feb
Mar
Apri
Jun
Q3
July
Planning
Research
Design
Implementation
Follow-up

THREE-POINT ESTIMATION

The first is the most likely or *best-guess estimate*, which is the average amount of work the task might take if a team member performed it 100 times. The second is the *worst-case estimate*, which is the amount of work the task could take if possible negative risks occur. The third is the *optimistic estimate*, which is the amount of work the task could take if relevant positive factors occur.

4. *Three-point estimating:* This includes best-guess, optimistic and worst-case scenarios.

5. Consider the details and possible risks for the task.

Time constraints and the critical path

The critical path is the longest sequence of tasks that must be completed to finish a project. Tasks on the critical path are critical because, if they become delayed, the whole project will be delayed.

The critical path method can be used to define the least amount of time necessary to complete each task with the least amount of slack. This uses a network diagram to represent the sequences of tasks needed to complete a project.

The duration of each task is estimated by using information from past projects and other sources of information, such as experts in their field.

The example below is an activity-on-node diagram showing a project with tasks A–G. The critical path, shown by the arrows in red, is A-B-C-D-H. Each of these tasks depends on the previous one being completed before it can be started.

Tasks F, G and E are non-critical and have 'slack' or float. They can therefore be completed in parallel to other tasks (because they don't depend on any previous task beyond the first, A, having been completed).

The network diagram (and the estimated duration of each task) can be used to determine the earliest start (ES) and earliest finish (EF) for each task.

The ES of any activity is equal to the EF of the one before, and its EF is determined by the formula EF = ES + t (t is the duration of the activity). The EF of the last activity shows the expected time required to complete the whole project.

The float or slack of each task is determined by taking the last start of each task and the earliest start and looking at the difference. Therefore, the float = LS − ES.

The critical path diagram template.

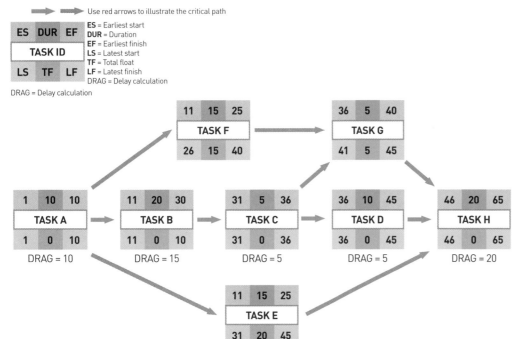

The activities with a zero float are those that make up the critical path. All these critical path activities are dependent tasks except for the first task in the schedule. If a task has positive slack, it is a parallel task to the critical path activities.

Critical path drag is the time that an activity on the critical path is adding to the total duration of the project. Put another way, it is the maximum amount of time that the activity or task can be shortened by before it is no longer on the critical path or before the duration of the task is zero.

The drag of an activity on the critical path is equal to whichever is lower: the remaining duration of the task or (if there is at least one parallel activity) the total float of the parallel activity that has the lowest total float. In the example for task B, although the duration is 20, the parallel activity with the least float is F, at 15. For task C, the duration is 5, and as that is lower than the float of F or E, that is the drag.

Scheduling with resource constraints

A *resource constraint* is a risk or limitation that is related to the resources allocated to a project. Part of the planning process for a project is identifying these restrictions as they can delay or disrupt a project.

Resource constraints

Constraints can be things like cost, time, quality or resources. To try to avoid these impacting your project you can use the approaches below:

- *Recognize what the constraints are:* Identifying the constraints before dealing with them involves examining who, what, when, where, why and how much the project might suffer due to the constraint. Various strategies can then be used to mitigate the effects – risk analysis, resource levelling, analyzing cause and effect and communication with key stakeholders.
- *Educate the key stakeholders:* Communicating with the key stakeholders also involves educating them on the possible limits of the project resources. They need to know what is included in the scope, but also what is excluded. Resource availability is something that needs understanding across sponsors, clients and stakeholders.
- *Approach these constraints positively:* Constraints are not necessarily limitations or restrictions. Some constraints may not be entirely negative as they can help to mitigate risks or, by reframing the issue, be viewed as 'guidelines' for the project management process that help you achieve a successful project.

MANAGING RISKS

A *risk* is anything that might impact the timeline, costs or success of a project. *Risk management* is the process of identifying, categorizing, assigning priority and planning to mitigate them.

Risk managementt

Risk management strategies on a large project might involve detailed plans for each identifiable risk to allow for mitigation, whereas for a smaller project it might mean creating a simple, prioritized list of low-, medium- and high-priority risks and some potential solutions.

MANAGING COSTS AND CLOSING A PROJECT

Closing a project is the final phase of project management. This is when a project manager checks that the client or stakeholder has accepted the project based on what it was promised would be delivered. It may also involve setting up a process for ongoing maintenance.

To determine that a project has been completed you need to establish that the following have been secured:

- sign-off that all the required work has been completed
- sign-off that all project management processes have been carried out
- formally recognizing project completion – there is agreement that it is completed

Along with determining that these requirements have been met and the stakeholders have signed off, it should also involve the following steps:

- *Arrange a 'post-mortem':* A post-mortem is the process of looking back at what went wrong and what went right during a project. Usually, the core project team will meet to give feedback about what worked and what didn't. The idea is that by documenting the mistakes and the successes of a project, it builds a resource that can be referenced for future projects.
- *Complete paperwork:* A project sign-off may have legal requirements, safety certificates or handover documents as a part of the closing process. It would also include settling invoices or fees.
- *Release resources:* Teams that have been working on a particular project are now free to have their time reallocated, or if the project involves other capital resource (such as the use of machinery), this can now be allocated to another project.
- *Archive documents:* A project file with all the documentation from the project, including plans, initial and final budgets, notes, etc. should be created. This allows for future projects to draw on the current experiences.
- *Celebrate success:* Even a small gesture to recognize the completion of a project and give credit to the team responsible can help create closure, and can also help to build team spirit for future projects together.

WHAT IS AGILE?

Agile methodology originated in software development. It involves managing a project by dividing it into several phases. It uses continuous improvement and constant collaboration with team members and stakeholders at each stage. Tasks are not necessarily sequential.

Once a project has started, teams cycle through a process of planning, executing and evaluating.

The word 'agile' is now commonly used to refer to these values in addition to the frameworks for implementing them. These include scrum, kanban, extreme programming and the adaptive project framework.

It is most commonly used in software development but is becoming more popular as a project management technique in other industries.

Waterfall project management

An alternative to agile project management is the *waterfall model*. This is a sequential or consecutive development process that goes through all stages of a project, with each phase completing before the next phase begins.

Succeeding with this methodology depends on accurately documenting everything in advance, including all the variations and outcomes of features. It also requires estimating the time needed for each requirement before the project begins. However, with this project management method, if the parameters change during the project, it can be more difficult to adapt the project to suit than it is when using agile methodology.

How agile works

Agile works by using a process of fast iteration, breaking up larger projects into small units of work. It also means

THE MANIFESTO FOR AGILE SOFTWARE DEVELOPMENT

'We are uncovering better ways of developing software by doing it and helping others do it.
Through this work we have come to value:
Individuals and interactions over processes and tools
Working software over comprehensive documentation
Customer collaboration over contract negotiation
Responding to change over following a plan
That is, while there is value in the items on the right, we value the items on the left more.'
Source: https://agilemanifesto.org/

The waterfall method is an alternative to the agile system.

THE ANDON CORD

The *Andon Cord* was introduced as a part of the Toyota Production System. It was a cord or button on the production line that any worker could activate (without any blame being apportioned) to stop production and warn management of a significant issue. This stopped faulty units from being produced and dealt with problems as quickly as possible. Agile benefits from the same kind of blame-free culture, as well as clear collaboration and communication to stop problems at source and prevent them becoming bigger issues.

listening to all the stakeholders and team members – whether that is engineers or user experiences.

As a part of working like this, teams need to accept that change will happen and have a consensus in the team on 'how to adapt to change'. There also needs to be a consensus on 'what good looks like' and 'what counts as done' to be able to complete each unit of work. It is a process of small teams moving quickly and agreeing upfront how to adapt to inevitable change.

Using the scrum framework (as an example of agile methodology)

Agile is a set of principles, whereas *scrum* is a specific framework for getting things done.

The sprint

Key to this framework is the concept of the *sprint*. A sprint is a short, time-limited period when the team works to complete a set amount of work. Because sprints are so fundamental to the scrum framework, they are often confused with the overall agile methodology.

Scrum masters and product owners

The *product owner* oversees the product backlog (the work that has not yet been started). They are in charge of making sure that the business gains the maximum value from the product.

The *scrum master* is the leader of the agile development team, facilitating the use of the scrum framework, supporting the product owner and communicating updates to relevant employees or other stakeholders.

Backlog

A *backlog* is a prioritized list of work that is derived from the requirements of the roadmap. The most important items are shown at the top of the list to indicate what should be delivered first. At its most simple, it is a list of all the things left to do.

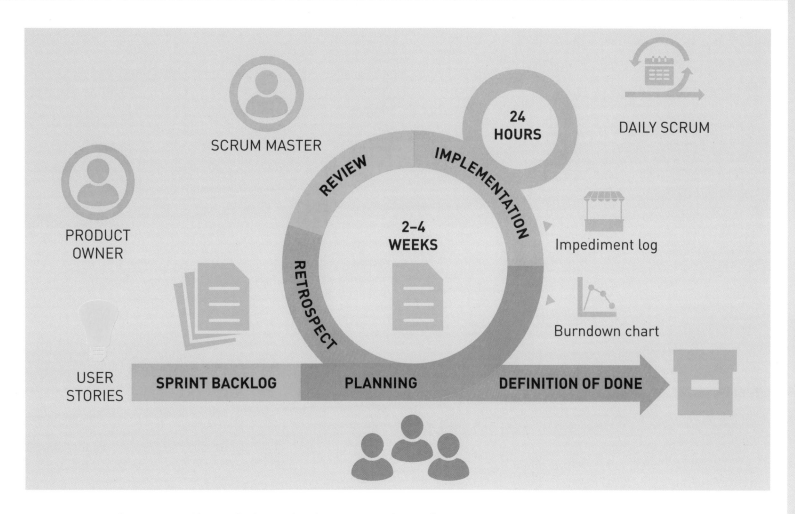

A diagram of scrum ceremonies

In scrum, the team pulls work from this list iteratively as there is capacity for it in a sprint. Alternatively, in the kanban framework, items are pulled continually from this prioritized list as it is focused on measuring work in progress and keeping it to a minimum.

Stand-ups (and other ceremonies in scrum)

Just as in some team sports, a scrum team huddles before each 'play'. This helps make sure the team is informed, aware of any issues and collaborating successfully.

A *stand-up* in scrum for software development (sometimes known as a daily scrum) is a short, daily meeting that involves the core team of product owner(s), developers and the scrum master. It is known as a stand-up because it should be short enough to be completed with everyone standing up.

This part of the framework is known as a *ceremony*.

An example of the kinds of questions raised and answered by each participant in each stand-up might be:

- What did I work on yesterday?
- What am I working on today?
- What issues are blocking me?

These kinds of questions help to show where progress is being made and highlight any issues that are blocking progress. The sharing of progress also helps to build the sense of a team working towards a common goal, when each individual may be working on their own most of the time.

This is only one of the ceremonies in scrum. Other ceremonies are also commonly used, such as the retrospective or sprint planning, etc.

Sprint planning

Sprint planning

The ceremony of *sprint planning* is what helps kick off or start a sprint. The intention is to define what it is possible to deliver in this sprint, and how to achieve this. The whole scrum team is involved. It defines the following elements:

- *The what:* The product owner describes the goal of the sprint and what units of work on the backlog will contribute to that goal. The whole team decides what can be done within the time frame of this sprint and what they will do to make that happen.

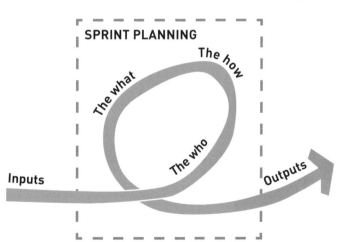

- *The how:* The development team The what plans the work necessary to deliver the goal for the sprint. The sprint plan is created through negotiation between the development team and product owner.

- *The who:* The product owner is required to define the goal based on the value required. The development team has to understand how they are able to (or not able to) deliver that goal. Both sides are needed to plan a sprint.

- *The inputs:* The starting point for a sprint plan is often the product backlog. This provides a list of things that could be part of the current sprint. The team also looks at existing work that needs to be completed in the increment and must be aware of total team capacity.
- *The outputs:* The sprint planning meeting is designed so that the team can clearly describe the goal of the sprint and how it will work towards that goal. This is shown visually in the sprint backlog.

Retrospectives and sprint reviews

A *retrospective* is another ceremony in the scrum framework. It is when a team reflects on the past to help improve the future. These can often happen at the end of a project, or at major milestones on a roadmap.

A *sprint review* is about showing the hard work of the team, as well as showcasing progress. At the end of each sprint, team members can get together to discuss the work achieved during the sprint, demonstrate new features, gather feedback from colleagues or describe the work that has been completed.

TRACKING PROGRESS

There are various ways of *tracking progress*. Boards with each unit of work displayed, alongside its status, estimated time or difficulty can help to manage the backlog and show what has been completed. A *burndown* chart shows the team progress made after, or during, every iteration.

Another key part of agile is the breakdown of the work into *epics* and *user stories*, which are added to the backlog. Epics are a collection of user stories that are related and combine to form one overall large story.

Each user story is then broken down into user cases, which are assigned an estimated number of *story points* (a measure of how difficult, risky or unknown a given user story is to implement).

Using these story points, the *velocity* can be calculated. This is the amount of work that a team can achieve in a time frame, measured by the number of story points completed. Estimates for story points and velocity tend to improve as a project continues.

USER STORIES

What are user stories?

The smallest unit of work in an agile framework is a *user story*. It's the end goal – not a description of a feature – expressed from the perspective of the user of the software. It is an informal description in simple language of how a user (or customer) interacts with a feature or achieves the desired outcome. It doesn't contain requirements or much detail as these are added later by the team.

It is important to note that when writing user stories, the writer is not the user. Stories always try to keep the focus on the user. The product owner or product manager will generally write the user story and then submit it to be reviewed.

It is a way of ensuring that each feature of a product, or unit of work, delivers value back to the customer. This customer could be internal (colleagues using internal software) or external.

User stories also create momentum. With each story that is completed, the team can see how they are solving problems for real users. Small challenges and small wins build together and gather momentum.

In the *sprint planning meeting* (or *iteration planning*), the team decide which stories to tackle during the sprint. At this point, the team discusses requirements and functionality for each user story. Once they are agreed, these more specific requirements are added to the story.

When writing user stories, the following should be considered:

- *What counts as done?* Usually, a story is done when the user can complete the goal as outlined. Therefore, this needs defining.
- *What are the subtasks?* What steps need to be completed to achieve this goal, and who is responsible.
- *Who is it for?* If there are multiple user personas, consider dividing into multiple stories.
- *Go step by step.* Each step in a larger process requires a story.
- *Gather feedback.* Listen to users and capture the problem or need in their words.
- *Make them small enough.* Stories that might take a long time to complete need to be broken up into smaller stories so they can be slotted into sprints.

USER PERSONAS ▶ *These provide a summary of the details of an idealized customer or user. They include demographic traits as well as behaviours, feelings, needs and challenges. They are fictionalized users, usually based on real, aggregated, user data, that are helpful in constructing more specific user stories. They can sometimes be given names to help give them more of a character.*

How to write a user story

'As a [persona], I [want to], [so that] ...': To help 'define what done looks like', user stories can be written in this format. Each step can be filled in with the relevant user persona, goal, action or result.

'As a [persona] ...': This describes who this is being built for. Because there is a detailed user persona, the team has a shared understanding of how that person might think, how they might behave, and their feelings.

'... I want to ...': This describes the intention of the user, rather than the feature they use to do it. This shouldn't describe how it might be implemented or how it works. It should only describe the user goal.

'... So that ...': Where does this fit into the bigger picture? Why is this user doing this? What is the overall benefit they want? This helps highlight where things fit in the bigger picture but can also surface bigger problems that need solving.

For example, if you have personas called Garrett (an existing user of a party organizing website) and Hamzad (a new user of a news alerts app), some example user stories might look like this:

- As Garrett, I want to *invite my friends,* so we can enjoy this party together.
- As Hamzad, I want *to set how many notifications I receive from this app* so that *I don't get overwhelmed.*

An example using a broader user internal persona might be:

- As a manager, I want to be able to *see my colleagues progress on a project,* so I *can better allocate resources.*

When a user persona can capture their desired value as expressed in the story – achieve their goal – then the story is complete.

What is marketing? • The marketing mix • Segmentation and targeting • Value propositions • Marketing in practice • Brand development and management • Brand identities and messaging • Communicating value • Pricing • Understanding consumer need • Agile methods in product management • Fundamentals of digital marketing

TONE OF VOICE

MEASURING BRAND PERFORMANCE

USE VALUE EXCHANGE VALUE PRICE

YIELD MANAGEMENT AND DYNAMIC PRICING

ONLINE AUCTION PRICING

SUBSCRIPTION PRICING

BRAND IDENTITIES AND MESSAGING

VALUE-BASED PRICING AND COST BASED PRICING

PRICING METHODS

E-COMMERCE PRICING

BRAND VALUE

BRAND DEVELOPMENT AND MANAGEMENT

PSYCHOLOGICAL DIFFERENTIATION VALUE

PRICING AND VALUE

PRICING PRACTICES AND SEGMENTATION

PROMOTIONS

MARKETING IN PRACTICE

BRAND EQUITY

MARKETING AND SETTING PRICES

PRICE VERSIONING

PRICE FENCES

CONSUMER PERCEPTIONS

SEGMENTATION

PRICE SENSITIVITY

SEGMENTATION AND TARGETING

THE MARKETING MIX

DEFINING MARKETING

COMMUNICATING VALUE

THE MARKETING FUNNEL

VALUE PROPOSITIONS AND POSITIONING STATEMENTS

THE FOUR Ps

SITUATION ANALYSIS THE FOUR Cs SWOT ANALYSIS

REFERENCE PRICES

PERCEIVED VALUE

WHAT IS MARKETING?

Marketing in business is not just adverts and sales techniques. It can also include other things, such as research, brand strategy and elements of product development. This is because it is not a good business strategy to make and sell products that people don't want, and it is hard to advertise a product that no one wants to buy.

The American Marketing Association (AMA) defines it as 'the activity, set of institutions, and processes for creating, communicating, delivering, and exchanging offerings that have value for customers, clients, partners, and society at large'.

Defining marketing

Creating value could also be called developing products, communicating value could be termed advertising, and delivering value could be another term for sales.

PERCEIVED VALUE

Perceived value is the value that people believe they will receive from a product. This is the reason why some people will pay more for some products. Things that can affect our perception of the value of something can include:

How customers perceive value

- brand name
- quality of packaging
- the advertising materials
- the benefits of the product
- peer pressure (if friends like the product)
- competing products

The perceived value of a product is largely influenced by the practical benefits it confers – this is the value we get from using the product.

The marketing mix

The marketing mix refers to the combination of factors that make up the marketing of a product or service. The first of these is the four Ps: *product*, *price*, *place* and *promotion*. They are the key elements that are used to achieve the marketing goals in a particular market. They can be affected by internal and external factors, and they often interact with each other:

- *Product* describes what you are specifically selling – this is different for each business, depending on sector.

An iconic brand such as Coca-Cola still needs to keep reviewing its marketing mix.

A large billboard for fashion house Saint Laurent keeps the promotion minimal and high-end.

- *Price* is how much the product costs – this can be impacted by competitor pricing, the volume of consumer demand, the costs to manufacture or pricing structures (i.e. subscription vs. one-time pricing).
- *Place* is where people buy the product – on the web, in a supermarket, through an app or via a sales representative.
- *Promotion* is the advertising or marketing activity that aims to reach the target market – for example, this could be billboards, email newsletters, PR campaigns on social media or trade shows.

The four Ps model can be useful at every stage of a business, whether planning a new venture, reassessing an existing offer, optimizing sales or testing a current strategy.

There are some other tools that you can use to provide information and data to launch, sustain or improve your marketing approach. The first of these is about assessing the situation as a whole.

Situation analysis, the four Cs and SWOT analysis

A situation analysis involves examining the activities of competitors, trends and other aspects of the marketplace. It usually aims to help assess these specific areas:

Purpose of situation analysis

- Defining the target market and target audience. Identifying new targets and new audiences that aren't currently being targeted by competitors.
- Understanding competitors' weaknesses and strengths – which can then help determine the best approach to access the target market.
- Spot opportunities and threats to the product you are selling. This helps to mitigate challenges and avoid potential obstacles along the way to successfully selling your product to consumers.

The four Cs

Another set of key factors to bear in mind in a marketing mix is the four Cs: *consumer* wants and needs, *cost*, *convenience* and *communication*.

- By looking at wants and needs, rather than the product itself, the first of these elements focuses on filling a gap in the *consumer's* life.
- The *cost* of a product does not mean the same thing as its price. Cost includes the price of the item but may also include things such as the time it takes for the customer to get to the purchase location. It can also include the product's benefit, or lack thereof, to a consumer.
- In the four Ps, place refers to where a product will be sold. *Convenience* is a more customer-oriented approach to this strategy.
- *Communication* is about the narrative that you tell the consumer. What message are you sending them (this can include advertising and copy, but also overall elements such as the message a brand conveys).

SWOT analysis

Conducting a SWOT analysis is about understanding the external and internal factors that will help achieve a marketing goal. It stands for *strengths*, *weaknesses*, *opportunities* and *threats*. It is comprised of:

- Internal assessments (your available, or potential, resources):
  Strengths: support an opportunity or combat a threat to create an advantage
  Weaknesses: mean an opportunity can't be taken or make create a vulnerability to a threat
- External assessments (the overall market, competition, etc.):
  Opportunities: external elements which are not controlled by you but are helpful (ie a competitor leaving the market).
  Threats: external elements which are harmful (i.e. a new competitor entering the market)

Both threats and opportunities can be tangible (ie a product) or intangible (ie reputation).

It involves honestly assessing these elements and using the information to make useful and strategic decisions when planning marketing spend, or other business activities.

THE MISSION STATMENT
A mission statement is a sentence which explains why a company exists: what its purpose is for the audience it serves. It is about the current purpose, unlike vision statements which are about the future. For example:
IKEA: to create a better everyday life for the many people.
Tesla: To accelerate the world's transition to sustainable energy.

| S | W | O | t |
| STRENGHTS | WEAKNESSES | OPPORTUNITIES | THREATS |

INTERNAL | EXTERNAL

A brand such as Rolex will have a limited market size but a number of customers with potentially unlimited spending power.

Segmentation and targeting

The process of choosing customers to sell a product to often involves *segmenting* the overall group of potential customers into sections. This groups customers with similar needs together and looks to discover the shared characteristics of these customers.

The next step is *targeting*, which is choosing which segment to focus on. The segment a company chooses will depend on various factors, such as market size, potential competition or profitability. By aiming resources more selectively, a company can then aim to create value for these targeted customers in a more specific – and hopefully efficient – manner.

Customers are often segmented by characteristics such as geography, behaviour (such as loyalty or usage rate), demographics, lifestyle, interests, or needs and desires (such as convenience, price or status associated with a product).

Some products or industries operate in undifferentiated markets, particularly large companies selling products desirable to most consumers, such as mobile phone manufacturers or computer makers. These markets are usually served by mass marketing (although they may create different products for different segments and target them separately). Smaller, or more niche, businesses usually need to segment and target their customers more precisely with their marketing efforts.

When looking at the selection of a particular segment of businesses, consider the characteristics, competencies and resources, and competition. The characteristics include the identifying factors of customers in that segment, but also information such as how fast or slowly that segment is growing or its profitability.

Competencies and resources indicate how well the company itself can serve that particular segment – if it is a particularly large segment, do they have the resources or skills to serve all of the customers?

Existing and potential competitors in a segment will also impact selection. A large, growing segment may be profitable, but will also likely attract many competitors, which would act to reduce margins.

The promise of a product

Value propositions and positioning statements

Value propositions describe the overall *promise* of a product or service. It describes the job the product is being purchased to do. They should be clear and short – they are effectively the elevator pitch for a product.

Creating value propositions that appeal to a target customer segment is known as *positioning* (right).

An example of a value proposition, positioning and messaging for Starbucks would be the table below:

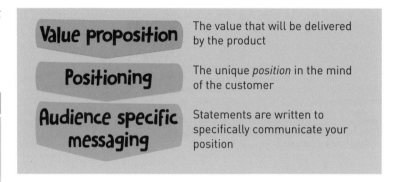

Value proposition	The value that will be delivered by the product
Positioning	The unique *position* in the mind of the customer
Audience specific messaging	Statements are written to specifically communicate your position

Value proposition	Live coffee
Positioning	Authentic coffee, great experience an quicker delivery
Messaging	Every name's a story

Other examples of some modern value propositions are:

Slack	Be more productive at work with less effort
Salesforce	Tools to help you find, win and keep customers
Zendesk	Keep it beautifully simple
PayPal	Make online payments safe and secure

You can see how each one promises something and positions the company in the customer's mind. Value propositions are designed to create (positive) perceptions about your product related to its value and competition.

Varied Nike trainers in a shop dedicated to the brand. The products themselves will have been designed for different parts of the market – and the promotional activity amended accordingly to appeal to that segment.

Positioning statements

Positioning statements are a kind of value proposition but are targeted to specific market segments or buyer personas.

Putting together a positioning statement

A positioning statement is a short description of a product and explains how it serves a specific need of that target market. The intention of a positioning statement is to make sure marketing efforts are aligned with the the brand and value proposition.

Positioning statements can include some or all of the following:

- what people actually buy – the offer your target market is buying into
- identifying the gap in the market the product fills
- demonstrating the product's competitive advantage (and sometimes leaning on the advantages of other products in the same market)
- showing the cost-benefit of the product

There can be more than one positioning statement for a value proposition as postioning is designed for each targeted segment or buyer persona and a product may serve a range of segments.

Marketing in practice
The marketing funnel

Turning leads into customers

This is a visual metaphor for the process of turning leads (potential customers) into actual customers from a sales and marketing perspective. It shows the stages of the customer journey.

It is shaped like a funnel because at each stage of the process the number of candidates to become actual customers reduces – in simple terms, some potential customers won't end up buying the product.

Ideally, a marketing strategy will maximize the number of leads that make it to each following stage. Although the names of sections can differ slightly in different versions, the stages are commonly divided into:

- awareness
- interest
- desire
- action

There are various ways of dividing and subdividing the stages. Here, it is divided into *awareness, interest, consideration, intent, evaluation* and *purchase*.

Awareness: This stage is where marketing campaigns try to make potential customers aware of the product and generate leads. This could be using techniques such as direct advertising, content marketing or consumer research. If contact information is gathered, potential leads are sometimes put into a system to help try to manage them through the remaining process.

Interest: At this stage, the leads who are now aware of the product are prompted by the company to learn more about what it does or the product offer (i.e. they could be sent an informational email after signing up to a newsletter). This stage is often about a brand beginning to develop a relationship with the leads they have gathered.

Consideration: By this stage, leads are now considered marketing qualified leads, and seen as prospective customers, as they are considering a purchase. Further information about the product or offers from the brand might be sent directly to leads, perhaps containing more detailed content, such as case studies, offers of free trials or other promotions.

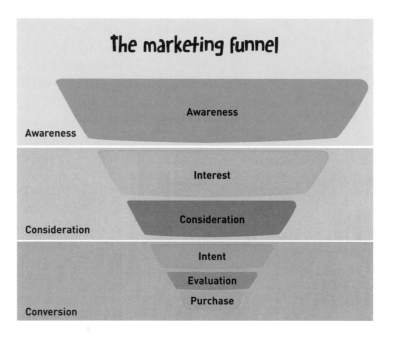

The various stages in the marketing funnel.

Intent: Prospective customers at this stage have shown that they are interested in purchasing the product. For instance, this could be given in a survey answer or by putting the product in an online basket. At this stage, marketing messages might include why this is the best choice for the buyer or indicate other forms of value.

Evaluation: A potential customer at this stage is making a final decision about purchasing the product, perhaps comparing it directly to competing products. Usually, sales and marketing will work together to nurture this decision-making process and demonstrate that this product offers the most value to the consumer.

Purchase: At this stage, the prospect or lead finally becomes an actual customer. It is also where a positive experience might prompt a satisfied customer to create referrals of new potential prospects, who are pushed towards the top of the funnel to start the process again.

When a lead becomes a customer

This multi-step process can be simplified by considering the funnel overall as three main stages – *awareness, consideration* and *conversion*. The function of any model of the marketing funnel is always to attract, engage and convert potential customers.

Key metrics to measure when assessing the effectiveness of a marketing funnel include:

- *Conversion rates:* This is at its simplest, how many leads convert to sales. It can also be analyzed in terms of how many leads move from a particular stage to the next one. For instance, how many website visitors sign up to a newsletter, or how many newsletter subscribers convert to customers.

Calculating the cost of acquiring customers

- *Cost per acquisition:* How much does it cost you in marketing spend to acquire each new customer? To calculate a simple version of this, divide the total marketing spend by the number of conversions in a period.
- *Customer lifetime value:* This is about retention. If a customer is likely to make another purchase after making the first or you have a subscription model.

THE VALUE OF A BRAND

Brand equity

This is the importance to a business of a brand – you could consider it the social value of a brand. It is comprised of brand associations and attributes, brand loyalty, perceived quality, and brand awareness. If it is positive, it can help increase revenue generated from any given opportunity. Brand equity can also be negative, and a liability to the business.

Products from brands with better brand equity are perceived as better than those from brands that are less well known. For instance, Adidas could charge more money for the exact same pair of shoes than a (theoretical) company called BasicallyTrainers because of their brand equity.

It is thought that brands can be assets that improve business performance over time. This concept helped change perceptions of what marketing does, who does it, and what role it plays across a business.

Brand value

Brand value is the financial value of the brand – how much the brand is worth in the market. However, a positive brand value does not necessarily mean that you will have positive brand equity.

Brand development and management
Key goals of brand marketing

The goal of *brand marketing* is to increase the *brand equity* or the *value* of a brand. Whereas *product marketing* is about promoting a specific product for sale, brand marketing promotes the brand itself. It creates a relationship between a brand and their consumers.

Creating a strong identity for the brand, raising brand awareness, establishing the position of the brand and encouraging customer loyalty are all aims of a brand marketing strategy. It usually has longer-term goals than product marketing efforts.

Brand identity (sometimes called *brand image*) could also be considered the personality of a brand. This identity includes brand names, taglines, tone of voice, logos, colour palettes, design styles and anything else that might be regularly associated with the brand. Usually, there are guidelines created for designers or managers to help with consistency across these for a given brand.

Brand recognition is a metric that assesses how familiar consumers are with a brand name. Increasing this often involves brand messaging tailored to target customers in a specific segment.

Brand positioning is about differentiation – demonstrating why a brand is unique or has more value helps to capture larger market share from competitors.

It means that when target customers think of your brand, they know what benefits you offer.

Brand loyalty is the long-term goal of brand marketing. Conversion of new customers is often harder and more expensive than repeat purchases from existing customers. By building trust between customers and a brand, retaining customers becomes a key component of the overall marketing strategy.

Brand identities and messaging

Almost all brands have an associated symbol, visual identity or logo. Symbols to identify religious groups, guilds or military units go back thousands of years, and personal maker's marks have existed for equally as long. But the practice of having a brand identity for a business began in earnest in the Industrial Revolution when mass production of household goods became widespread. This was a way to differentiate a product from competitors' and brand logos or marks have become one of the most important aspects of brand identity.

The Apple logo.

The Apple logo of an apple with a bite taken out is one example of a visual identity very strongly connected with the brand. However, their choice of typefaces, colours and overall aesthetic also help to express their brand identity. Even without the logo, you can often identify the company involved, if the messaging is from a brand that has a very strong visual identity.

Tone of voice

This is about how a company communicates through the language it chooses to use. It includes all the words used across the content connected with a business, from the website copy to the headlines on presentation, the scripts used by the helpdesk and the information in product manuals.

The importance of tone in marketing

Tone of voice is about the distinct flavour or style your communication demonstrates. The company voice can be a crucial part of the brand identity. It isn't necessarily about good writing, or the best words, it is about how a brand communicates its personality.

Consider these two examples of a slogan painted on the wall of a coffee shop:

'Just the best coffee, ever'
or
'Single origin, ethically sourced, highest-quality beans'

They may be serving the exact same product from the same supplier, but it is likely their tone of voice is different because their target markets are different – they have very different brand identities and this helps to frame that.

Measuring the performance of a brand

To measure brand performance, there are some key metrics that can be used. Brand awareness is one of these measurements, and can be divided into three key types:

1. *Unaided brand awareness or top-of-mind:* Where customers think of this brand immediately when they think of that particular market.
2. *Spontaneous brand awareness:* Where this brand would be mentioned in a post or discussion about this market or product type, without any prompting.
3. *Aided or prompted brand awareness:* This might be referrals or recommendations from your existing audience.

There are also measurements that can be made of *brand sentiment* – how an audience feels about the brand or perceives it overall; *purchase intent* or *consideration* – whether a brand is considered as part of a customer journey; and *brand loyalty* – if customers repeatedly purchase from the brand.

Pricing and how it relates to value
Value-based pricing and cost-based pricing

Cost-based pricing is where a set profit margin is added to the overall cost of production to determine the price. *Value-based pricing* is a strategy that involves setting the price mainly based on the perceived value of the product by the customer – how much the customer thinks it is worth.

Cost-based pricing tends to apply to companies that operate in markets for products that are already commoditized. Value-based pricing usually applies to markets where the brand of the product might give value to the customer, or it offers unique experiences. So, the perceived value reflects the worth of the product, and the price that is paid.

This kind of pricing can be determined using marketing techniques such as customer feedback or market research, which quantifies the perceived value of the experience of a particular product.

To use value-based pricing, the product needs to be differentiated from the competition, should be focused on customer needs and desires, and tends to be high quality.

A branded item of clothing like these jeans will probably be priced according to perceived value rather than pure cost plus margin.

Use value, exchange value and price

The *use value* of a product includes its functional benefits, plus the amount of satisfaction it gives the consumer. This is what is used for value-based pricing.

Exchange value (sometimes called *economic value*) is a way of expressing value in reference to another commodity – this could be any other item or it could be money. So, if someone were prepared to exchange two pairs of trousers for one coffee maker, then the exchange value of the coffee maker would be two pairs of trousers. Similarly, when expressed in money form, the exchange value can be said to be the price, so the exchange value of the coffee maker could be expressed as $150.

This exchange value is still ultimately based on use value – the value comes from the consumer understanding of its usefulness.

The subjective theory of *value* indicates that the value of a product is not intrinsic or based solely on the labour and resources used to create it; it can be influenced by context. For instance, *necessity* (an umbrella has more value to you when it is raining) or *scarcity* (rare baseball cards can fetch huge sums of money) can alter a product's value.

One of the other elements important to value-based pricing is the next best alternative. This is the product that the consumer is most likely to purchase instead. Usually, this means that the essential features are likely to be the same, the brands are alike, and it offers the same benefits. For instance, the *next best alternative* (in terms of small cars) to a Toyota Yaris might be a Ford Ka.

Companies can use this alternative price to set their own value-based prices. As a reference from which to deviate – if it has more features then value is added and the price can be higher; alternatively if it has fewer features, then the price might be lower. This difference in prices is known as the *differentiation value*.

Pricing practices and segmentation

There are many different pricing practices that companies can use to maximize the number of customers they attract and increase their profitability.

Price segmentation is the differentiation of prices for a product (or subsets of a product) based on the maximum amount they are prepared to pay. Because different customers can have different levels of price sensitivity, it allows a

OTHER PRICING METHODS
Competitive pricing

For readily available products, *competitive pricing* is an option. That said, it is a good idea to differentiate a business on something other than a competitive price, in case costs suddenly go up.

Cost-based pricing

Cost-based pricing is often used when the manufacturer of a product also retails the product. Cost-based (or cost-plus) involves adding the production costs to a fixed profit margin to decide the final price of the product.

Markup pricing

Markup pricing is a kind of competitive pricing. It involves a set percentage, the markup, being added to the wholesale product cost.

Demand pricing

Demand pricing can also be known as *customer-based pricing*. A retailer uses data about consumer demand to determine the price that should be set.

An umbrella's perceived value is largely dependent on the weather.

PSYCHOLOGICAL DIFFERENTIATION VALUE

Psychological differentiation value is the amount of innate satisfaction a product gives a consumer when compared to another. For example, a Ferrari has greater psychological value than a Fiat because it's a faster, better-engineered car and a higher status symbol.

Although difficult to quantify directly, psychological differentiation value can be measured through surveys, testing or other indirect methods.

business to offer a range of prices for the same, or similar, products, which in turn means they don't lose out on the more price-sensitive consumers.

Communicating value

The key to price management is *communicating value*. This means making sure that the differentiating benefits of a product are communicated in monetary terms. A company needs to establish the value provided to the customer early in the transaction and link it directly to a monetary price.

Consumer perceptions

A consumer's concept of quality and value for money come from the consumer's perception of price. Consumers will often assume that a higher price means the product is higher quality, but equally that it involves a greater sacrifice in terms of money spent. The trade-off between these two perceptions results in perceived value. As this increases, so does willingness to buy.

One of the functions of marketing and product teams is to establish the balance between perceived quality and perceived sacrifice when setting prices.

Reference prices

If a consumer has previously seen a set of prices for a product or service, then this will have an impact on how they perceive the price of the product in front of them. They are comparing this to their internal *reference price*.

Price anchoring

Price anchoring helps to mitigate this by trying to increase the internal reference point. This can be done by exposing the consumer to higher price points, whether by offering a higher-priced alternative, ensuring that cheaper products are not displayed when a customer is looking for a premium product, or presenting prices in descending order (this is because presentation order affects which price is weighted more).

Segmentation by price sensitivity

Charging different prices to different customers for the same (or a very similar) product is called price segmentation.

Price sensitivity

Price sensitivity is a measure of how the price of a product affects consumer desires. It is demonstrated by demand changing in response to a change in the price of a product.

By separating target markets by their relative price sensitivity, companies can offer tailored discounts to those more price-sensitive groups of consumers, while making sure they receive the maximum possible price for the product from all other groups.

Price fences

This strategy is used, for instance, when senior citizens get a discount on products, student prices are offered at the cinema, or people might take coupons to the store to save money on a specific product.

These ID- or effort-led discounts are both versions of *price fencing*, because they 'fence off' those groups that might not be willing to pay more, making sure that those who can afford to pay more don't pay the lower price.

Another version of price fencing has historically existed in the travel industry. Offering different classes of rail tickets – first-, second- and third-class carriages. Each effectively offered the same service (a trip from A to B) but by adding premium features to first class that were valued by wealthy individuals, ensuring second class was moderately priced to the mass market. In some instances in the early days of rail travel, by removing the roof from the third-class carriages to reduce value they were able to prevent those who could afford second-class tickets from being tempted by the lower prices.

Price versioning

Price versioning is a tactic long used by the long-haul airline industry. There are usually two or three different kinds of seat available (economy, business and first class, or their equivalents). These different classes escalate in price.

Examples of price fences	
Regional pricing	Wine is cheaper in France than in Iceland.
Channel pricing	Water is more expensive at music festivals.
Group pricing	10% off with Senior Citizen ID.
Time-based pricing	Cocktails are discounted at happy hour.
Volume discounting	Cupcakes are £1 each or 10 for £6.
Coupons	Peach yoghurt is half price with a coupon.

The experience first-class train travel is designed to offer higher value to the customer to offset the higher cost.

Customers who can and want to pay for the extra services will then pay more for business class to gain some additional value, or even more for first class to gain even further value.

This kind of versioning is a form of *quality discrimination*. All the passengers are on the same flight, they receive the same basic utility for their ticket, but the quality of the service is higher the more they pay. It works best when there are large fixed costs but small variable costs. It also happens in a wide variety of industries. You can see examples in the car industry, the smartphone market, software subscription services, or various food products.

One of the other versioning tactics commonly employed is a *good-better-best strategy*. This ensures that there is a middle version of a product (in terms of price and features) that avoids the extremes – it isn't too cheap and low quality, and it isn't too expensive but of unnecessarily high quality.

Price bundling

How prices are 'bundled'

Price bundling is the technique of combining two or more products together in a single 'bundle' that then sells at a lower price than if those same products were sold individually. This can help get potential customers to buy products they otherwise might not be persuaded to purchase. If there are items in the bundle that are particularly desirable, or in demand, then they can have a leverage effect, enhancing the customer perception of the value of the other items.

There are various kinds of price bundling:

- *Pure bundling:* Only the bundle of products is available. They cannot be purchased separately.
- *Mixed bundling:* Products are available separately as well as in a bundle.
- *Feature bundling:* This combines features into one product (e.g. a portable power-bank that is also a torch).

Promotions and markdown pricing

Many retailers offer promotional prices on products when they are looking to get rid of end of season stock.

Promotions are temporary reductions in price, designed to boost demand in the short term and increase revenue, whereas *markdowns* are permanent price reductions in response to a decline in demand.

Promotions or discounts can have longer-term effects, too. They can tempt consumers of competitor products to switch or increase the overall number of consumers in the product category.

Markdowns can help clear slow-moving inventory but to work successfully, the strategy needs to ensure that those customers who are willing to pay full price do so. They are incentivized to do this if they think that there is a limited supply of the product, or the value of the product reduces over time (for instance, it becomes less fashionable or less useful).

An early markdown involves gradually reducing the price after a given period of offering it at full price. This can increase customer traffic overall as the regular discounts tempt customers to return regularly.

Late markdowns involve heavier discounts but after a longer period of being sold at full price. Clearance sales are an example of this and tend to lead to an increase in customer traffic for the sale itself but not necessarily over time.

E-commerce pricing

The rise of online retail has created a massive new environment in which companies can exploit existing and novel pricing and marketing strategies. It has increased consumer price sensitivity as well as competition. However, it has also enabled firms to maximize revenue, efficiently manage price testing, collect and analyze consumer data, and respond swiftly to changes in demand.

Although there is an increase in price transparency (it is easy to find out the range of prices available), the actual range of prices paid for products – the price dispersion – is greater online than offline.

Newer companies can often combat high competition for prices by differentiating their products for niche markets, because the number of potential customers is so much greater online, or by using temporary discounts.

Yield management and dynamic pricing

When companies change prices in real time to respond to increases or decreases in supply and demand they are operating *dynamic pricing*.

Dynamic pricing

Yield management is a method of dynamic pricing that increases prices as the date by which a product must be used gets nearer. It aims to maximize short-term revenue. This model is usually only used when the product:

- has a limited supply and must be used by a certain date
- is reserved or bought before it is used
- has different fare classes
- has the capacity to alter the number of units available in each class

There are two main ways of managing prices for a product with different fare classes, for instance when selling plane tickets.

1. In *fixed allotment pricing*, all available units are assigned a price relative to their fare, and they are sold at that original price. This sets a fixed number of tickets available for each class based on predicted demand. Every time a ticket is sold, the number remaining in that fare class reduces by one.

   Fixed allotment pricing vs dynamic nesting

2. Using *dynamic nesting* means that a reserve count of each fare class is set, based on predicted demand. Every time a ticket is sold, the total number available (the booking limit) in all fare classes is reduced by one using a booking control system. This means that if more than the expected demand is willing to pay for a premium ticket, then they can, as the reserve can be allotted to that class as needed. This kind of dynamic pricing means that customers don't pay less than they are willing to.

Auctions are a good way to discover how much customers will pay for certain products.

Customer retention

Online auction pricing

There are many online retailers that use an *auction model* for retail sales. Auctions help discover the maximum price consumers are willing to pay.

The main kinds of auctions are:

- *English auctions:* Where a product starts with an opening price, and this price is raised until only one bidder is remaining. The current highest bid is always visible, and it can drive up prices through engagement.
- *Dutch auctions:* These set an opening price and then drops the price at fixed intervals. This is efficient as bidders will accept the highest amount they will pay.
- *Sealed-bid or blind auctions:* Where each person bidding offers a single hidden bid. This tends to get closest to the top-price bidders will pay as they are incentivized to make their maximum bid. The highest bid wins.
- *Second-price sealed-bid auctions* (also known as a Vickrey auction): This is where the highest bidder pays the price of the second highest bid. This encourages bidders to submit higher bids as even if they win, they will pay less than that.

Subscription pricing

It is now possible to subscribe to thousands of products and services online. Everything from pet food to coffee, gin to washing powder is being offered as a subscription service.

Some of the reasons these models can work well is that they aim to maximize customer lifetime value, they reduce uncertainty in revenue streams, they decrease the marketing and transaction costs per customer, and businesses receive the money up front.

Businesses are incentivized to try to retain customers for as long as possible, as their lifetime value increases the longer they remain a customer – this is the recurring revenue multiplied by the length of the customer relationship in time.

By comparing this value to the cost of acquiring a customer (and the likelihood of retaining them) you can easily calculate the profitability of a given customer over their lifetime.

STEVE JOBS: APPLE

Steve Jobs was an American entrepreneur who was the co-founder, CEO, and chairman of Apple Inc. Throughout his career, Jobs was known for his impeccable attention to detail and his insistence on design simplicity. Under his guidance, Apple became the world's most valuable company.

Jobs dropped out of college and co-founded Apple with his friend Steve Wozniak, first building the Apple I, a computer that was hand-built by Wozniak and sold by Jobs. They understood that the computer could appeal to a wide audience. The success led to the Apple II, one of the first commercially successful personal computers. In the early 1980s, Jobs oversaw the development of the Macintosh, the first personal computer to use a graphical user interface.

After a power struggle with the board, Jobs was forced to resign from Apple in 1985. He went on to found a new computer company, NeXT, and acquired the computer graphics division of Lucasfilm, which he renamed Pixar Animation Studios. In 1996, Apple purchased NeXT, and Jobs returned to the company he had co-founded.

Under Jobs' second period of leadership, Apple introduced a number of groundbreaking products, including the iMac, iPod, iPhone, and iPad. He was a master of product marketing, and his ability to generate excitement for Apple's products was a major factor in the company's success. He was also known for his confrontational management style, and was both revered and reviled for his perfectionism and his temper.

In *The Innovator's Dilemma*, Clayton Christensen explains one aspect of Steve Jobs' strange brilliance is that when he went back to Apple he repeatedly disrupted his own company.

Steve Jobs died of pancreatic cancer in 2011, at the age of 56. He left behind a legacy as one of the most successful and innovative entrepreneurs of his generation.

WHAT IS PRODUCT MANAGEMENT?

Being a *product manager* (sometimes referred to as a *product owner*) normally means looking after a specific product (or products) within a company. This product could be the main website the company runs, an app they have developed and support, or a physical product.

Within this role, the needs and desires of customers must be balanced with the requirement to deliver value to the business as well as what it technologically and operationally possible.

It involves developing product strategy, helping direct product development, managing the

Role of product manager

A product manager will help to define what a customer will be looking for when choosing to buy a particular kind of product.

building of the product, and aspects of product marketing and sales.

Product managers need a broad range of skills. They must understand how to manage projects, research, define and describe customer needs, communicate with stakeholders and teams, and think creatively about the product and ways to most profitably bring it to market.

METHODS TO HELP UNDERSTAND CUSTOMER NEEDS
Buyer personas and feedback

A *buyer persona* is a detailed, but fictional, representation of the target audience. This is based on researching existing audiences, customers of your competitors, and other analyses. These fictionalized target customers help to guide product development to suit the needs of the persona(s) and help align the work a business does towards fulfilling those needs.

Competitor analysis

Researching the major competitors in the market helps to provide insight into their product strategy, sales approach and marketing tactics. This kind of competitive analysis can allow a business to create a profitably differentiated business strategy, capture market share with a different approach or compete directly.

A *competitor analysis* can also help define the unique value proposition of a product – what makes it different from those offered by competitors. This can be important in informing marketing efforts.

Identifying those things that a competitor is successful at means you can define how to meet or exceed industry standards. Conversely, if you can highlight where the competition is not succeeding, these may be areas of opportunity where you can use strategies they haven't yet used and so gain an advantage. It also provides a basic benchmark against which to measure growth.

Customer needs statements

A *customer needs statement* helps to define exactly what a specific buyer persona is looking for, helping to align the whole company from marketing to production, and from sales to development with a clear goal in mind.

These statements should be consistent over time, useful to the customer (it needs to describe how this product is better than that of the competition), have utility for the business (all departments should be able to understand how it helps direct their efforts), and simple, clear and accurate in their writing.

AGILE METHODS IN PRODUCT MANAGEMENT

Agile product management sets product strategy and aims to create roadmaps in an agile environment. It is about having an adaptive approach to planning products and implementation so that the business can respond to feedback swiftly.

The importance of flexibility

Traditionally, new products are planned, designed and tested in a step-by-step process. This means that any new functions are delivered sequentially. Because all requirements are defined in advance, it can be difficult to make changes. This was particularly a problem for large software projects, and therefore many software teams moved to an agile methodology. The flexible approach of agile allows for the adjustment of the plan along the way.

Design thinking

Design thinking is a way of bringing the methods and processes of the world of design and ways of thinking creatively about a problem into other areas of business, such as product management.

It is an iterative process that challenges assumptions, and seeks to understand users, redefine problems and create new solutions as prototypes that can be tested. This means that at any stage, you may need to go back to a previous stage with new information, or a new idea or direction. It can be useful when approaching problems that are poorly defined or unknown.

These ways of thinking are represented by these five stages: *empathize, define, ideate, prototype* and *test* (right).

Empathize and define

This is about trying to put yourself in the user's position (*empathizing*) to best understand that perspective. This understanding can be achieved through role play, user interviews, observations or surveys, or similar.

Defining the problem is the process of gathering all the information that has been created to indicate what a new design should accomplish. This might include a vision board containing notes, images, research and other pieces of inspiration.

It might also include the following:

Ideal user: A user who shows the behaviours, desires and concerns of the people most likely to use the design.

Problem statement: An explicit, short statement that outlines the problem and points towards its solution.

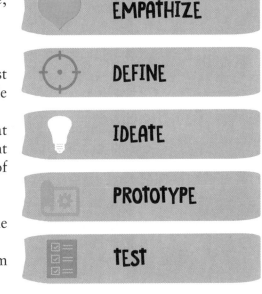

EMPATHIZE

DEFINE

IDEATE

PROTOTYPE

TEST

Ideate and prototype

Ideation is all about freeing up ideas that might help craft a solution. This could start with a brainstorming session, or a similar exchange. Most importantly, it needs to be a collaborative exchange, with no wrong ideas, to help maximize potential solutions. The quantity of ideas is more important than the quality, and people are encouraged to build on the ideas of others.

Ideation

Once there are some ideas for a solution, *prototypes* can begin to be built, whether through sketching them on paper or using a computer to quickly lay them out. This allows everyone to explore the potential product. Doing this may result in new ideas or even new insights into the user experience that will then feed back to the previous stage in the process, and this can lead to a revised prototype.

Test (and repeat)

Once there is a functioning prototype or a simple working model, end-users can be introduced to the revised product in an environment that is controlled (so that they can be observed but also so that limitations of the prototype can be mitigated).

Testing

Usually, this will involve allowing users to get hands on with a prototype, asking for feedback and trying to simulate how the product will work in the real world. This stage can sometimes be run concurrently with prototyping to quickly incorporate feedback.

Crucially, each stage can happen in parallel if necessary. They can be repeated, and a previous stage can be revisited at any point in the process – they don't have to be accomplished in a strict order.

DIGITAL MARKETING AND SEO

THE FUNDAMENTALS OF DIGITAL MARKETING
Inbound and outbound marketing

Outbound marketing is the process of putting a message in front of a large number of people. Printed posters, TV adverts, adverts in magazines, cold calling, direct mail and mass emails are all examples of outbound marketing. The idea is to aim at a large audience, the majority of whom won't be looking for the product being marketed, therefore it is usually concerned with the product itself and the reasons why people seeing the advert should buy it.

Inbound marketing, on the other hand, is designed to be 'magnetic'. It aims to attract the best prospects – those who are already looking for solutions online – and then once these leads have arrived at your site, provide guidance, information and help directly related to what they were searching for.

Magazine advertising is a classic example of outbound marketing.

The primary focus of inbound marketing is content. This could be written content, such as a blog or article, video content or downloadable ebooks, images or PDFs.

When a company is attempting to leverage inbound marketing, they are attempting to match up with various points in the buyer's journey. This overlaps with the concept of the marketing funnel, introduced earlier.

At the start of a buyer's journey, they are familiarizing themselves with the problem and the possible solutions. In the middle, they are evaluating a set of solutions, and at the end of the journey, they are undertaking research, or due diligence, to make a decision.

Each stage has different kinds of content that align with the needs of a potential customer, so by providing this content on their website (usually discovered via search), a company is attracting the customer to come directly to them by providing relevant answers at each stage.

A buyer's journey – an example
The awareness stage

The buyer is experiencing a problem, and their goal is to stop it happening. They might be looking for information to better understand, contextualize, and put a name to the problem.

Example search: *'Why does my foot hurt all the time?'*
Example content: *A blog post on common types of foot pain.*

The consideration stage

The buyer has defined and found a name for their issue, and now they are researching the possible solutions for this specific issue.

Example search: *'How to treat plantar fasciitis?'*
Example content: *An article and video about best treatments for plantar fasciitis.*

The decision stage

The buyer has chosen a solution. The aim is now to find where it is available, choose a supplier and make a purchase decision.

Example search: *'Where can I get custom orthotics? Which are the best custom orthotics?'*
Example content: *A review of the best orthotics, with links to buy.*

Key tools for digital marketing
Social media platforms

Most customers now have access to social media via their phones, offering a powerful marketing channel.

A major part of most integrated marketing strategies is using *social media platforms* such as Instagram, Facebook, Snapchat or Twitter. These are a way in which companies can engage with audiences as well as create buzz around a product or brand. Most of the major platforms have dedicated features or apps for managing marketing activities and tracking performance, and there are also third-party tools for scheduling, measuring and managing content.

Email marketing tools

Email marketing tools help companies to create email campaigns that use content that is designed to encourage users to be more engaged with the brand than just being on the email list – like signing up for events and buying products. There are email marketing platforms such as MailChimp or Sendinblue, which provide tools to build email lists and automate campaigns. They also offer analytics for the campaigns, meaning that testing and optimization are straightforward.

Software for design

Whether creating nice images of a product to put on Instagram, laying out ads or designing images for the company website, *design tools* are a key part of the digital marketing process. There are many programs that allow users to make good-looking designs fairly simply, such as Canva or Photoshop.

Analytics tools

Tools to analyze the traffic on your website, assess the impact and engagement of social media posts, or optimize digital advertising are an essential part of the toolkit. These tools include services like Google Analytics or Heap for website statistics, Facebook Insights and Twitter Analytics for social media (along with many third-party tools), as well as a range of other tools and internal dashboards for analyzing user behaviour, conversion metrics and site searches.

Content marketing tools

If there is a particular focus on content marketing, then there are tools that can help identify opportunities and create content that is suitable for a specific audience. Currently, CoSchedule and HubSpot and both examples of this kind of tool, whereas tools such as Buffer are designed to show what fans of a brand are talking about on social media to help target content.

Lastly, and crucially, there is also the success of the customer experience itself, which can help turn customers who are genuinely delighted with a product or service into active promotors of a product or brand.

SOCIAL MEDIA MARKETING

Marketing via social media is usually focused on raising brand awareness and driving traffic to a website for conversion.

The direct contact with followers allows companies to reach large audiences without high costs, sell products and services directly, target particular demographics or specific audiences (such as those interested in a trending topic or hashtag), provide direct customer support, create a community around a brand, and analyze sentiment (whether people are positive or negative) about a brand.

Strategies such as inviting users to submit content (user-generated content) for use in campaigns or marketing activities, spreading awareness of a product or creating a strong brand personality are all useful ways of using social media in a marketing context.

Many companies use planning tools designed specifically for social media to schedule content, analyze engagement and respond effectively to user questions.

Paid digital advertising

Paid digital advertising is a form of marketing where a company pays an online publisher (such as a website, social media platform or a search engine) to display advertising content to their audience or users.

These kinds of adverts are paid for in two main ways, whether based on *visibility* – the number of people who get shown the advert, referred to as *impressions* – or *activity* (usually a click, or some other action).

Visibility vs activity

Adverts that are based on impressions don't take into account how many people click on the advert, or subsequently purchase a product (though these things can still be measured). These kinds of ads are therefore usually placed on high-traffic websites. The size of their audience is the main factor in pricing.

Paying based on an action is where you are charged a price decided by the publisher for every click, usually in an automated auction process (a company says the maximum they are prepared to pay for a single click and this offer goes into an auction with other bidders for that advertising space). The action of the user is tracked, either as a click or through to a successful conversion. This is known as *pay-per-click*, or *cost-per-click*.

Ad impressions are about visibility, whereas pay-per-click means paying for engagement.

Normally, digital adverts are priced one of three ways:

- *Cost-per-thousand* (CPM – which stands for 'cost per mile'): This is the cost per 1,000 impressions of the advert.
- *Cost-per-click* (CPC): The advert is paid for only when it's clicked.
- *Cost-per-action* (CPA): The cost per completion of an action (for instance, a conversion into a purchase or subscription).

CPM-style ads are about high traffic and large numbers of views of the advert, so often take the form of display ads, whereas CPC channels are about driving traffic, so it helps if they are more carefully targeted to users with specific interests or intentions (for instance paying to display an advert for pet food when someone searches for toys for their dog).

Affiliate marketing

Another form of digital advertising is *affiliate marketing*, where the publisher of the link earns a commission for each successful conversion as a result of one of their users clicking on it. For instance, a blogger posting an affiliate link to Amazon could receive a small commission if a user clicked a link to a product on their blog and went on to purchase the product from Amazon.

Targeting and retargeting

To make sure that adverts are shown to the right audience – a particular demographic, location or those interested in a specific topic – digital advertising services use *targeting* and *retargeting*.

Targeting allows advertisers to choose who to show their content to, and can separate audiences into groups to be shown the advert that are more likely to be interested in a product or service.

Retargeting is the process of reaching people who have already indicated some interest in a product, maybe by visiting a company webpage or clicking on an advert. This means that purchasing intent can be converted into a sale.

Online advertisers sometimes do this by placing a small pixel on a webpage that inserts a cookie into a web browser. This tracks how someone interacts with webpages or services and means that the ads they then see can be targeted to them more accurately.

Another method for retargeting is to use a list of identifiers, such as an email address, to target people who have previously indicated interest.

Email marketing

Email marketing is a kind of *direct marketing*, using email to promote the products or services a company provides. Because of the direct connection, it can be a way to regularly engage with existing customers and resell, advertise sales or offers, move potential customers further along the marketing funnel or maintain brand awareness.

This regular engagement can also help to build a relationship with the audience, drive traffic to content on a website or perform automated retargeting – such as emailing customers who put something in their basket but didn't fully check out to remind them to complete their purchase.

Often, a third-party service is used to manage the process of email marketing, and most offer some kind of all-in-one package with email design tools, optimization suggestions, list and audience management and analytics built in.

The first challenge for any email marketing campaign is to build and grow an audience of interested people. This often needs to rely on other forms of digital marketing to drive this traffic, though it is also possible to sign people up at in-person events.

AVOIDING SPAMMING PEOPLE

The *CAN-SPAM Act* is a US law that sets some rules around email marketing. Even if a company is not based in the USA, they may have to comply if their software provider is based there or some of their customers reside there.

CAN-SPAM basic requirements:

- Make it possible to unsubscribe simply.
- Don't pretend the email comes from someone else.
- Don't use deceptive subject lines.
- Clearly identify who sent the email (and include a contact address).
- Identify the email as an advert when necessary.
- Remove emails from your list promptly, when asked.
- Monitor any third parties or subcontractors with respect to these requirements.

Building an audience via email

Key digital marketing metrics

When assessing the success or failure of any digital marketing campaign, there are some important metrics that need collecting so that proper comparisons and informed decisions can be made. These metrics need measuring before, during and after a marketing campaign.

Metrics

Basic metrics include: overall traffic (how many visitors were there to the website?); which channels this traffic came from; how many conversions there were (whether to a sale, sign-up or something else, how much revenue was generated?); what the bounce rate was (how many people immediately left after landing on the page, presumably because they weren't interested?); and what people are searching for most frequently.

A/B TESTING FOR MARKETING

A/B testing (also called *split testing*) is a method of experimenting where the audience is split to test a number of variations, usually two different options, and then decide which performs better. Version A is shown to one half of the audience and version B is shown to the other half. This is possible because websites can choose what to show to particular users based on demographics or unique identifiers using cookies.

The changes are made to only one variable, shown to similar-sized and sufficiently sized audiences and for a long enough but limited period, then statistically analyzed to determine which performs better. There are online calculators to help determine how big an audience is and how long a test needs to be run to have a minimum sample size.

The method can help marketers decide which piece of content works better. A marketing team may want to find out if changing the colour of the buy button on the website can increase the click-through rate. To run this test, an alternative buy button in a different colour would be designed, but it would lead to the same page as the original, or control in the experiment. If this new version or variation leads to a better click-through rate, then it may be worth changing the colour.

The two conversion rates that result from this test might look something like:

Control 15% (+/− 2.1%)
Variation 18% (+/− 2.2%)

This would mean that 18% of the audience clicked through on the new colour button, with a margin of error of 2.2% at a p-value (measurement of statistical significance) of 0.05.

This p-value would mean that if you ran this A/B test many times, 95% of the time this range will capture the true conversion rate – the conversion rate falls outside the margin of error 5% of the time.

Of course, it doesn't guarantee that level of conversion, but with a large enough sample audience size you can be fairly confident that the metrics for the change suggested above would suggest the new colour will increase click-through rates.

If there are significant costs involved in the change or variation, then the decision about what constitutes enough of an improvement will probably be decided by other concerns, such as potential return on the investment vs. the cost of the change.

Companies with more specific requirements or particular campaigns may need to use additional metrics, such as new vs. returning visitors, what search queries are leading visitors to their site, which pages on their sites are being visited most from searches, the demographics of their users or what the sentiment around their brand is.

Once the key metrics for a campaign have been chosen, they can be used to evaluate it as a KPI, based on the overall aim of the campaign.

Digital marketing teams will also want to know the *return on their advertising spend* (ROAS), which is the revenue generated from a campaign, divided by the total cost of the campaign.

SEO and content marketing

SEO

Search engine optimization (SEO) is the practice and process of improving the appearance and position of a website – the ranking – in organic search results (the unpaid listings on a *search engine results page* or SERP). It is designed to increase the quality of traffic and attract the largest number of visitors to a website.

Because most people search for things online via a search engine, ensuring that a website appears near the top of the list of results can have a big impact on overall traffic.

Search engines want to accurately match the intent of a user's search to the list of webpages on the SERP, so SEO can help with the quality of these results.

Search engines use *bots* (sometimes called *crawlers* or *spiders*), to index the information they find on the internet. These bots examine the content on the pages of a site and follow all the links to other pages, or external sites. This helps determine the semantic connections between pages and other sites and then allows the search

Comparing organic and paid results on a search engine.

SERP organic vs paid

GENERIC SEARCH ENGINE

Ad

Paid results
The accounting businesses pay to appear here

Ad

Organic results
Nobody can pay to appear here

engine's own algorithm to determine where to place a website in a page of search results.

When a user searches for something, this algorithm decides what websites to display, and what order to display them in based on how useful and accurate it decides they might be as a response to a user search query.

The quality of the content on a website, the speed of the site, keywords, the number of links to that website from another website (particularly well-regarded ones) and other elements and connections can determine the final ranking of a site on a search engine.

Strategies for SEO

The specifics of the search engine algorithms that determine rankings change regularly, so the best strategies for SEO are based around good user experiences, non-manipulative ranking tactics (i.e. not using unrelated content to garner traffic that doesn't connect to your product or service), technical optimization such as accurate tagging of headers (these are the HTML header tags H1-H6), and most importantly, high-quality, relevant content.

Content marketing

One aspect of this kind of optimization is the approach to the content on a website. *Content marketing* is a strategic approach to increasing traffic that is primarily about creating and publishing relevant, high-quality and consistent content (such as articles, blogs, videos, ebooks or infographics) to attract, retain and ultimately convert a clearly defined target audience.

A longer-term approach

Rather than promotional content directly about the benefits of a specific product, this kind of content is usually a longer-term approach that offers solutions or information that a target audience might want, often only tangentially connected to the actual product, with the intention of building a relationship with this audience. This builds loyalty to a brand, and therefore when a purchasing decision is made, this audience is more likely to prefer it over the competition.

Examples of content marketing could be a cosmetics company providing comprehensive how-to video tutorials on their site or social media channels, or a company that makes trainers creating free, professional training schedules and injury recovery guides for runners. In both instances, the content they've created builds trust in the brand, and should increase the possibility they can convert that audience into paying customers.

Earned and unearned media

Paid media is what is usually referred to as *digital advertising*.

Earned media is publicity or other material about a business that hasn't come from paid advertising or has been created in-house.

Owned media is anything that the company controls, such as websites, social media accounts, newsletters or catalogues. One way of thinking about earned media is as a kind of online word-of-mouth. This could be in the form of mentions on social media, coverage on third-party sites, reviews, recommendations or *viral content* (an example of owned media that becomes earned media).

Having a strong SEO strategy and a good organic SERP ranking (ideally, the first page of search results) as well as high-quality, relevant, consistent content is the most effective way of driving positive earned media.

How these three kinds of media interact helps determine the overall digital marketing strategy for a brand or product (below).

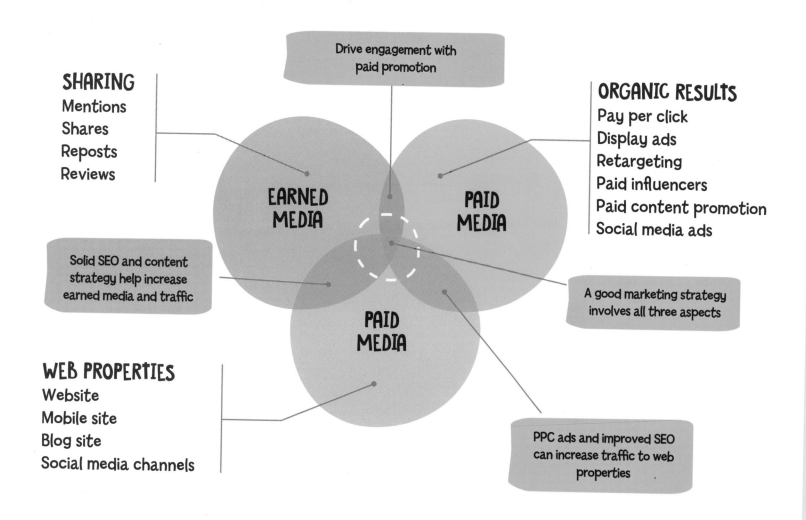

Drive engagement with paid promotion

SHARING
Mentions
Shares
Reposts
Reviews

ORGANIC RESULTS
Pay per click
Display ads
Retargeting
Paid influencers
Paid content promotion
Social media ads

EARNED MEDIA

PAID MEDIA

PAID MEDIA

Solid SEO and content strategy help increase earned media and traffic

A good marketing strategy involves all three aspects

WEB PROPERTIES
Website
Mobile site
Blog site
Social media channels

PPC ads and improved SEO can increase traffic to web properties

Chapter Six

STOCKS, SHARES, MANAGERIAL ACCOUNTING & VALUING COMPANIES

Stocks and bonds • The stock market • Managerial accounting • Artificial intelligence, machine learning and deep learning • FinTech • What is a blockchain? • What is cryptocurrency?

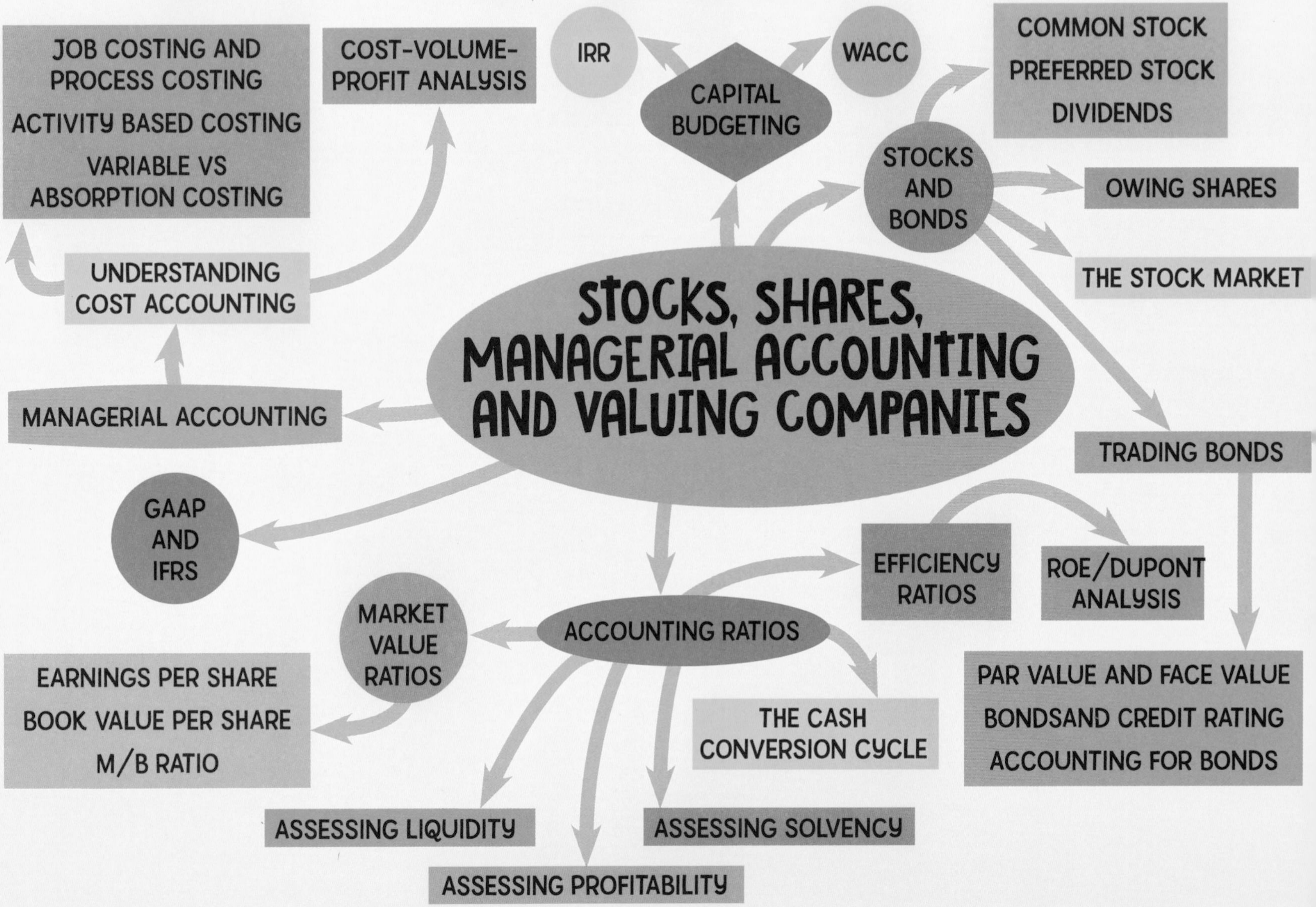

STOCKS, SHARES, MANAGERIAL ACCOUNTING AND VALUING COMPANIES
JOB COSTING AND PROCESS COSTING
ACTIVITY BASED COSTING
VARIABLE VS ABSORPTION COSTING
COST-VOLUME-PROFIT ANALYSIS
IRR
CAPITAL BUDGETING
WACC
COMMON STOCK
PREFERRED STOCK
DIVIDENDS
STOCKS AND BONDS
OWING SHARES
THE STOCK MARKET
UNDERSTANDING COST ACCOUNTING
MANAGERIAL ACCOUNTING
TRADING BONDS
GAAP AND IFRS
EFFICIENCY RATIOS
ROE/DUPONT ANALYSIS
MARKET VALUE RATIOS
ACCOUNTING RATIOS
PAR VALUE AND FACE VALUE
BONDSAND CREDIT RATING
ACCOUNTING FOR BONDS
EARNINGS PER SHARE
BOOK VALUE PER SHARE
M/B RATIO
THE CASH CONVERSION CYCLE
ASSESSING LIQUIDITY
ASSESSING SOLVENCY
ASSESSING PROFITABILITY

STOCKS AND BONDS

Stocks are a form of partial ownership of a company – they represent equity. When you buy stocks, you are effectively purchasing a small piece of the company. You can receive a return on your investment if the value of the stock goes up (if the value of the company increases). Obviously, you can also lose money if the value of the company decreases.

Stocks are a general term for part ownership of one or more companies whereas a share is an individual unit of ownership in a company. Investors buy shares in specific companies, which means they are invested in a share of a company's stock. However, the two terms are commonly used interchangeably.

Bonds are in essence a form of loan from you to a company (or a government). You don't receive any equity, but you do receive interest payments (known as *yield*) over a set period, and at the end of that period you receive the initial amount back – this is called *reaching maturity*. These interest payments are a source of fixed, predictable income. Though there are still risks – the company could go bankrupt, and you would stop getting interest payments and maybe lose the money you paid at the beginning.

Traders at the New York Stock Exchange.

The stock market

The *stock market* is where the shares of publicly listed companies are traded. The stock market refers to all the places where this can happen, mostly in *stock exchanges* such as the Nasdaq, the New York Stock Exchange or the FTSE.

Stock markets are designed to be a secure and regulated environment in which trades can take place on both the primary and secondary markets with low operational risks. The *primary market* is where companies are offering their shares to the public for the first time – known as an *initial public offering* or IPO, to help raise capital from investors. The *secondary market* is where these company shares are bought and sold to and from other investors.

In the USA, the stock market is regulated by the *Securities and Exchange Commission* (SEC); in the UK it is the *Financial Conduct Authority* (FCA).

WHAT OWNING A SHARE MEANS

As a shareholder, you own a small piece of the company, in proportion to the number of shares you hold. There can be just one shareholder in a company, or many.

The price paid for a share can increase (or decrease) over time, and if a shareholder sells their shares at a higher price than they bought them for, they will make financial gain. Over time, particularly longer periods, this can be a straightforward method to generate income from capital.

Shareholders are entitled to receive a share of the profits, known as *dividends*, with the amount depending on the number of shares they own.

Owning shares in a company may also give the shareholder *voting rights*, such as voting for the board of directors.

Shareholders have limited liability, so they are not responsible for the debts or obligations of a company. They are only responsible for the value of their shares, which can decrease or increase.

Common stock, preferred stock and dividends

There are different kinds of stock available to different investors. Common stock will usually allocate voting rights to a shareholder (usually allocated as one vote per share), but it is usually the last kind of stock to be paid any dividends.

Preferred stocks have priority over the income of a company, so they are paid dividends first, or allocated assets first – for instance if the company goes into liquidation. However, they have no voting rights. Preferred stock can be converted to a fixed number of common stock in certain situations, but common stock cannot.

Treasury stock is formerly outstanding stock that is bought back from stockholders by the company that issued it. It reduces the shareholders' equity on the balance sheet, and means the company increases its ownership of itself.

Dividends are the distribution of a proportion of net company profits to the relevant shareholders. The payment and value of dividends are determined by the board of directors and usually approved by shareholder vote. Not all companies issue dividends; some keep their earnings to reinvest in the growth of the company.

Types of bonds

There are a number of different types of *bonds*, but the main four are government, municipal, agency and corporate. They represent a form of loan from the bondholder (the investor) to the government or company who issued the bond. They are used to raise money for projects, maintain operations or sometimes refinance existing debts.

The *issuer of the bond* (i.e. the company) issues a bond that states the terms of the loan, the interest payments that will be made and the date when the bond principal (the initial amount loaned) must be paid back – the *bond maturity date*.

The *bond yield* is the return (the amount of money made or lost) for the investor. It refers to the expected earnings on the investment over a specific period, usually expressed as a percentage or interest rate. This interest rate is known as the *coupon rate*.

Par value and face value

Bonds are usually issued with a *par value* of $1,000 (or sometimes $100). If an investor buys a bond with a par value of $1,000 and a maturity date set for five years, then when those five years have passed, the issuing entity must pay the bondholder $1,000.

Face value

The par value of a bond is this price that the issuer pays at maturity, whereas the *face value* of a share is the price of the stock when it is first issued.

Bonds and credit ratings

Bond ratings are used to measure the creditworthiness of a bond. These ratings are normally given with letter grades that indicate their credit quality – the cost of borrowing for an issuer.

Creditworthiness

The highest-rated bonds are known as *investment grade bonds*, and they are given AAA or BBB ratings (if using S*tandard & Poor's* ratings). These are seen as safer, more stable investments. These kinds of bonds normally see bond yields increase as ratings decrease – the riskier the investment, the higher the yield.

Trading of bonds

Investors can buy and sell bonds in the secondary market after they have been issued. This can be publicly through exchanges, or via broker-dealers acting for clients.

Bond trading

The price of a bond moves in the opposite direction from its yield. The price of a bond reflects the value of the income that it provides from regular coupon interest payments as well as the repayment of the principal. When interest rates are dropping, older bonds become more valuable because they were sold when interest rates were higher, which means they will have higher coupons and a premium can be charged for them. When interest rates rise, older bonds become less valuable and may have to be traded at a discount.

Because bonds repay the principal (the par value) at maturity, they appeal to investors who don't want to risk losing capital or need to meet a liability in the future.

Accounting for bonds

When a company issues a bond, they receive cash from the investor and record a liability for the bonds issued – the issuer is now liable to pay back the principal of the bond. This is what it looks like in accounting terms:

	Debit	Credit
Cash	1,000	
Bonds payable		1,000

The interest payments on a bond are a debit to interest expense and a credit to cash.

At maturity, there is a debit to the bonds payable account and a credit to the cash account.

Accounting ratios

Various accounting ratios

Accounting ratios are an important kind of financial ratio. They are metrics that rate the efficiency and profitability of a business based on their financial reports. These ratios take two specific line items from the financial statements of the business and compare them.

You can use these ratios to assess the financial health of a given company and look at their fundamentals over a particular period (a quarter or a fiscal year, for instance). Some of the most commonly used ratios are the *debt-to-equity ratio*, the *quick ratio*, *return on assets*, *net profit margin* and *operating margin*.

Both investors and companies themselves use ratios to monitor progress and determine the most valuable investment option. Different ratios are used for assessing different elements of a company's performance.

Assessing liquidity

Quick ratio

The *quick ratio* (or *acid-test ratio*) is useful for looking at a company's short-term liquidity because it measures the ability of a company to meet its short-term obligations with the assets available that are most liquid (this means the easiest assets to turn into cash, so it doesn't include inventory).

$$Quick\ ratio = \frac{(Current\ assets - inventory - prepaid\ expenses)}{Current\ liabilities}$$

The *current ratio* is similar and looks at the ability of a company to pay off the liabilities due within one year using its total current assets, such as cash, accounts receivable and inventory. A higher ratio is better.

$$Current\ ratio = \frac{Current\ assets}{Current\ liabilities}$$

Assessing solvency

Assessing solvency

Ratios to *assess solvency* are about the ability of a company to meet its long-term debts. It is commonly used by prospective lenders when loaning money to a business. They have a longer outlook than liquidity ratios, but both measure the financial health of a company.

The *debt-to-equity* ratio (sometimes referred to as the D/E ratio) shows how a company is funded – the higher the ratio, the more debt the company has, the higher the risk of default. It looks to see how much of the debt can be covered by equity if the company were to have to liquidate.

$$Debt\text{-}to\text{-}equity\ ratio = \frac{Debt\ outstanding}{Equity}$$

Other ratios for assessing solvency are a *debt-to-assets ratio,* where debt-to-assets equals total assets divided by total debt. This looks at how much of a company's assets are financed by debt.

Whether a ratio is good or bad also depends on the type of company. It is usual to compare companies to their peers when assessing ratios and deciding if they are acceptable, as certain industries may have more debt than others due to the nature of their business.

It is necessary to balance equity against debt when working out a company's risk.

Assessing profitability

When looking at the most basic element of a company's health, its profitability, there are some key ratios that are used. While solvency and liquidity ratios show you how well a company can cover its obligations (long term or short term), *profitability ratios* tell you about a company's ability to convert its assets into cash flows, and net income.

Net profit margin shows the net income generated as a percentage of the revenue the company has received. It is calculated by dividing net income (revenue minus all the associated costs) by *revenue.*

Net profit margin

$$Net\ profit\ margin = \frac{R - COGS - E - I - T}{R} * 100$$

where:
R = Revenue
$COGS$ = Cost of goods sold
E = Operating and other expenses
I = Interest
T = Taxes

Alternative (and slightly simpler) ratios for assessing profitability include the *return on assets*

121

(ROA) or the *earnings before interest and tax* (EBITDA) margin.

The return on assets is calculated by dividing the net income by the total assets.

$$Return\ on\ assets = \frac{Net\ income}{Total\ assets}$$

You can also assess the *return on equity* (ROE), but ROA factors in any debt the company may have, whereas ROE doesn't.

The EBITDA margin turns the EBITDA metric into a ratio, meaning you can then use it to compare a company's performance to others in the same industry. It focuses on operating profitability and cash flow.

$$EBITDA\ margin = \frac{(EBIT + depreciation + amortization)}{total\ revenue}$$

Efficiency ratios

The *operating margin* of a company is one of the best ways to quickly assess its efficiency. It looks in basic terms at the operational profit margin after taking away the variable costs of production and marketing the goods or services. It shows how well the management of a company can control their costs by demonstrating how efficiently the company can generate profit from its core operations.

$$Operating\ margin = \frac{Operating\ earnings}{Revenue}$$

Operating earnings is the same as EBIT (Revenue − COGS and regular costs).

One of the things that the operating margin can show is if a company is generating most of its income from its core operations or from other activities, such as investing.

The cash conversion cycle

The *cash conversion cycle* (CCC) is used to demonstrate how quickly a business can convert its initial capital investment into cash. If a business has a low CCC, it can be an indicator of good management, but a proper analysis of management efficiency means combining the CCC with other ratios, such as ROA and ROE, as well as comparing with industry competitors.

How the cash conversion cycle works.

ACCOUNTS RECEIVABLE

INVENTORY

CASH CONVERSION CYCLE

CASH

ACCOUNTS PAYABLE

Market value ratios

Market value ratios help to assess the financial health of publicly traded companies and can be used to identify specific stocks that might be overvalued, undervalued or priced correctly. There are a range of market value ratios that can be calculated, each of which measures a slightly different aspect of the company's financials and can be combined to give an overall picture. They can help to analyze stock trends – for instance a low price/earnings (P/E) ratio might mean that the stock is undervalued (in a stable industry context), or it could mean it is possibly a risky proposition. These ratios also give a sense of what investors think about the future performance of a company.

Here are some of the more common ratios and how they are calculated:

- *Earnings per share:* To calculate earnings per share you divide the net income of a company by the number of outstanding shares (the stock held by all the shareholders). For example, if a company has net income of $20 million and 4 million outstanding shares, the earnings per share would be $20 million divided by 4 million, which amounts to $5. This represents net income per share of outstanding stock and demonstrates profitability.
- *Book value per share:* To calculate this, you divide equity (not including preferred stock) by the shares outstanding in the market. So, if the total assets of a company equal $25 million and its total liabilities are $10 million, their total equity would be $15 million. If the company has $5 million in preferred stock, take that away to find the amount available to common shareholders, $10 million. Then, if there are 2 million outstanding shares, the book value per share would be $5, or $10 million divided by 2 million.
- *Market/book (M/B) ratio:* This is used to compare the market value of a company to its book value. To calculate this, you divide the market value per share by the book value per

M/B ratio

share. For example, if a company has a book value per share of $12 and the stock currently is valued at $15 per share, the M/B ratio can be calculated by dividing $15 (the stock price) by $12 (the book value per share). This gives a ratio of 1.25. Therefore, the market value of a share of this stock is 25% greater than its book value. Having a ratio of less than 1 could mean a company's stock might be undervalued, while a ratio greater than 1 might mean it is overvalued.

P/E ratio

- *Price-earnings (P/E) ratio:* This is calculated by taking the current price of the stock and dividing it by the earnings per share. Usually this takes into account the last four quarters of results. For example, if a stock is trading at $50 per share and its earnings per share are $5, the P/E ratio would be $50 divided by $5, which is a ratio of 10:1. The estimated P/E ratio for the next four quarters is known as the forward P/E ratio.

MANAGERIAL ACCOUNTING
Understanding cost accounting

Rent for premises is a key fixed cost for a business.

Cost accounting is a form of managerial accounting that looks to understand the total cost of production by taking into account the fixed and variable costs of each step of production.

It is used internally by company management to make informed decisions about the business. It is not the same as financial accounting as it does not provide information to external users of financial statements and therefore it is not required to stick to the same set standards and can be more flexible.

It usually considers all input costs, including variable and fixed costs. There are various kinds of cost accounting, including *standard costing*, *lean accounting*, *activity-based costing* and *marginal costing*.

Types of costs

Fixed costs don't vary dependent on production levels. So, a rent payment for an office would be a fixed cost as an increase or decrease of production would not cause this cost to change.

Variable costs change with the level, or amount, of production. For

GAAP AND IFRS

Generally accepted accounting principles (GAAP) and *international financial reporting standards* (IFRS) are the two main sets of basic accounting principles used in the USA (GAAP) and most of the rest of the world including the EU (IFRS). These principles must be followed by companies when creating their financial statements.

These systems aim to improve the consistency, clarity and ability to compare financial information. In the USA, if a company doesn't follow GAAP accounting, they are said to follow *pro forma accounting*.

The ten principles of GAAP

There are ten key concepts that show the mission of GAAP:

1. *Principle of regularity:* The company accounts have adhered to GAAP rules and regulations as a standard.
2. *Principle of consistency:* Companies apply the same standards throughout to enable financial comparisons between periods.
3. *Principle of sincerity:* Providing an accurate and impartial picture of the financial situation of a company.
4. *Principle of permanence of methods:* The procedures and methods used in the reporting must be consistent, allowing the company's financial information to be compared.
5. *Principle of non-compensation:* Negatives and positives should be reported transparently and without the expectation of compensation for debt.
6. *Principle of prudence:* Fact-based financial data should be presented, and not speculation.
7. *Principle of continuity:* It should be considered that the business will continue to operate for the purpose of valuing assets.
8. *Principle of periodicity:* Entries into the accounts should be made across the appropriate periods of time. For example, revenue must be reported in the accounting period to which it is relevant.
9. *Principle of materiality:* All financial data and accounting information should be disclosed in the financial reports.
10. *Principle of utmost good faith:* This comes from the Latin *uberrimae fidei*, which is used in the insurance industry. It assumes that all parties will be and have been honest in all transactions.

Differences between GAAP and IFRS

GAAP and IFRS are fairly similar, but despite inference of the names, GAAP can be considered rules-based and IFRS is more principles-based. Some key differences in implementation are that inventory cannot be reversed once written down under GAAP, whereas under IFRS, a write-down can be reversed in the future under specific conditions. Under IFRS, revenue can also be reported sooner, which could show a higher stream of revenue than the GAAP equivalent of the same balance sheet.

Operating costs

example, a shop that makes chocolates may have higher ingredient costs (because it buys more ingredients from suppliers) if it increases production for Valentine's Day.

Operating costs are those that are associated with the day-to-day running of a business. They can be fixed or variable.

Direct costs are those that are specifically associated with the product. If a carpenter spends five hours making a chair, then the direct costs of the finished product include the hours of labour to make the chair, as well as the cost of the raw materials.

Indirect costs are those that cannot be directly linked to a product. With the example of the carpenter, this could be the electricity costs to run the electric sander and table saw. These are indirect because they are not exact and can be complicated to attach to an individual product.

Job costing and process costing

Job costing is when production costs are attributed to a particular unit. In the example of a carpenter and upholsterer (or a team of such craftspeople) making a chair, all the hours worked on that item would be recorded on a cost sheet, along with any raw materials or other component parts that would be charged to the production job linked to that specific chair. This can then be used to create a bill for the customer or to track profits on that particular job.

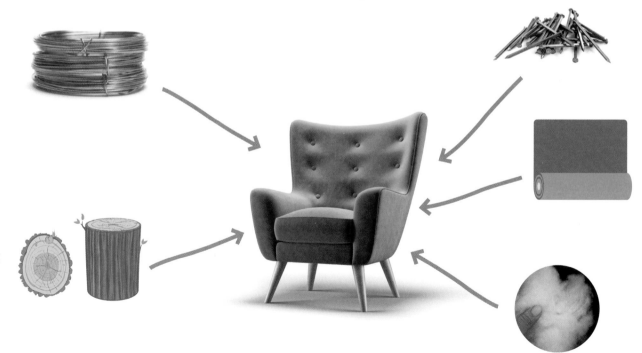

All of the components that go to make up a chair have to be accounted for when costing such an item.

Process costing is where costs are accumulated over longer-term production runs of mass-produced products. For example, the manufacture of 200,000 packets of spaghetti would require that all the flour used in the process, as well as all the labour in the factory, would be added to a cost account, and then divided by the number of packets produced to give the *cost per unit*.

Activity-based costing

This is a form of costing that takes the overhead costs from each department and assigns them to particular cost objects, such as products or services. It assigns both direct and indirect costs. The *activity-based costing* (ABC) method uses activities, which can be any event, unit of work or task with a particular aim – designing products, operating machines, setting up production processes or distributing products.

For example, if a spaghetti-extruding machine requires periodic maintenance, then these maintenance costs are ultimately assigned to the products produced. If after every 10,000 hours, the machine needs £500 worth of maintenance time and materials, then every hour that it runs costs £0.05 (500/10,000). These machine hours would then be considered a *cost driver* – as it affects the cost of the product being manufactured.

The maintenance of machinery is one of a number of costs incurred in the production of spaghetti

Variable vs. absorption costing

If only variable production costs are included in the product cost, then this is considered *variable costing*, whereas in absorption costing, all the absorbed costs are taken into account – fixed and variable production costs are first deducted, and then fixed and variable selling expenses are deducted.

Variable costing is also known as *marginal* or *direct costing*, and absorption costing is also known as *full costing*.

Other differences include:

Basis	Variable costing	Absorption costing
Internal/external use	Generally used for internal reporting purposes. Management decisions are taken on the basis of variable costing.	Used for reporting to external stakeholders as well as for filing taxes. It is in line with GAAP and IFRS.
Relevance	Used to compare profitability of different product lines. The business can analyze based on costs, volumes and profits.	Used for calculating per-unit costs based on all costs (including fixed overhead costs).
Reporting	Based on internal specifications of reporting and presentation.	Based on external reporting standards given by external agencies.
Inventory	Only involves variable production costs to be assigned to inventory, work-in-progress and COGS.	Considers all production costs and includes them in inventory and work-in-progress..
Contribution	Calculates difference between sales and variable cost of sales.	Used to calculate net profit.
Profit	Profit can be easier to predict as it is a function of sales.	More difficult to predict the effect of change in sales on profit.

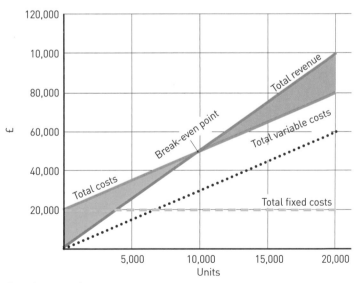

Break-even chart

Cost-volume-profit analysis

Cost-volume-profit analysis looks at the effect of sales volume and product costs on operating profit of a business. It demonstrates how the operating profit is impacted by changes in fixed costs, variable costs, the price per unit sold and the sales mix across multiple products.

The graph at left demonstrates the relationship between total costs and total revenue. The area in between the two lines, and below the break-even point, represent losses whereas the area above the break-even point indicates the total profit. This kind of graph helps to show profit at different levels of production output – in this example, the company would need to be producing more than 10,000 units to make a profit.

Capital budgeting

Capital budgeting is a planning process that is used to determine which of a company's long-term potential investments are worth pursuing. The most common approaches to choosing a project are payback period (PB), internal rate of return (IRR) and net present value (NPV).

- *Payback period* demonstrates how long it would take to have sufficient cash flows to recover the original investment.
- *Internal rate of return* is the return expected for a specific project – if this rate is higher than the cost of capital, it's considered to be a good project.
- *Net present value* indicates how profitable a project should be vs. potential alternatives.

In the following example of PB, it would take four years to recoup the initial investment from cash flows:

Investment	Cash inflows				
Year 0	Year 1	Year 2	Year 3	Year 4	Year 5
-1,000,000	250,000	250,000	250,000	250,000	250,000

This ignores the time value of money and doesn't account for cash flows at the end of the project, such as equipment salvage value.

Alternatively, to calculate the *internal rate of return,* you need to determine the discount rate (the amount that each cash flow needs to be discounted to account for its present value) that would result in a *net present value* (NPV) of zero. The rule is:

IRR > Cost of capital = Accept project
IRR < Cost of capital = Reject project

You can use Excel or online calculators to help you determine the discount rate that will set NPV to zero.

NPV discounts after-tax cash flows by the weighted average cost of capital. The

OPPORTUNITY COSTS AND SUNK COSTS

When one decision is made over another, the benefits of the alternative decision that have been given up (the one not chosen) are the *opportunity cost.*

It is most relevant for two mutually exclusive events and can be used in planning by management. For example, if a farmer chooses to plant quinoa, the opportunity cost is the possibility of sowing a different crop, or an alternate use of the resources (such as renting out the land and machinery). In investing, it is the difference in the return between an investment that was made and one that was not made.

Sunk costs are costs that have already been incurred, so they shouldn't make any difference to current decision making. They are unrecoverable or unavoidable costs and as such are excluded from future decisions. An example could be the amount spent by a company on a previous marketing campaign. Other areas of expenditure that could sometimes be considered sunk costs include historical wages, research, equipment or past rent.

rule is that an investment with a positive NPV should go ahead, and a negative NPV means it should be rejected. One of the benefits of NPV is that you can compare mutually exclusive projects. In the table below, assuming a discount rate of 10%, both projects have a positive NPV, but project B has a better return and should be preferred.

	Investment	Cash inflows				
Project A	Year 0	Year 1	Year 2	Year 3	Year 4	Year 5
	-1,000,000	250,000	250,000	250,000	250,000	250,000
Project B	Year 0	Year 1	Year 2	Year 3	Year 4	Year 5
	-1,000,000	250,000	-250,000	250,000	250,000	2,500,000

Weighted average cost of capital

Measuring how much it costs a company to borrow money is another way of assessing their profitability. The *weighted average cost of capital* (WACC) looks at the cost of capital where each category of capital is weighted proportionately.

Included in the WACC calculation are all sources of capital – common and preferred stock, bonds and any other kind of long-term debt. Each source of capital is multiplied by its relevant weight by market value, and then added together to determine the total.

Capital asset pricing model

The *capital asset pricing model* (CAPM) can be used to estimate the cost of equity. This needs the rate of return (RoR) for the general market, the beta value of the company stock, and the risk-free rate:

$$Cost\ of\ equity = Risk\text{-}free\ RoR + Beta \times (Market\ RoR - Risk\text{-}free\ RoR)$$

Using publicly available financial documents, we can give a real-world example of WACC for the US retailer Walmart.

In April 2021, the risk-free rate (as represented by the annual return on a 20-year treasury bond) was 2.21%.

Walmart's systemic risk compared to the market (known as the beta) was 0.48 as of 14 April 2021. The average return on the market (using the S&P 500) is roughly 8%. The cost of equity can be established with the capital asset pricing model. Using this, Walmart's cost of equity is 4.99%.

The market cap for Walmart was $394 billion as of 14 April 2021. The long-term debt was $44 billion at the end of the 2021 fiscal year and the average cost of debt for Walmart was 3.9%. The corporate tax rate is assumed to be 33.3%.

WARREN BUFFETT: BERKSHIRE HATHAWAY

Warren Buffett is an American business magnate, investor, and philanthropist. The chairman and CEO of Berkshire Hathaway, he is considered one of the most successful investors in the world. Buffett is known for his value investing strategy, and his ability to identify undervalued companies and turn them into profitable investments.

Buffett was born in 1930 in Omaha, Nebraska. He began his investing career at the age of 11, when he bought shares in a local utility company. In 1956, Buffett started his own investment partnership and over the next decade, he made a number of successful investments in companies such as Coca-Cola, Washington Post, and GEICO. In 1965, Buffett took control of Berkshire Hathaway, a textile manufacturing company.

It was struggling at the time, but Buffett turned it into a highly successful conglomerate.

Buffett is sometimes known as the 'Oracle of Omaha' for his uncanny ability to pick stocks that outperform the market. He follows a value investing strategy, which involves buying stocks that are undervalued by the market and holding them for the long term. This has proven to be a very successful strategy, as Berkshire Hathaway's stock portfolio has outperformed the S&P 500 index by a wide margin over the past several decades.

Today, Berkshire Hathaway is a holding company that owns a number of businesses, including GEICO, BNSF Railway, and Duracell. The company has a market value of over $500 billion, and Buffett is worth an estimated $84 billion.

A philanthropist all his life, he has pledged to give away 99% of his fortune to charitable causes.

The WACC is calculated as follows:

$$(E/V * Re) + (D/V * Rd * (1 - Tc))$$

where:

E = Market value of the firm's equity
D = Market value of the firm's debt
$(V = E + D)$
Re = Cost of equity
Rd = Cost of debt
Tc = Corporate tax rate

Using the figures on Walmart's financial reports, the calculation is as follows:

$$V = E + D = \$394 \text{ billion} + \$44 \text{ billion} = \$438 \text{ billion}$$

The equity-linked cost of capital for Walmart is:

$$(E/V) \times Re = (394/438) \times 4.99$$

The debt component is:

$$(D/V) \times Rd \times (1 - Tc) = (44/438) \times 3.9\% \times (1 - 33.3\%) = 0.0026$$

Using the figures above, the WACC for Walmart can be determined as:

$$0.045 + 0.0026 = 4.76$$

On average, Walmart can be assumed to be paying around 4.76% per year as the cost of overall capital raised through a combination of debt and equity.

AI, ML AND FINTECH

ARTIFICIAL INTELLIGENCE, MACHINE LEARNING AND DEEP LEARNING

Artificial intelligence, machine learning and deep learning are three related fields of study that focus on the development of computer programs that can learn and work on their own.

Artificial intelligence (AI) is the process of creating computer programs that can think for themselves. This can be done in a number of ways, but the most common and simplest version is to create algorithms, or sets of rules, that can sort, process and analyze data.

An *algorithm* is a set of instructions for carrying out a process (or a calculation). It is functionally a step-by-step guide for solving a problem or completing a task. In AI, AI algorithms can be programmed in by the person creating it or built to change and adapt. Evolutionary algorithms, artificial neural networks and reinforcement learning are all examples of algorithms that create themselves.

Machine learning (ML) is a type of AI that focuses on giving computer programs the ability to learn from experience. This is done by feeding the program datasets that it can use to learn from. For example, a machine learning algorithm might be given a dataset of images of animals, and it will learn to identify different animals by looking for patterns in the data.

Deep learning (DL) is a type of machine learning that uses a particular type of algorithm, called a *neural network*. Neural networks are modelled after the way that the human brain learns. They are made up of many small processing units, called *neurons*, that are connected to each other to create layers. Deep learning algorithms learn by adjusting the connections between the neurons and layers in the network.

The neural networks in deep learning are comprised of many layers of neurons. Illlustration by Jamillah Knowles (www.jemimahknightsudio.com).

What is AI?

AI is an umbrella term that encompasses various methods of creating intelligent systems. ML is a subset of AI that focuses on learning from data.

Alan Turing (1912–54).

Deep learning is a newer approach that uses neural networks to learn complex patterns in data.

Alan Turing's seminal 1950 paper 'Computing Machinery and Intelligence' marks the start of conversations about AI in earnest. Turing, sometimes referred to as the father of computer science, essentially asked: *'Can machines think?'* Turing created a test, now known as the 'Turing test', where a human questioner would try to tell the difference between a computer and human text response.

The field of AI, at its most basic, combines computer science and large datasets, which enables problem-solving. It also contains the sub-fields of machine learning and deep learning. These are often AI algorithms that look to build systems capable of classifying, predicting or calculating creatively based on inputted data.

As expected of any emerging and novel technology in the market, there is some significant hype around AI and its current and future capacities. As expressed in *Gartner's hype cycle*, product innovations follow 'a typical progression of innovation, from overenthusiasm through a period of disillusionment to an eventual understanding of the innovation's relevance and role in a market or domain.'

THE TURING TEST

The *Turing test* is a test of a machine's intelligence. It is named after Alan Turing, the English computer scientist, cryptanalyst and mathematician, who first proposed it in 1950. A human questioner interacts with a machine and a human subject. The questioner asks questions and gives commands, and the machine and human respond in turn. If the questioner cannot tell which is the machine and which is the human, then the machine is said to have passed the Turing test.

Turing's idea was that you could say a computer possesses artificial intelligence if it can present what seem like human responses under specific conditions. However, given the current abilities of ML language generation models, the Turing test is likely to be too simplistic to accurately determine anything more than effectively 'human-like' responses, and is not a useful measure of intelligence, thought or behaviours other than language.

DeepMind

DeepMind is a London-based artificial intelligence company founded in 2010 by Demis Hassabis, Shane Legg and Mustafa Suleyman. It is part of the Alphabet (Google) family of companies. Rather than focus on specific applications, the company's aim is to 'solve intelligence' and build *artificial general intelligence* (AGI).

DeepMind has made a number of significant achievements since its formation. In 2016, the company's AlphaGo artificial intelligence program defeated a

professional human player at the game of Go (being played by humans in the picture opposite) – a game that had long been considered too complex for machines to master. This was a major milestone in the field of AI and demonstrated the power of their technology.

Other areas that DeepMind has had success in include 3D video game environments, creating programs that are able to beat human players at a number of different games; using AI to improve the efficiency of energy use; and to develop new methods of early detection for disease.

More recently, it built a program that can predict the three-dimensional shapes of proteins. These shapes are important because they determine how the proteins function. DeepMind's program, AlphaFold, was able to correctly predict the shapes of more than 100 proteins that had been previously studied.

DeepMind is probably getting closer to what most people imagine when they think of AI – the kind that tends to be presented in fiction and films. An 'intelligence' that can learn, compared to the more limited ML algorithms or other more rudimentary versions of AI.

Machine learning and some current models

The following text (in bold) was generated with GPT-3, OpenAI's large-scale language-generation model. It was given these two prompts:

'An article giving a broad overview of what Machine Learning is, explaining it step by step.'
And then:
'Write an article explaining how the XXX algorithm works, explaining it step by step.'

Upon generating draft language, this content was reviewed and very lightly edited for formatting. The prompts were run a few times until a satisfactory text was produced for each section and that text was then used without changes:

Machine learning is a subfield of artificial intelligence (AI) that is concerned with the design and development of algorithms that can learn from and make predictions on data. The result is that, instead of being explicitly programmed to perform a task, a machine learning algorithm can automatically improve its performance by learning from experience.

In general, there are three types of machine learning algorithms:

1. *Supervised learning*: In supervised learning, the algorithm is given a training dataset of known inputs and outputs. The algorithm then learns to map the inputs to the outputs.
2. *Unsupervised learning*: In unsupervised learning, the algorithm is given a dataset of unknown inputs and must learn to find patterns in the data.
3. *Reinforcement learning*: In reinforcement learning, the algorithm is given a task to perform and a feedback signal indicating how well it is doing. The algorithm then learns to perform the task by trial and error.

GPT3

GPT3 is a machine learning algorithm that is used to predict the next word in a sentence. It is based on a statistical model that is trained on a large corpus of text. The algorithm is able to predict the next word with a high accuracy.

The GPT3 algorithm works by firstly taking in a sentence as input. It then tokenises the sentence into a series of words. Each word is then vectorised, which means that it is converted into a numerical representation. The algorithm then looks at the context of the sentence, and predicts the most likely word that will come next.

The GPT3 algorithm is a powerful tool for predictive text, and has a wide range of applications. It can be used to improve the accuracy of machine translation, and to generate text responses in chatbots.

PaLM

The PaLM algorithm is a text-mining algorithm that can be used to find and extract important information from text data. The algorithm works by first identifying and then extracting the most important words and phrases from a text document. The PaLM algorithm is designed to work with a variety of different languages, and it has been shown to be effective at extracting information from a variety of different types of text data.

OpenAI's Codex 12B

OpenAI's Codex 12B is a computer system designed to read and comprehend text documents. It does this by breaking down the text into a series of smaller pieces, each of which is then processed by a separate "reader" module.

The Codex 12B system is designed to be scalable, so that it can be used to process large volumes of text quickly. It is also designed to be accurate, so that it can correctly identify the meaning of a text even if it is poorly written or ambiguous.

To test the system, OpenAI used it to read a set of Wikipedia articles. The system was able to correctly identify the main topic of each article, and also to identify the relationships between different topics.

The Codex 12B system is an important step forward in the development of artificial intelligence. It shows that computers can be used to understand complex text documents, and that they can be used to extract useful information from them.

DALL-E2

OpenAI's DALL-E2 is a computer system that has been designed to generate images from textual descriptions. The system is based on a neural network that has been trained on a large dataset of images. The system is able to generate realistic images from textual descriptions.

You can create ML-generated texts from a prompt using GPT3 at beta.openai.com

Neural networks

Artificial neural networks have nodes called 'neurons', which are given data and then co-operate to solve problems. A neural net adjusts these networks of nodes and the links between them to see if the resulting behaviour is more successful at finding a solution. As the network discovers more efficient patterns that are better at producing solutions, it makes these the default setting for the next set of problems. This is similar to the way in which the human brain works. A neural network is 'deep' if it has many layers of neurons.

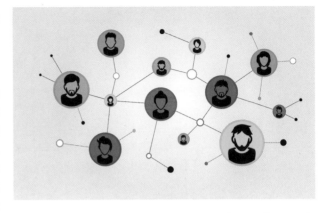

A neural network.

These kinds of neural networks are already being used to look at medical scans, and to power some features of autonomous driving, but they have some serious limitations. There is evidence that tiny changes in the input data can lead to wildly different outcomes, making these models potentially dangerously unstable – for example, researchers found that changing a single pixel on an input image could make the AI think that a picture of a horse is a picture of a frog.

Very small data changes can lead to very different outcomes in recognition.

Despite building ever bigger language-processing systems, the same weaknesses still show up in many ML models: they often generate toxic, biased and inaccurate text. They can also generate racist remarks, produce misinformation or store personal identifiable information.

One of the arguments against continuing to increase the size of these models is that the software can't understand language and is only regurgitating patterns it sees in the training data. Smaller and more focused models may help to mitigate this problem, as well as better and more open use of training data so that source texts and the basic information a model uses is open to increased scrutiny.

The current state of soft vs. hard AI

There are several examples of *soft AI* that are in use today, such as *chatbots* and *digital assistants*. These AI applications are designed to perform relatively simple tasks that require little to no human input and need only a series of input-output algorithms to make them function.

Significant progress has also been made in the development of so-called *strong* or *hard AI* – that which is able to autonomously learn and understand complex tasks, such as drive cars or beat humans at complex games. This technology is still largely in its infancy, and there are significant concerns about its potential impact on society, particularly with regard to job losses to automation or the risks posed by AI-powered weapons.

If an AGI starts to be able to learn, evolve and develop by itself, it could become very complicated for humans to comprehend or even control its actions. Therefore, it is crucial to make sure that AI is developed cautiously and responsibly, in order to avoid negative consequences for society.

FINTECH
What is FinTech?

New technologies and software that improve or automate the way in which financial services are delivered or used are commonly referred to as *FinTech*, a portmanteau of financial and technology.

This relatively new industry tends to be focused on the management of financial operations, processes or consumer financial activity, and often uses smartphones to deliver new software-based solutions to end-users.

FinTech sectors

There are various sectors within FinTech, from retail banking apps, to education, fundraising, and savings and investment management.

Many of the firms in the FinTech space have unbundled some specific service or offer from the incumbents in the industry (for instance, creating a bespoke, automatic saving app, operated on your phone, but independent of your bank account). Usually, these firms are using technology to help cut down on operating costs as well as to create efficiencies they can pass on to the consumer in the form of cheaper or more convenient products.

Early iterations

The beginnings of the modern FinTech industry were in reinventing and improving the back-end services that help large institutions to operate. One such example would be Paypal in the early 2000s, which created secure software for consumer or business transactions on computers, in multiple currencies. It was a platform that allowed people to use their existing financial tools (credit cards, banks accounts) to transfer money online.

In the developing world, M-Pesa launched in 2007 and allowed users in Kenya to transfer or store money using text messages on their mobile phones. This was particularly important for this market, as many consumers did not have a traditional bank account.

Financial inclusion (in the case of M-Pesa, serving the unbanked, or underbanked) aims to help consumers who don't have access to traditional banking services for geographic, economic or technological reasons. By making these kinds of transactions possible for end-users using existing technology that many already had access to,

M-Pesa was a leapfrog technology for Kenya, building a successful FinTech platform even before widespread wifi or internet access became available.

Challenger banks and regulatory changes

The most well-known examples of modern FinTech companies in Europe and America are probably *challenger banks*. These are new institutions that offer traditional banking services (and extra features), but do not have physical branches and usually operate mostly or entirely through an app.

Monzo, *Starling* and *Revolut* are all established players in the UK market whereas *Chime* and *Current* were the most downloaded banking apps in the USA in 2021.

In the UK, these banks are regulated and authorized by the UK financial regulator to accept retail deposits and allow them to be referred to as a bank.

The impact of challenger banks and the degree to which many customers have embraced banking by smartphone has encouraged traditional banks to adopt some of their practices.

In addition to the basic services a traditional simple bank account provides, challenger banks often offer services that high street banks don't provide with basic accounts – automatic budgeting, notifications about your spending or opportunities to simply invest your money, as well as fee-free transactions when abroad. Incumbent banks are starting to respond to these challenger banks by matching their features and improving their apps and online interfaces.

Open Banking

In Europe and the UK, there is now an *Open Banking Standard* that enables customers to securely share their account information online, down to the transaction level, with third-party providers.

This data can then be used to provide bespoke services or analysis for the consumer, such as automated saving apps like *Plum,* which assesses recent and upcoming transactions and the overall balance to determine how much you can afford to set aside in savings that week, and then automatically moves that money into a savings account for you.

Other examples of FinTech using the Open Banking Standard are money management tools such as *Mint,* or budgeting and deals apps, such as *Snoop.*

Insurance, payments and other services

Most FinTech companies are seeking to out-compete existing service providers in the industry by offering more efficient operations, faster or better service, or by serving segments of the population who are not currently targeted by incumbents.

Sectors embracing FinTech

Stripe is an Irish-American FinTech company providing an easy-to-use payment processing platform to physical businesses as well as APIs that allow e-commerce websites and apps to process transactions. Recent strategic additions to their offering have included: capital financing for SMEs; creating and managing company credit cards; and fraud and risk tools.

Affirm and *Klarna* are providers of short-term, immediate loans for consumer purchases. Their interest rates are often high, but they say they can safely offer loans to users with poor or no credit ratings (which in turn, helps to build their credit history).

In 2022, there are FinTech applications trying to streamline the mortgage application process (*Better Mortgage*), improve the process of getting large home improvement loans (*GreenSky*), simplify stock trading (*Robinhood*), offer peer-to-peer lending (*OnDeck, Lending Club*), provide business with capital (*Funding Circle, Lendio, Kabbage*) or help with brokering insurance (*Oscar, Anorak*).

B2B FinTech

Although the most obvious FinTech companies are in the consumer space, there are a number of offerings in the business to business (B2B) market for FinTech, too. These look to improve spend-management, real-time payment processing, underlying infrastructure or even helping with cash flow for supplier payments.

These are all services that previously existed, but often they were either only available to large organizations, not small businesses, or they were inconvenient and inefficient to access through existing financial institutions. The FinTech era has used software to help democratize access to the full range of financial tools and products, giving greater flexibility to businesses of all types.

BLOCKCHAIN AND CRYPTOCURRENCIES

A *blockchain* is a kind of digital database that stores information and shares this information across a network of distributed computers, or *nodes*.

The best-known examples of blockchains are probably those that power cryptocurrency systems such as Bitcoin. What the blockchain does in this situation is maintain a secure and decentralized record of transactions.

One of the main benefits of a blockchain is that they can guarantee the fidelity and security of a data record, and they can provide trust without the need for a third party to provide validation. It achieves this by having the network validate the transactions as they are requested.

Most databases put their data into tables, but a blockchain structures data in blocks that are then joined together, and each block contains the 'fingerprint' of the block before it. This then effectively creates an immutable timeline of data once it is stored in a decentralized manner.

A 'block' in a blockchain has a certain capacity – once it is full, this is closed and linked to the previous block. This is what creates the *chain* part of the blockchain. All new information is added to the end of the chain as it fills up each block in turn.

One of the main structural advantages of a blockchain is that the information on it can be recorded and distributed, but not edited. This means it is good for creating ledgers of information that cannot be altered, deleted or destroyed.

To stop dishonest users validating a bad transaction

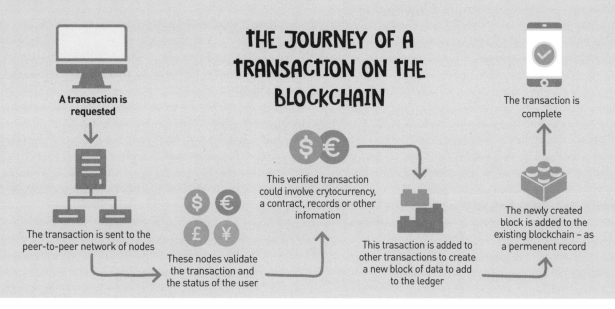

THE JOURNEY OF A TRANSACTION ON THE BLOCKCHAIN

A transaction is requested

The transaction is sent to the peer-to-peer network of nodes

These nodes validate the transaction and the status of the user

This verified transaction could involve crytocurrency, a contract, records or other infomation

This trasaction is added to other transactions to create a new block of data to add to the ledger

The newly created block is added to the existing blockchain – as a permenent record

The transaction is complete

– for instance, approving a transfer of money a user doesn't actually have – blockchains use mechanisms such as proof of work, or proof of stake, to disincentivize this. This process of auditing transactions and being rewarded for it is known as *mining*.

PROOF OF WORK ▶ *Where a network user competes with others to solve an extremely complex mathematical problem, which gives them the right to then be the node that adds the next block to the chain. In return for adding the next block to the chain, they receive payment.*

PROOF OF STAKE ▶ *This has a similar intention to proof of work but requires putting up money (a stake) to compete for the right to add the next block to the chain.*

What is cryptocurrency?

Cryptocurrency is a form of digital-only money that uses cryptography to verify and authenticate transactions and secure supply. It uses the peer-to-peer system of nodes on a blockchain that allows anyone to send and receive payments. When money is transferred between users, these transactions are all recorded in an append-only blockchain describing the details in this public ledger. Users store cryptocurrency in digital wallets that allow people to receive cryptocurrency and store the codes that enable them to send it to others.

The best-known example of a cryptocurrency, and the first to be created, is Bitcoin. This is often abbreviated as BTC. There are many different cryptocurrencies, though only a few are currently particularly widely used and traded.

Bitcoin uses a blockchain as a way to transparently record a public ledger of payments, but blockchain can theoretically be used to record other kinds of datapoints in a permanent, public and uneditable way. This could be things such as votes in an election, product inventories, personal identity documents, etc.

Mining

Cryptocurrency *mining*, using Bitcoin as an example, is a highly complex computing process that uses a large amount of computing power. Miners compete using proof of work to be the first to verify transactions, and earn rewards paid in that currency.

Once a new block is successfully verified, the block is distributed to all other miners and devices with a full copy of the blockchain. Miners are then paid with transaction fees from the users and newly created – or *minted* – digital currency.

Servers at a Bitcoin cryptocurrency mining farm.

BITCOIN VS. ETHEREUM

Bitcoin

Created in 2009, *Bitcoin* – also referred to as BTC (example below) – was the first cryptocurrency and is still the most common. It was developed by a figure known as Satoshi Nakamoto – whose real identity is still unknown.

Ethereum

First launched in 2015, *Ethereum* is a blockchain platform that has its own cryptocurrency, called Ether – also referred to as ETH. It is the second most popular cryptocurrency as of 2022.

The most important difference between the two is that the Ethereum network is a *programmable* blockchain that can hold information that isn't just about currency; it can be applied in numerous areas, including Decentralized Finance (DeFi), smart contracts, dApps and NFTs.

Smart contracts

Smart contracts are a kind of computer program stored on a blockchain that contain instructions that are carried out only when certain conditions are met. The term was coined by Nick Szabo, a computer scientist involved in the early development of cryptocurrencies.

A smart contract can automate the execution of an agreement, meaning that all the participants can be certain of the outcome without the need for a trusted third party to intervene. As such, these kinds of contract are known as *self-executing*.

Among the terms a smart contract needs to define are how transactions and data are represented on the blockchain, what the 'if/when/then' rules that govern the transaction are, explore exceptions and define how disputes can be resolved. They can usually send and receive cryptocurrency as a part of their execution.

Because they are created in computer code, they can be used to manage complex transactions with multiple parties over a long period of time and because they don't involve third parties, such as lawyers or notaries, they can be executed very quickly once the conditions are met.

However, because of the immutable nature of a blockchain, errors, bugs or flaws in smart contracts can be difficult to fix even after they are found.

DAOs and dApps

Decentralized applications – which can also be known as *dApps* – are digital applications that use smart contracts on a blockchain to run, instead of on a single computer or server. Because such dApps are decentralized, they are free from censorship interference, have the resilience of the network and are relatively transparent.

NON-FUNGIBLE TOKENS AND WEB 3

The existence of digital objects other than currency on the Ethereum platform in particular has led to the rise of non-fungible tokens, or NFTs (below).

These are unique, digital tokens that exist on a blockchain and cannot be replicated. They can represent real-world items, or more commonly, pieces of digital art. One of the advantages is that as these tokens are part of a blockchain, a smart contract can allow the original creator to receive residual payments whenever it is sold on to another user.

However, NFTs don't stop the digital assets they represent from being copied for free. They merely represent ownership of the asset. It is the token that is bought and secured, not the asset itself.

This is a very young market, and most of the transactions have so far taken place among a very small subset of the users. However, some analysts point to the NFT market as an example of the *greater fool theory* – the idea that someone can still make money on an asset that is overvalued as long as you can find one more person who is a 'greater fool' who believes it is worth even more.

Web 3 is an idea still in the early stages that a blockchain could be used to restructure the internet as a whole. One of these ideas is to register ownership for the assets that make up the internet (everything from the colours on a website to the font used for an article). One of the benefits of this is that the principles of residual payment for the creator or owner could be built in using smart contracts.

However, among numerous other obstacles, the lack of consumer need, the immaturity of the technology itself and the inherent structure of the web – effectively free information at the point of use – could make it difficult for these ideas to gain traction.

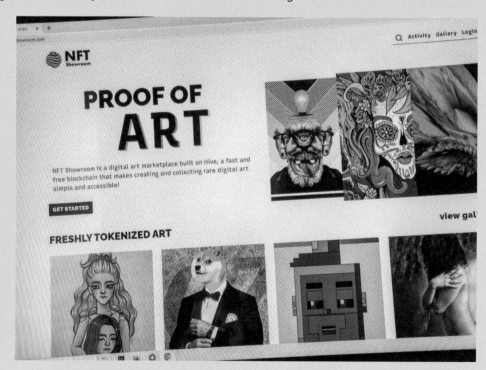

A *decentralized autonomous organization*, or DAO, is effectively a kind of dApp. It's a complex structure of smart contracts that operates as a business using these contracts to automate its essential and non-essential processes including the governance of the organization.

A DAO allows for different forms of governance from existing businesses as they don't require centralized leadership but are collectively owned and managed through smart contracts.

Because a DAO can be spread across global jurisdictions, and there is currently no legal framework for them, any legal issues that arise might need solutions that involve numerous different regional laws.

Downsides and issues with the blockchain

- Scalability of the technology can be an issue as it contains inefficiencies and bottlenecks. The network can become congested, and transactions can take a long time to complete, and even when at full speed it is slower than traditional systems. Bitcoin can process about seven transactions per second, whereas VISA processes around 1,700 transactions per second on average.
- As a blockchain ledger grows, it gets larger and more difficult for each node to store and process. The Bitcoin blockchain is already hundreds of gigabytes.
- When using a blockchain for data records such as identity, it doesn't stop people lying about their inputs. Although the blockchain itself does stop middleman attacks, these are effectively encouraged by the structure itself.
- The immutability of the blockchain means reversing errors can be very difficult, and in addition, the public nature of the ledger could potentially affect privacy rights.
- The regulation around cryptocurrencies and blockchains remains uncertain and varies considerably by jurisdiction, which has possible legal ramifications.
- There are significant energy resources required to maintain a blockchain, with huge amounts of electricity and computing power required to mine, mint and verify transactions.
- The blockchain doesn't have interoperable standards that would allow different networks to co-operate with each other.
- Lastly, as an immature technology with little existing regulation, it is a market that is vulnerable to scams.

Environmental and energy issues

Bitcoin and other cryptocurrencies that use proof-of-work need huge amounts of energy to run the computations required for mining.

Bitcoin alone has been estimated to generate annual emissions of carbon dioxide at around 22 megatons, according to a Technical University of Munich study. This is about the same as the total annual emissions of Las Vegas or the nation of Jordan. The same study suggests including other cryptocurrencies would likely account for double these emissions.

Although spread around the world, the majority of Bitcoin mining as of 2022 occurs in China, which accounts for 65% of Bitcoin mining activities.

However, there are new methods being designed for validating cryptocurrency transactions that may help reduce energy requirements.

Chapter Seven
ORGANIZATIONAL BEHAVIOUR AND LEADERSHIP

Working in groups and teams • Organizational structure and culture • Corporate governance • Theories of leadership • Different types of negotiation

GROUP ROLES AND NORMS

TYPES OF TEAMS

THREATS TO GROUP EFFECTIVENESS

LEADERSHIP VS MANAGEMENT

LEADERSHIP AND POWER

CULTURE AND LEADERSHIIP

TEAMS

WORKING IN GROUPS AND TEAMS

TEAMS IN ACTION

TRANSFORMATIONAL, TRANSACTIONAL AND SERVANT LEADERSHIP

THEORIES OF LEADERSHIP

TRAIT AND PROCESS APPROACHES

TUCKMAN'S MODEL OF GROUP DEVELOPMENT

ORGANIZATIONAL BEHAVIOUR AND LEADERSHIP

FIEDLER'S CONTINGENCY THEORY

THE SITUATIONAL APPROACH

CREATING AND MAINTAINING CULTURE

CORPORATE GOVERNANCE

THE BOARD

STRUCTURE

ORGANIZATIONAL CULTURE

ORGANIZATIONAL STRUCTURE

MODERN ORGANIZATIONAL STRUCTURES

PROCEDURES AND DUTIES

MODELS OF CULTURE

MANAGING ORGANIZATIONAL CHANGE

STRUCTURAL FORCES IN ORGANIZATION

COMPANY VISION AND BUSINESS PHILOSOPHY

SELECTION, COMPENSATION AND EVALUATION

CEO COMPENSATION AND SUCCESSION

WORKING IN GROUPS AND TEAMS

A group is more than two people who share goals and norms and have an identity in common. Teams are a specific kind of group, whereas groups are the simplest arrangement of multiple people with some sort of shared aim or intention. These are the smallest arrangements found in an organization and tend to be focused on projects or smaller tasks and activities.

Groups and teams

Groups and their life cycles

There are a series of stages to the development of a group, defined by the psychologist Bruce Tuckman as:

1. *Forming:* The group get acquainted with each other and the task at hand.
2. *Storming:* The group tests the limits of the leader and other members, and the boundaries of their own power and influence.
3. *Norming:* Group norms, goals and processes are established, and roles for each member are defined.
4. *Performing:* The group is now solving problems and achieving their aims.
5. *Adjourning:* The group has completed the tasks it intended and disperses.

Group roles and norms

Groups have norms, which are shared attitudes that guide the behaviour of all members. Group roles are an informal set of expected behaviours for a member in a particular position.

Some examples of the roles found in groups are:

- An *initiator* suggests new ideas or aims.
- A *co-ordinator* pulls together suggestions and concepts.
- A *recorder* reports the discussions and outcomes.
- A *harmonizer* deals with conflict between group members.
- A *gatekeeper* encourages and keeps track of participation.

Initiators, co-ordinators and recorders allow the group to define common goals, set tasks and enact them. Harmonizers and gatekeepers help to create constructive relationships between group members.

However, there is often ambiguity about these roles – group members may be uncertain about the behaviours, expectations or consequences for a particular role. There are also times where there is role conflict if a group member believes they are responsible for more than one role, and these roles are incompatible or too demanding.

The five stages of Tuckman's model of group development.

Initiators, co-ordinators and recorders

A team meeting drawing in colleagues from inside and outside the office.

Teams – their components and characteristics

A team is a particular kind of group. In a team, members hold themselves mutually accountable, and have a common purpose, common goals and a common approach.

Three examples of the main kinds of tasks tackled by teams are:

1. *Production* tasks: Building a product, making something or creating a marketing plan.
2. *Idea-generating* tasks: Brainstorms, creating new processes.
3. *Problem-solving* tasks: Creating action plans and decision making.

Teams often have a great deal of task interdependence; this is a mutual dependence between team members undertaking a task. This can be divided into three kinds of interdependence:

1. *Pooled*: This is the interdependence between team members and happens when they make separate contributions to a common goal.
2. *Sequential*: This describes the output of one team member becoming the input of another team member.
3. *Reciprocal*: This is when team members work together on inputs.

There are sometimes roles in teams that span boundaries, for instance to connect the team to the wider organization. However, these roles are not always necessary – in self-managed teams, the members plan and manage their own activities but do not have direct supervision.

Teams in action

When working as a team, there are four key components to help with effective teamwork. These are cohesiveness, co-operation, communication and trust.

When there is a *cohesiveness* to a team, members feel bound together with a common purpose. This can be

TYPES OF TEAMS

Advice team: This makes proposals or recommendations for decisions by management.

Production team: This is focused on day-to-day operations and provides goods or services (such as a customer support team or a bicycle assembly team in a factory).

Action team: This is a specialized team that carries out specific actions on demand.

Project team: This is usually about creatively solving problems with specialized skillsets.

Virtual teams: This is a team that usually meets online. This can be very flexible but suffers from a lack of opportunity to foster social bonding, and it can be harder to build trust.

generated from a *socio-emotional basis*, where members stick together because they like each other. It can also be *instrumental cohesiveness*, which comes from the mutual dependence needed to achieve the task.

Co-operation is the process of working together, and not against each other, to achieve common goals. This is usually more productive than using competition and individual effort to attempt a task.

The most important predictor of a team's success is *how* team members *communicate* (even more than *what* they communicate). Teams are most productive when they have valuable interactions outside of formal settings, and when each team member communicates to the same level as all other team members.

The last element to effective teams is trust. This is when members have reciprocal faith in the intentions and behaviours of others. In successful teams, each member trusts that all the other members will put as much effort in as they will.

ORGANIZATIONAL STRUCTURE AND CULTURE
Organizational structure

The way in which responsibilities and roles are arranged within a company determine the *organizational structure*: who works with whom, how reporting is structured, etc. When an organization groups employees together, this is referred to as *departmentalization*. There are usually two ways in which a company structures departments – a functional or divisional structure.

A *functional structure* is one where activities are divided by skillset, for instance a customer support department or an engineering department. A *divisional structure* is one where the departments are divided by region or a set of products or services (for instance, the motorbike department vs. the car department).

Organizations are considered *formalized* if employees are strictly governed by many rules and regulations, and they are considered *centralized* if the authority for decision making is concentrated at the higher levels of the organization.

There are also different levels of hierarchy between organizations. Some companies have lots of employees

Employees in a hospital are organized via a formalized functional structure; often indicated by the colour of their uniforms.

reporting to a single manager, whereas others have much smaller groups reporting to each manager. This is the *span of control*. If there are fewer employees reporting to one manager – a smaller span of control – then the height of the organization is said to be *tall*, whereas if there are many employees reporting to a manager, the hierarchy is said to be *flat* – it has a greater span of control.

If a company is very formalized and highly centralized, they are normally rigid bureaucracies. An example of this would be McDonald's with its extremely tightly controlled operations.

Structural forces in organizations

Two major structural forces can have an impact on organizations – differentiation and integration.

The division of work into various distinct or specialized types causes differences in the behaviour of the employees and alters their perspectives. This is *differentiation*. If there is too much differentiation in an organization it can lead to *miscommunication* (employees fail to understand each other's perspectives), *inefficiencies* (employees' efforts in one area slow down work in another) and *conflict* (where one area of work directly harms or stops work in another).

By contrast, *integration* is where specialized employees are co-ordinated to achieve a goal together. Forming matrix structures is one such integration strategy designed to deal with the problems caused by differentiation.

Ideally, a balance is found between these two forces.

Identifying the reasons for organizational change

Some change is inevitable in the life of any organization, but successful change must be managed. Identifying the reasons for change, and then planning the process, are important steps in successfully navigating this.

Changes happen in organizations for all kinds of reasons, but there are five key external forces that tend to contribute to change:

MODERN ORGANIZATIONAL STRUCTURES

A matrix organization is a modern organizational structure that combines functional and divisional structures. It groups employees from different departments into project or product teams.

Boundaryless organizations are those that look to remove the dividing lines between employees, such as hierarchy, geography or job function. It empowers those employees who are closest to the root of a problem to make decisions about it. It is constructed of self-managing and usually cross-functional teams that are organized around core business processes.

The three main types of boundaryless organizations are:

1. *Virtual organization:* This is a network of independent companies or contractors sharing skills, market access and costs. They are flexible and adaptable as each partner contributes to its area of core competency.
2. *Modular organization:* This looks to get rid of the boundaries with suppliers. They perform a few key functions and outsource other activities to suppliers and specialists. This keeps unit costs low and allows for the rapid development of new products.
3. *Learning organization:* This is an organization that is structured to continuously adapt by focusing on the creation and transfer of knowledge. All members have an active role in identifying and resolving issues. Communication and sharing of knowledge are key across all levels and functions of employee.

1. *Market conditions:* Recession in the economy, increase in competition.
2. *Societal values:* If customers care strongly about sustainability, the company may wish to alter its practices.
3. *Technology:* New products, ideas or capabilities may increase the need for change.
4. *Globalization:* Geographical changes to supply chains, overseas competitors, etc.
5. *Labour force demographics*: Age, education, etc. may create change in employment circumstances.

There are also internal catalysts for change, such as a reduction in productivity or a decline in staff morale, which could cause the company to alter aspects of the business.

Managing organizational change

Change management

It is important for the success of any change management that employees co-operate with the process. If change is mismanaged, then the chance of achieving business goals declines, the capacity to retain employees reduces and resources go to waste.

There are many possible reasons why employees may be resistant to change in an organization, but commonly they reflect concerns about their own capabilities to manage the changes proposed, or anxiety about their status or the security of their job. It is easier to manage the process of change if employees are clearly communicated with, brought on board, and can see that the overall benefits outweigh any personal cost to them.

As a useful way of thinking about how to manage these processes, psychologist Kurt Lewin outlined a three-step change model for implementing organizational change:

- *Unfreezing:* Ensure that employees are ready for and receptive to change.
- *Change:* Executing the change.
- *Refreezing:* Reinforcing these changes so that they become normalized.

Informal structures and entrepreneurship

Alternatively, more informal, organic structures – with lower centralization – allow for more entrepreneurial thinking. Companies such as 3M have used these kinds of structures to foster innovation across the company.

Lewin's change model.

Lewin	Kotter
Unfreeze	1. Create a sense of urgency
	2. Form a coalition.
	3. Create a vision for change
	4. Communicate the vision
Change	5. Eliminate obstacles to change
	6. Create small wins
	7. Build on change
Refreeze	8. Make change a part of culture

Also useful is Harvard Business School Professor John Kotter's eight steps for leading change. This builds onLewin's change model and the eight steps all fit within the three broader stages.

Organizational culture

The culture of an organization is the set of shared values and beliefs that underpin the identity of a company and guide behaviour. It means that members of the organization have a concept of what the company represents as well as a sense of their place in the organization.

The three layers of organizational culture are:

Shared values and beliefs

1. *Basic assumptions:* These are the values that are entrenched within the organization over time. They are often taken for granted and members may not be explicitly aware of them.
2. *Values:* These are the beliefs that the organization expresses. They give an organization a behavioural compass either from the values espoused by management, or the enacted values from what employees actually do.

The competing values framework (CVF).

3. *Artefacts:* These are the tangible and visible elements of culture. These could be things like symbols used, organizational traditions or the physical layout of an office.

Models of organizational culture

One of the most used frameworks for categorizing organizational culture is the *competing values framework* (CVF). There are two axes: *degree of control and direction of focus.*

It outlines four archetypes to categorize an organization, each with different strengths:

1. *Clan culture:* A family-like, collaborative environment.
2. *Adhocracy culture:* Fosters innovation and can adapt quickly.
3. *Hierarchy culture:* Formalized structures, efficient, stable.
4. *Market culture:* Primarily results-oriented, driven by achievement.

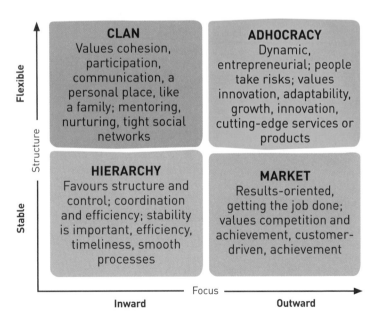

CLAN
Values cohesion, participation, communication, a personal place, like a family; mentoring, nurturing, tight social networks

ADHOCRACY
Dynamic, entrepreneurial; people take risks; values innovation, adaptability, growth, innovation, cutting-edge services or products

HIERARCHY
Favours structure and control; coordination and efficiency; stability is important, efficiency, timeliness, smooth processes

MARKET
Results-oriented, getting the job done; values competition and achievement, customer-driven, achievement

Flexible / Stable — Structure
Inward / Outward — Focus

Another tool used to assess companies when preparing for cultural change (such as a merger or other large change) is the *organizational culture profile* (OCP). It represents the culture of an organization across seven values:

1. *Stable* cultures are highly structured, which helps create constant levels of output.
2. *Innovative* cultures are good at adaptability and enable risk-taking.
3. *Aggressive* cultures are driven to succeed by any means necessary.
4. *Outcome-oriented* cultures value achievements and results.
5. *People-oriented* cultures are respectful of individual rights and value fairness.
6. *Team-oriented* cultures are co-operative and encourage collaboration.
7. *Detail-oriented* cultures are precise and rigorous.

The organizational culture profile (OCP).

Creating and maintaining organizational culture

The culture of an organization changes over time, but the foundations are largely set by the founders, as well as the context for the business and the initial assumptions, goals and values.

Once an organization has established the basic tenets of their culture, the maintenance of it is spread across a number of areas of responsibility.

The people who apply for jobs at a particular company (and those selected for employment) tend to align with existing company values. Culture mismatches tend to leave – this is the process of attrition.

When onboarding new employees, they are introduced to the values of a company as well as their practices and processes, which helps to demonstrate the cultural expectations.

Introducting the company culture

Leadership should always model appropriate behaviour to their employees, as well as providing a reward mechanism that supports the continuation of positive cultural attributes and prioritises ideal outcomes (see page 154).

Having a strong organizational culture can be a positive or negative asset for an organization, depending on the specific values that are shared.

For example, a company that is strongly outcome-oriented and has employees who are a match to this could perform well and outperform the competition. This would mean their culture is an asset as long as the company is behaving in ethical ways.

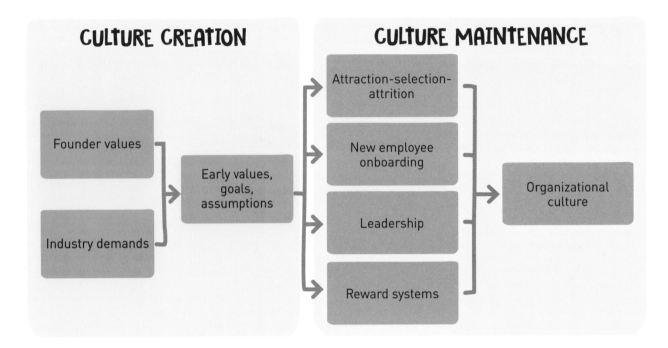

CULTURE CREATION

Founder values

Industry demands

Early values, goals, assumptions

CULTURE MAINTENANCE

Attraction-selection-attrition

New employee onboarding

Leadership

Reward systems

Organizational culture

The creation and maintenance of a company culture.

However, the same strong outcome-oriented culture combined with unethical behaviour and an obsession with targets could be a negative asset and even a liability. Enron is a recent example of this kind of dysfunctional strong culture.

CORPORATE GOVERNANCE

The structure of rules, practices and processes by which companies are controlled, managed and directed is called *corporate governance*.

Usually, a board of directors is responsible for the governance of a company. The role of shareholders is to appoint the board of directors (as well as auditors) and to ensure that an appropriate structure of governance is in place.

The purpose of corporate governance

Corporate governance is intended to enable effective and prudent management to deliver on the long-term success of the business.

The board of directors has a series of responsibilities including hiring the CEO, setting strategic aims, providing leadership to enact this, overseeing the management of the business and reporting back to shareholders on their activities. It is not the same as the day-to-day operational management of a business by senior staff.

Structure of the board of directors

At the early stages of a company, as a start-up, it is not unusual to have one director, as this is the minimum required to establish a company in most jurisdictions. They may also hold most or all of the shares and be the person who runs the business day to day.

As a business grows, a single director may not have time to cover all the necessary responsibilities. If this happens then it can make sense to appoint a board of directors with each of the directors having responsibility for a certain area of the business.

They then may have a defined reporting structure for those parts of the business – for instance, the sales team reporting to the director responsible for strategic planning in that area.

The need for a board of directors

Board structure

In a larger company, the board structure can sometimes look something like this:

- *Chair or president:* Oversees the whole business, usually a non-executive role.
- *Managing director or CEO:* They run the business and report to the chair as well as overseeing the board of executive directors. This is a role employed by the company.
- *A team of executive directors* (sometimes called inside directors): These can be senior employees of the company. They sit on the board, take a salary and manage the main areas of the business.
- *Non-executive directors:* They advise on strategic direction and decide remuneration of executive directors. They can be paid fees.

  A non-executive director is not an employee of a company – they don't engage in the day-to-day management of an organization. Most non-executive directors are independent advisors and undertake planning and policy setting.

  The idea is that they can understand the interests of the company with more objectivity than executive directors, as the latter can have an agency problem – a conflict of interest between management and shareholders.

A board meeting in progress.

Selection, compensation and evaluation of the board

In the USA, members of the board of directors are elected by the shareholders for publicly listed companies.

Candidates for the board can be nominated by the board's nomination committee, or by investors seeking to change the membership and policies of a board. Directors can be removed in elections or in instances where they have violated their fiduciary responsibility.

Identifying specific needs

When recruiting new or replacement board members, the nominating/governance committee will be looking to identify the specific needs of the company and any gaps in their current capabilities before they put candidates to the shareholders for a vote.

Board members are compensated for their time spent on board matters, but also for the need to keep their schedule flexible enough to accommodate any urgent issues and the possible risks to their reputation from lawsuits or corporate scandals.

The board is evaluated regularly for its effectiveness in carrying out responsibilities, but directors do not require individual evaluations. The board evaluates itself in these matters.

These evaluations look at the existing composition and skillset of the board, the process of meetings, the effectiveness of strategic plans, how well performance is being monitored and the quality of director relationships with stakeholders (senior management, shareholders, each other).

Replacing directors

A director can be replaced for a wide variety of reasons, for instance: ill heath; age; performance; retirement; the need for new skills. However, shareholders don't always know why a member has left the board. Removing directors usually means waiting until the next annual meeting or other board members encouraging them to resign. Shareholders have some limited rights to remove directors either by special resolution or at an election (if it is conducted by majority voting).

Procedures and duties of the board

One of the main functions of the board of directors is to hire the CEO (or most senior overall manager of a business), along with setting strategy and direction. The CEO is then responsible for day-to-day operations and the hiring of all other employees. Management is not responsible for the overall decisions on policy and the board is not responsible for the day-to-day operations, and the system works most smoothly when this separation is respected.

The major responsibilities and duties of a board of directors are the following:

- Recruitment, supervision, retention, compensation and evaluation of the CEO.
- Strategic functions and providing direction. For instance, defining or improving the mission, vision or goals of an organization. Usually, these are established in partnership with the CEO and senior management team.

- Developing a governance system based on policy for this particular business. There are standard articles of governance that provide a basic framework, but the board needs to develop its own policies specific to the company defining how the board functions and to help guide the actions of the CEO.
- Governance of the organization and building a strong working relationship with the CEO. This is usually through monthly board meetings, though the schedule depends on the company.
- The board has a fiduciary duty to protect the assets of the organization and the investors' interests. This includes all the assets or resources, including human capital (employees).
- The auditing process, as well as other monitoring responsibilities. The hiring of auditors is done by the board (or the auditing committee of the board). They then assess areas such as the reliability of financial statements, effectiveness of risk management, compliance with legal or regulatory requirements and the corporate governance process itself.

Company governance

CEO compensation and succession

When trying to recruit and retain a CEO, boards of directors try to use compensation contracts to make sure that the incentives of the executive(s) are the same as those of the company. This is sometimes known as *pay for performance,* as the CEO's compensation reflects the overall performance of the company itself.

Planning for a successor

In the USA, the compensation information for a CEO (and often some of the other highly paid executives) of a publicly traded company must be filed with the US Securities and Exchange Commission (SEC). This shows what form the compensation takes (shares, cash, options) and how any bonuses are determined.

Investors often prefer to see more compensation as bonus, rather than salary, as the theory is that this can better align incentives.

Succession planning is the preparation for a transition from one CEO to the next. It is important to identify any potential internal successors and make sure they are getting the proper experience.

Usually, the board oversees this process, as well as the CEO. However, internal recruitment is not the only option for succession.

There are four main types of CEO succession processes: *crown heir* (someone has been picked to succeed); *horse race* (there are various internal candidates who are in competition for the role); *coup d'etat* (the CEO is asked to leave and the board have a replacement lined up); or *comprehensive search* (the board and other stakeholders seek a candidate who matches their requirements).

Who decides	Not planned	Planned
Incumbent	*Crown heir* • Led by CEO • Long time frame • Information symmetry • Limited time spent • Single candidate	*Horse race* • Led by CEO • Long time frame • Information symmetry • Lots of time spent • Multiple candidates
Non-incumbent	*Coup d'etat* • Not led by CEO • Short time span • Information asymmetry • Limited time spent • Single candidate	*Comprehensive search* • Not led by CEO • Short time span • Information asymmetry • Lots of time spent • Multiple candidates

THEORIES OF LEADERSHIP

Leadership vs. management?

While *management* is about controlling a group to accomplish a particular goal, *leadership* is about an individual's ability to motivate, influence or enable other people to contribute to the success of the organization. The important factors that set leaders apart from managers are influence and inspiration, whereas power and control are often held by both.

Counting value vs. creating value

One way of thinking about managing people is the process of *counting value* – a large part of management can be assessing and collecting metrics. While this gives a view of progress towards a goal, it doesn't add value to the process itself (and can even subtract value due to the time taken to report the metrics).

A leader who is focused on *creating value* would minimize this kind of metric-collection and might look to have someone handle problem X while they handle problem Y.

Circles of influence vs. circles of power

The difference between managers and leaders when it comes to how they interact with groups is that leaders have groups they influence whereas managers have groups they hold power over. Managers have subordinates but leaders have followers.

One quick way of assessing the current status of a leader or manager is to count the number of people outside of their defined reporting hierarchy who approach them for advice. The more people who do that, the more likely it is they are already perceived to be a leader.

Trait and process approaches to leadership

There is one theory of leadership that states that certain innate characteristics or traits make someone a leader. They could be factors of personality, intelligence, physical factors, or similar. The main assumption is that if the person with the right set of traits can be found, then their leadership will help improve the performance of an organization.

However, this focuses entirely on the leader, and does not take into account the behaviour of followers. It also limits the potential pool of leaders, as it overlooks social, economic or other inequities that might limit a person's potential to lead.

An alternative theory is that of *process leadership*, which says that leadership is a process that involves the interaction between the follower and the leader. It is open to the idea that anyone can be a leader, not just those with certain qualities. It means that leadership can be 'observed, learned and trained'.

The situational approach to leadership

The *situational approach* to leadership emphasizes that a leader's style and behaviour should depend on the characteristics of their followers; that there is not a singular, best way to lead.

It suggests that a leader will encourage the best performance from their followers when the behaviour of the leader is tailored to the ability level of the follower, their willingness to try and their level of confidence.

When a follower is at the start of their career or new to a role they would still be developing their skills and

LEADERSHIP AND POWER

Power is the ability to influence the behaviour of others. *Positional power* is the influence that someone has because of their position (such as Jeff Bezos below), whereas personal power is the influence someone has independent of their position.

Bases of power are the sources that allow leaders to influence the attitudes and actions of others.

Bases of power	
Referent power	based on how much a person is liked and respected
Expert power	based on a person's perceived knowledge about a subject
Legitimate power	derived from a formal position held in an organization's hierarchy
Reward power	based on one's ability to give a reward as a means to influence others
Coercive power	ability to force others to follow an order by threatening punishment

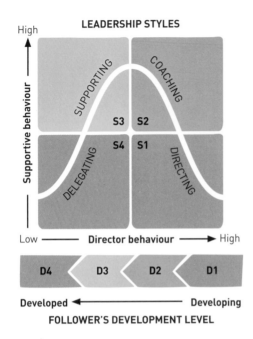

LEADERSHIP STYLES

High

Supportive behaviour

SUPPORTING

COACHING

S3 S2

S4 S1

DELEGATING

DIRECTING

Low ——— Director behaviour ——→ High

| D4 | D3 | D2 | D1 |

Developed ←————————— Developing

FOLLOWER'S DEVELOPMENT LEVEL

Diagram illustrating the situational approach to leadership.

require leadership that is primarily about directing them specifically in what to do but does not require as much specific support.

As the follower gains in confidence and skill, the leader can move on to coaching them more intensively and then supporting them in what they've learned (these two phases require more support from the leader).

Finally, as the follower is fully developed in their role, the leader can move to a process of delegation and the need for support is less frequent as the follower continues to gain confidence and ability.

Culture and leadership

Culturally endorsed implicit leadership theory (CLT) is the idea that beliefs about leadership can be different between cultures. It identifies six dimensions of leadership, some of which are stronger in certain cultures than others:

1. *Participative leadership* involves others in the process of decision making or encourages active participation.
2. *Autonomous leadership* is about taking action based on the leader's own ideas and beliefs.
3. *Team-oriented leadership* prioritizes team building, collaboration and diplomatic behaviour.
4. *Self-protective leadership* is concerned with status-aware and face-saving behaviours.
5. *Human-oriented leadership* values compassion and supportiveness.
6. *Charismatic* or *value-based leadership* aims to inspire people with a vision – using this passion to improve performance.

Fiedler's Contingency Model

Fiedler's Contingency Model states that for a leader to be effective, the style of their leadership must fit the situation. It establishes that a leader's ability to succeed rests on two factors: *natural leadership style* and *situational favourableness*.

The least-preferred co-worker scale (LPC) helps to determine leadership style. It asks participants to describe the co-worker they least prefer to work with.

The more positively they rate their least preferred co-worker (high LPC), on a range of criteria, the more *relationship-oriented* their leadership style is. If they are a low LPC leader, the more task-oriented their leadership style is.

Leaders who are relationship-oriented are good at managing conflict, facilitating collaboration (or creating synergy) and building relationships. Leaders who are task-oriented tend to be good at organizing teams and running projects efficiently and effectively.

The other half of the theory is about what is happening. *Situational contingency* or *situational leadership* requires different kinds of leadership for different situations. Fiedler then establishes how favourable the situation is, given the influence and power the leader has.

This situational favourableness is determined by three variables:

Situational favourableness

1. *Leader-member relations:* Does the team trust them as a leader? The more trust there is, the higher the degree of leader-member relations and the more favourable the situation.
2. *Task structure:* This is about the clarity of the tasks required to complete a project. The more clear-cut the tasks are, the higher the task structure – alternatively, the more vaguely they are defined, the lower the task structure.
3. *Position power:* This is the authority the leader has over their team. The capacity to reward or punish, or the ability to direct means position power is high. Higher position power makes the situation more favourable.

The diagram below outlines the connections between these elements and circumstances where different kinds of leaders might perform best.

SITUATION	FAVORABLE		MODERATE				UNFAVORABLE	
Category	1	2	3	4	5	6	7	8
Leader-member relations	Good	Good	3 Good	Good	Poor	Poor	Poor	Poor
Task structure	High	High	Low	Low	High	High	Low	Low
Leader position power	Strong	Weak	Strong	Weak	Strong	Weak	Strong	Weak

Fiedler's contingency theory of leadership

Transformational and transactional leadership

The four 'I's' of transformational leadership.

Transformational leadership is primarily interested in inspiring people to make a difference, whereas *transactional leadership* is focused on the task itself. Transactional leadership is about getting the work done, and transformational leadership is about motivation and inspiring teams to get the work done (and be engaged with the work).

This means that transactional leadership is useful in emergency and crisis situations, which are not situations that usually need creativity but benefit from clear tasks being set and rules being followed. It is appropriate when the projects, policies or tasks need to be performed a particular way.

The proactive style of transformational leadership is useful in situations requiring creativity, gathering ideas that add to the culture of the company or for facilitating longer-term changes. It is described as a 'pull' style of leadership.

Psychologist Bernard Bass established four elements of transformational leadership (*the four Is*):

- *Idealized influence:* Is the leader a role model? Does their behaviour reflect the vision? Are they consistent in their behaviour? This sets a standard and helps engage followers with the vision.
- *Intellectual stimulation:* Challenging the existing situation. Enabling creative thinking, a growth mindset and innovation in products and services to help the business progress.
- *Inspirational motivation:* Creating a compelling vision, bigger than the individual tasks. Setting challenging goals and inspiring and supporting personal development.
- *Individualized consideration:* Treating each person according to their needs, desires and fears. This is about understanding and empathy to get the best out of everyone.

Servant leadership

Servant-leaders

In Robert K. Greenleaf's 1970 essay *The Servant as Leader,* he states that: 'The servant-leader is servant first… It begins with the natural feeling that one wants to serve, to serve first. Then conscious choice brings one to aspire to lead.'

This is different from a someone who identifies as a leader first and foremost. The servant-leader tends to ensure that other people's highest priority needs are dealt with – they are concerned with the well-being and growth of people and communities that they lead.

The servant-leader is less focused on power, or being at the top, but is in fact happy to share power, put others' needs first and aims to help people develop and perform to the best of their ability.

COMPANY VISION AND BUSINESS PHILOSOPHY

The foundations of a strategic plan are often built around mission, vision and values statements. They are designed to express the purpose, direction and core principles of an organization.

Many organizations will have a public mission statement – a concise explanation of the reason that the business exists. It is a way of communicating purpose and direction to employees, customers and other stakeholders. It operates in support of the vision of a company.

When creating a mission statement, the key questions to think about are:

- What is the purpose of the organization?
- Why does the organization exist?

Some examples of mission statements are included in the table below.

Vision statements are expressly designed to be future-oriented. They talk about what a company wants to achieve and tend to be aspirational and/or challenging. The kinds of questions that they try to answer are:

- What problem is the company looking to solve?
- Where are we heading?
- And what could we look like in ten years?

Explaining the core principles of an organization is the purpose of a values statement. They create an internal framework, acting as a moral compass for leadership and employees, establish standards and help to guide decision making.

The kinds of questions values statements look to answer are:
- What are the values that are unique to our company?

HOW TO WRITE A MISSION STATEMENT

- Explain the product or service offer.
- Identify the core values of the company.
- Demonstrate how the company's offering connects with their values.
- Make these statements into one, shorter, more condensed version.
- Aim for a statement that is clear, concise and without jargon.

Company	Mission statement
Tesla	'To accelerate the world's transition to sustainable energy.'
LinkedIn	'To connect the world's professionals to make them more productive and successful.'
Patagonia	'Build the best product, cause no unnecessary harm, use business to inspire and implement solutions to the environmental crisis.'
Nike	'Bring inspiration and innovation to every athlete* in the world. *If you have a body, you're an athlete.'

- What values do we want to guide the way our company is run?
- What standards of conduct should our employees be held to?

Along with the values statement, some companies have a code of ethics that codifies the procedures that ensure company values are kept to.

By themselves, a mission, vision or values statement will not change a company immediately – but they can help to structure change and shift company culture towards where it wants to be.

URSULA BURNS: XEROX

Ursula Burns is the chair and CEO of Xerox Corporation. She is the first African American woman to head a Fortune 500 company.

In her early career, Burns worked as a summer intern at Xerox and joined the company full-time in 1981. She rose through the ranks, holding a series of increasingly responsible positions, including engineer, product manager, and manufacturing manager.

In 2000, Burns was named vice president of corporate strategic services, responsible for the development and execution of Xerox's long-term growth strategy. In this role, she took charge of the company's transformation from a hardware-focused business to a services-led enterprise.

In 2007, Burns was named president of Xerox, and in 2009, she was named CEO, succeeding Anne Mulcahy. As CEO, Burns has led Xerox through a period of significant change, including the global financial crisis and the transformation of the company's business model.

Under her leadership, Xerox has emerged as a leader in the global document management and business process outsourcing industry. The company has also made significant progress in reducing its environmental impact, becoming the first major company to commit to carbon neutrality.

Burns has been recognized for her leadership, receiving numerous awards and honours.

NEGOTIATION SKILLSETS

Negotiation styles need to be adapted to the situation in hand.

DIFFERENT TYPES OF NEGOTIATION

Negotiation is the process of reaching agreement through dialogue. The main concern in any negotiation is whether to co-operate or compete.

In a *zero-sum* (or *distributive*) *negotiation*, both parties are competing for the most gain out of a situation, whereas in an *integrative negotiation* the two parties collaborate to create value for both sides.

Your position: BATNAs and ZOPAs

When starting out in a negotiation, one of the first things you need to decide is what your *best alternative to a negotiated agreement* (BATNA) is. This is the best possible outcome if you don't come to an agreement. This helps to decide what the desired outcome is and allows you to assess the relative strength of different offers.

Just as in an auction situation, there is a reservation price – which is the worst deal that the other side of the negotiation will accept and still complete the agreement. This reservation price might be the same as your BATNA, or it may be that there are other elements that are important and need considering.

The *zone of possible agreement* (ZOPA) is the range within which both parties to a deal can agree – the boundaries of the ZOPA are set by either side's reservation price.

Agents, conflicts of interest and information asymmetry

Agents are anyone who is representing a stakeholder or a principal in a negotiation, for instance an estate agent acting for the homeowner in a real estate deal or a lawyer speaking on behalf of their client. Agents can be independent or non-independent – but both may have conflicts of interest either with their own personal agenda or with the organization they are negotiating for.

An imbalance in knowledge between two negotiating parties is considered *information asymmetry*. This asymmetry usually means that the party with more information has a competitive advantage in the negotiation.

Types of challenging opponents

Existing relationships: If there is a relationship that already exists between the parties in a negotiation, this can result in larger concessions – the value of the relationship becomes a part of

FRAMING AND REFRAMING

The way in which an issue is presented and the communication of information to all parties is called *framing*. This framing can impact the natural conclusion of a negotiation, or the *focal point*. This focal point is also based on the expectations each party has of the other, the amount of communication and their incentives to achieve an agreement.

Reframing involves shifting some of these elements. One example might be reframing a negotiation from competitive to collaborative by changing the language used – referring to 'we' rather than 'I' and 'you'.

Other options include reframing the question being asked, so that both parties can change their approach, or reframing the offer by making multiple different offers (*multiple equivalent simultaneous offers*, or MESOs) at once to better indicate relative value.

A 1992 Stanford study by Simonson and Tversky looked at the impact of price framing by Williams-Sonoma for a specific bread maker. Their first bread maker was priced at $275, then after a while they introduced a higher-priced machine for $429. There were some sales of the more expensive machine, but the sales of the cheaper model doubled. Once it was in direct comparison to the more expensive machine, it seemed a better deal.

In negotiations, this contrast effect can be used strategically. By asking for more than expected, and then accepting when this offer is rejected, the other party may then find a reasonable offer more appealing than they would otherwise.

the negotiation itself as it may be more important to keep the relationship healthy than to get the best possible deal.

Untrustworthy opponents: These are parties involved in a negotiation that have a poor reputation, offer misleading information, make suspicious requests or lie. Dealing with untrustworthy opponents can involve using non-compliance penalties, increasing transparency measures and demanding documentation for all claims. Recognizing bluffs or intimidation tactics is also important.

Die-hard bargainers: This kind of opponent is very focused on claiming value and is often unwilling to co-operate.

Spoilers: This is when an opponent actively doesn't want a deal, despite being party to the negotiation – potentially because they believe it would have a negative impact. Sometimes, spoilers can be persuaded to see that some control over the terms may be to their benefit, and they need to engage in good-faith negotiation to achieve this.

Coalitions: If more than one party joins one side of a negotiation, there is a coalition. There are natural coalitions where there are broad shared interests, and single-issue coalitions that join forces to deal with a specific problem.

Other tactics

Before opening a negotiation, there are three important things to consider: resources, interests and differences. *Resources* are what each party has, *interests* are what each party wants, and *differences* are what each party can offer the other.

The first offer helps sets the parameters in which the negotiation happens. This is known as the *anchor*. If the anchor is not favourable to one party, they can try offering a counter anchor to move the negotiation into a better range.

Even in a single-issue negotiation, putting together a package deal may help to achieve an agreement between parties.

The final step in any negotiation is both parties committing to the agreement.

Do	Don't
Be enthusiastic and kind to try to encourage collaboration.	Be misled by flattery or charm.
Use your anger strategically to convey your passion or determination.	Be bullied or dissuaded by a show of anger or fury.'
Listen to and respond to your feelings	Be arrogant, too confident or unprepared.

Emotions and irrationality

When in the middle of a negotiation, *emotions* can be heightened and need handling carefully so as not to undermine any possible agreement.

The emotions you feel and the emotions that you express (or choose to show) are not necessarily the same. These expressed emotions can be used strategically to create or claim value.

If the other party has an emotional outburst, take some time to determine where the emotion is coming from and then proceed once you've assessed the underlying motivation.

Other irrational behaviours can include a negotiating party overestimating their own abilities or the strength of their bargaining position. This can lead the same party to fall prey to *confirmation bias* – drawing a conclusion first and then only recognizing facts that support this, and ignoring any contradictory information, even if it is correct.

Cultural and gender differences

Men initiate negotiations more often than women, and women are more likely to receive lower amounts when they do initiate a negotiation.

Perceptions and stereotypes can impact how negotiators interpret what is being said, screen and select information, and understand both what is stated and what they think should be stated. Generalizing based on the attributes of one individual can lead to a *halo effect*.

When negotiating across cultures there are three main cultural dimensions it is useful to be aware of:

- *Goals*: In this culture, is the focus on the individual or the collective?
- *Influence*: Are the parties hierarchical or equal?
- *Communication*: Does communication occur explicitly or tacitly?

When negotiating across cultures, it is important to be sensitive to possible concerns, behavioural norms, and differences in values, perceptions and moods. Active listening, always being respectful and keeping these variations in mind can help to navigate these situations.

Chapter Eight
DATA ANALYSIS AND STATISTICS

One variable statistic • Five number summary • Probability basics • Probability distributions • Two variable statistics • Regression analysis • Data collection methods • Using data and statistics in business

CORRELATION COEFFICIENT

HYPOTHESIS TESTING

P-VALUES

USING DATA AND STATISTICS IN BUSINESS

DATA VISUALIZATION

CORRELATION AND CAUSATION

CONFIDENCE INTERVALS AND HYPOTHESES

DATA COLLECTION METHODS

DATA NARRATIVES

DATA ANALYSIS AND STATISTICS

T-TESTS

TWO VARIABLE STATISTICS

ONE VARIABLE STATISTICS

STANDARD DEVIATION

BAYES' THEOREM

FREQUENCY DISTRIBUTIONS

FIVE NUMBER SUMMARY

REGRESSION ANALYSIS

VENN DIAGRAMS AND PROBABILITY

PROBABILITY

HISTOGRAMS

BOXPLOTS

LINEAR REGRESSION

MULTIPLE REGRESSION

THEORETICAL AND EXPERIMENTAL

PROBABILITY DISTRIBUTIONS

THE COMPLEMENT RULE

CONDITIONAL PROBABILITY

NORMAL DISTRIBUTION

BINOMIAL DISTRIBUTION

POISSON DISTRIBUTION

THE EMPIRICAL RULE

DEPENDENCE AND INDEPENDENCE

ONE VARIABLE STATISTIC

Statistics allow you to *analyze* and describe data in different ways.

By accurately describing and analyzing datasets you can determine details and better interpret data. This helps you make better-informed business decisions, or to calculate the likelihood of different future events occurring.

One variable analysis is the simplest way of analyzing statistical data. It *describes* but does not take into account causes or relationships between data. For example, if you were interested in the scores of students who took an exam, you might be interested in how varied the results are.

You can use *single variable statistics* to make summaries of the data, which give you a series of key metrics that measure the performance of the whole group that took the exam. The most basic of these are mean, median and mode. These are sometimes called *central tendencies*.

Mean is the average of all the results – the total of all the exam results added together and divided by the number of students who took the exam.

The *median* is the result that lies in the middle of all the exam scores when they are in ascending or descending order. This is more useful than the mean when there are outliers in the data that might skew the results (if one student gets 100% but all the others get between 40–50%, the mean will be skewed higher by that single result).

Examiners compare overall exam results to achieve a mean, while judges at a dog show assess against agreed physical standards.

The *mode* is the most frequently occurring number in the dataset. The mode of the series 5, 2, 5, 3, 2, 2 would be 2 because it occurs more than any number.

Standard deviation

Standard deviation is a measure of how spread-out numbers in a dataset are. It is usually represented by the symbol σ (the Greek letter sigma).

The formula for standard deviation is the square root of the variance. Variance in this instance is the average of the squared differences from the mean.

To work out the variance, calculate the mean and then for each datapoint, subtract the mean and square the result (this is the squared difference). Next, calculate the average of those squared differences.

An example of standard deviation

You and four friends have just measured the heights of your dogs (in millimetres):

The heights are: 500 mm, 370 mm, 170 mm, 420 mm and 300 mm.

The first step is to find the mean by adding the datapoints and dividing by the number of points: the mean height is 352 mm.

$$Mean = \frac{500 + 370 + 170 + 420 + 300}{5}$$

$$= \frac{1760}{5}$$

$$= 352$$

Now we calculate the difference of each datapoint from the mean by subtracting 352 from each one.

And then to work out the variance, take each difference, square it, and average the result. Negative numbers won't make a difference once squared, as it is the difference between the numbers that matters here.

$$\sigma^2 = \frac{148^2 + 18^2 + (-182)^2 + 68^2 + (-52)^2}{5}$$

$$= \frac{21904 + 324 + 33124 + 4624 + 2704}{5}$$

$$= \frac{62680}{5}$$

$$= 12536$$

So, the variance is 12,536. And the standard deviation is the square root of variance:

$$\sigma = \sqrt{12536}$$

$$= 111.964$$

In normal distributions, data is what is called *symmetrically distributed* with no skew. Most of the datapoints will be around a central region, with the number of each of these datapoints tapering off as they are further away from the centre. The standard deviation tells you how spread out from the centre of the distribution your data is on average.

Many scientific variables follow normal distributions, including height, standardized exam results and satisfaction ratings.

In any normal distribution, approximately 95% of values will be within 2 standard deviations of the mean. This is part of the *empirical rule* or the *68-95-99.7 rule*:

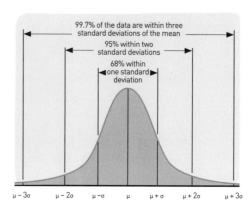

A normal distribution curve.

- about 68% of scores are within 1 standard deviation of the mean
- about 95% of scores are within 2 standard deviations of the mean
- about 99.7% of scores are within 3 standard deviations of the mean

FIVE NUMBER SUMMARY

A *five number summary* can give you a quick and rough sense of how your dataset looks. It contains your lowest value, the highest value the first quartile (the 25% point), the median and the third quartile (the 75% mark).

You can use these figures to discover further useful statistics, such as the *interquartile range* – also called the *middle fifty*.

To create a five number summary, you must have a single variable – it must be *univariate*, for instance a series of height measurements or ages. The data must also be *interval*, *ordinal* or *ratio*.

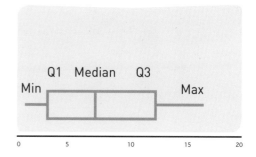

Using a boxplot to present a five number summary.

Boxplots

Using a *boxplot* to present data allows you to quickly see the five number summary – in the graphic above you can easily see the five key data points and their relationships.

Frequency distributions

A *frequency distribution* is a dataset displayed in a table that indicates how frequently a particular datapoint occurs.

For instance, the numbers of chocolate bars sold at a shop over the last ten days are: 20, 20, 25, 24, 20, 18, 22, 20, 18, 22.

You can show this as a frequency distribution, which will show how often a specific number of sales happened in the last ten days (see table overleaf).

Chocolate bars sold	Frequency
18	2
19	0
20	4
21	0
22	2
23	0
24	1
25	1

Histograms

Histograms are one of the most commonly used graphs to show frequency distribution. They are a graphical presentation of data that uses bars of different heights. Like a bar chart, a histogram groups numbers in ranges. It can be a useful way to display single-variable data.

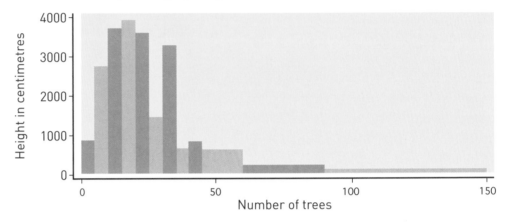

PROBABILITY BASICS

Probability is all about how likely something is to happen. Simple examples include rolling a set of dice or how playing cards are dealt, and it is also crucial to statistical analysis.

Probability can be expressed as a number between 0 and 1, where 0 is no chance of it happening and 1 is being certain that it will happen. It can also be expressed as a percentage or a fraction.

Theoretical and experimental probabilities

Theoretical probability is a description of how likely it is that a particular event is going to occur. For instance, a coin has an equal chance of landing heads or tails, so the theoretical probability of landing on tails is 50% (or 1/2 – described as 'one in two').

Experimental probability describes the actual frequency of an event occurring in an experiment. For instance, if a coin is tossed 40 times and lands tails up 16 times, then the experimental probability of landing on tails is 16/40, which could also be expressed as 2/5 (or 0.4 or 40%).

Theoretical probabilities will always be the same (presuming your information is correct), but experimental probability is affected by chance, so can have different results in different experiments. However, the more experiments that are carried out, the closer the result (the experimental probability) is likely to be to the theoretical probability.

Theoretical probability

Experimental probability

Basic probability rules

Venn diagrams and probability

When talking about probability, a *Venn diagram* is a graphic with at least one circle, inside a rectangle, which describes the logical relationships between events.

Using Venn diagrams

The rectangle represents the *sample space* – the set of all possible outcomes, whereas a circle inside this rectangle represents an event, which is a subset of the sample space.

For example, if a school year contains 100 students, and 70 like History, 60 like English and 40 like both, this could be represented in the Venn diagram below.

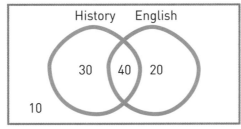

The overlapping region of the two circles in a Venn diagram represents the intersection of events. In this example, this is the 40 students who like History and English.

From this, we can work out the rest of the numbers to label the remaining portions of the diagram.

The number of students who like History only is 70 – 40 = 30. Similarly, we can deduce that 60 – 40 = 20 students like English only.

There are 10 students outside the circles, because we know that the sum of all values within the Venn diagram is equal to 100 (because the school year contains 100 students). We can from this determine the probability that a randomly chosen student likes History but not English. On the diagram below, the region of the Venn diagram representing this event is highlighted.

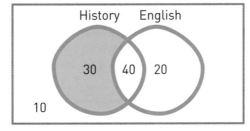

Therefore, the probability that a randomly selected student likes History but not English is 30/100 = 0.3 or 30%.

Finding the conditional probability of an event

In their exams, 40% of the students failed History, 25% failed English and 19% failed both History and English. What is the probability that a randomly selected student failed English given that they passed History?

As before, you can use the given information to calculate the relative proportion of each region. Since 40% of the students failed History while 19% failed both History and English, we can deduce that 40% – 19% = 21% of the students only failed History. And we can work out that 25% – 19% = 6% of the students only failed English. Then, we have the following data:

- 21% of the students failed History but not English
- 6% of the students failed English but not History
- 19% of the students failed both English and History

The remaining proportion (shown outside the circles) is the students who passed both subjects. Because the total of all the relative proportions must equal 100%, the percentage of students who passed both subjects is given by 100% – 21% – 6% – 19% = 54%.

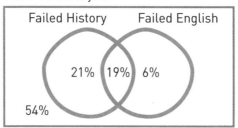

We can find the probability that a randomly selected student failed English given that he passed History. The percentage of students who passed History is shown outside of the circle labelled 'Failed History' in the Venn diagram. This is the area coloured grey on the right-hand diagram opposite. Also, we know that the area coloured pink represents the students who failed English and passed History.

Because we are choosing from the group of students who passed History (and not the entire year group) the sample space (or universal set) is the area coloured grey, not the whole rectangle.

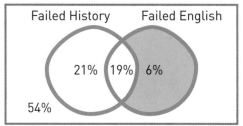

Class = school year

Failed History   Failed English

21% 19% 6%

54%

Students who failed History and passed English

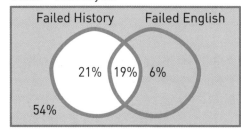

Class = school year

Failed History   Failed English

21% 19% 6%

54%

Students who passed History

The percentage of students who passed History is determined by adding the percentages in the grey area, which is 6% + 54% = 60%. Of the students who passed History, the percentage of students who failed English is found in the pink area (6%). Therefore, the probability of randomly selecting a student who failed English from the group of students who passed History is 6%/60% = 0.1 or 10%.

The formula to establish the conditional probability for event A given event B is:

$$P(A|B) = \mathbf{P}(A \cap B)P(B)$$

Below are examples that outline the various Venn diagram layouts for a series of possible outcomes – as well as the symbols that indicate their probability relationships.

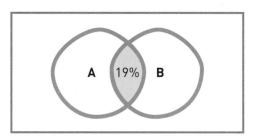

Intersection: A ∩ B

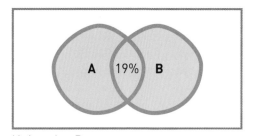

Union: A ∪ B

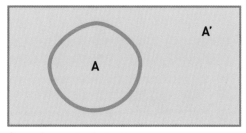

Complement of: A: A′

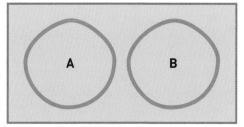

Mutually exclusive (disjoint)

How can you work out the probability of drawing two cards of the same colour?

The complement rule

This can be written as: $$P(A) = 1 - P(A')$$

A' (or A^c) means 'not A'.

For example, the probability that Azim will graduate high school is 0.9. What is the probability that he will not graduate?

$$P(\textit{not graduate}) = 1 - P\{\textit{graduate}\} = 1 - 0.9 = 0.1$$

Multiplication rules (also called joint probability)

Dependent events

Two events are dependent if the outcome of the first one affects the outcome of the second.

$$P(A \cap B) = P(A) * P(B \mid A) \textit{ if A and B are dependent}$$

∩ is the symbol for *intersection* (this is similar to saying 'and': A *and* B)
P(B|A) means the probability of B happening *given* that A has occurred
For example, if you draw two cards from a deck, *without* replacing the first, what is the probability that both cards are red?

$$P(\textit{red and red}) = P(\textit{red}) * P \,(\textit{red given red}) = 26/52 * 25/51 = 0.245P$$

Independent events

Two events are *independent* if the outcome of the first does *not* affect the outcome of the second.

$$P(A \cap B) = P(A) * P(B) \textit{ if A and B are independent}$$

If you draw two cards from a deck, and replace the first, what is the probability that both are red?

$$P(\text{red and red}) = P(\text{red}) * P \,(\text{red}) = 26/52 * 26/52 = 0.25P$$

Mutually exclusive events

Two events are *mutually exclusive* if they can't happen at the same time.

$$P(A \cap B) = 0 \textit{ if A and B are mutually exclusive}$$

If you roll a six-sided die, what is the probability of rolling a 3 and 5 at the same time?
$P(3 \textit{ and } 5) = 0$ because you can't simultaneously roll two faces of the same die.

Addition rules (the union of events)

∪ is the symbol for 'union' (this is similar to saying or: A *or* B). The formula for this is:

$$P(A \cup B) = P(A) + P(B) - P(A \cap B)$$

For example, there are 14 dogs and 10 cats in a pet behaviour class. 5 dogs and 6 cats got an A in the class. If a pet is chosen at random, what is the probability of choosing a cat or a pet with an A?

$$P(cat \text{ } or \text{ } A) = P(cat) + P(A) - P(cat \text{ } and \text{ } A) = \frac{10}{24} + \frac{11}{24} - \frac{6}{24} = 0.625$$

When the events are mutually exclusive:

Because the last part of the equation, P(A ∩ B) = 0 when A and B are mutually exclusive, you're left with P(A) + P(B).

So, if you roll a six-sided die, what is the probability of rolling a 3 or a 5?

$$P(3 \text{ } or \text{ } 5) = P(3) + P(5) = 1/6 + 1/6 = 0.333$$

Conditional probability

The likelihood of a particular event occurring, given that another event has already occurred. The formula for this is:

$$P(A \mid B) = \frac{P(A \cap B)}{P(B)}$$

This is only true when $P(B) \neq 0$

What is the probability that you will choose a pet that is an A grade achiever?

As an example, a teacher gave his class two exams. 70% of the class passed the first of the exams. 50% of the class passed both the exams. What percentage of those who passed the first exam also passed the second exam?

$$P(second \text{ } given \text{ } first) = \frac{P(first \text{ } and \text{ } second)}{P(first)} = 0.5/0.7 = 71\%$$

Bayes' theorem

This is the formula for Bayes' theorem. This is used when trying to assess the probability of an event based on previous knowledge of context or conditions that could be related to the event.

Crucially, it offers a way to revise existing predictions (by updating probabilities) once new or additional evidence comes to light.

$$P(A \mid B) = \frac{(P(B \mid A) \times P(A)}{P(B)}$$

For instance, imagine you had planned to play tennis outside today, but it's cloudy this morning and 50% of all rainy days begin cloudy. However, cloudy mornings are common; roughly 40% of all days start off cloudy (including non-rainy ones). It's also the summertime, and the chance of rain is only 8% this time of year. What is the probability of it raining today?

$$P(rain\ given\ cloudy) = \frac{P(cloudy\ given\ rain) \times P(rain)}{P(cloudy)}$$

$$= \frac{0.5 \times 0.08}{P(first)} = 0.1$$

According to Bayes' theorem, given the information above, there is a 10% chance of it raining today.

PROBABILITY DISTRIBUTIONS

Different kinds of distributions

To describe the likelihood of an event happening, there are functions called *probability distributions* that can display the possible values. These can be *discrete* – where the data can only have certain values – or *continuous,* where the data can take on any value in the available range (which could be infinite).

Normal distribution

One of the most important kinds of distribution in statistics is *normal distribution.* This is when the data as presented on a graph appears in the shape of a bell (it is referred to as a bell curve or Gaussian curve). This is because the data near the mean will occur more frequently than the outlying data points. One example of data that is normally distributed would be the heights of a large selection of people. The majority of people will be at or near average height, and there will be very few people who are extremely short or extremely tall, so the data will form a bell curve, peaking around the mean height.

Binomial distribution

Binomial distribution is used to measure probabilities for situations where there are only two potential outcomes, such as a coin flip.

Poisson distribution

Poisson distribution is used to calculate the probability that a given number of events will happen during a specific time frame – for instance, the number of ice creams sold per hour.

The empirical rule

Using standard deviation (how far dispersed data is from the mean) there is a basic rule for normal distribution that states that:

How many ice creams will be sold in a given time?

68.27% of data lies within one standard deviation of the mean
95.45% of data lies within two standard deviations of the mean
99.73% of data lies within three standard deviations of the mean

Because almost the entire dataset will lie within three standard deviations of the mean, outliers in the data are easy to spot, and this makes it easy to see if data is normally distributed.

Z-scores and the standard normal distribution

To analyze how close to the mean a datapoint is, *z-scores* measure how many standard deviations away from the population mean a particular datapoint is.

Z-scores

They are used to compare results to a normal population – for instance, it can tell you how a single datapoint such as someone's height compares to the mean height of a population.

The basic z-score formula is:

$$z = \frac{(x - \mu)}{\sigma}$$

If you have a quiz score of 240 (x), the quiz has a mean (μ) of 190 and a standard deviation (σ) of 28. Assuming a normal distribution, your z-score would be:

$$z = \frac{x - \mu}{\sigma} = (240 - 19)/28 = 1.79$$

This shows how many standard deviations from the mean your score is. In this example, your score is 1.79 standard deviations above the mean. If the number were negative, it would show how far *below* the mean it was.

T-TEST

A *t-test* is a statistical test used to compare the means of two groups.

The formula for the two-sample t-test (known as the *Student's T-test*) is as follows:

$$t = \frac{x_1 - x_2}{\sqrt{\left(s^2\left(\frac{1}{n_1} + \frac{1}{n_2}\right)\right)}}$$

t is the t-value
x_1 and x_2 are the means of the two groups to compare
s^2 is the pooled standard error
n_1 and n_2 are the number of observations in each group

If there is a larger t-value, it indicates that the difference between the group means is greater than the pooled standard error, meaning there is a more significant difference between groups.

The calculated t-value can be compared with the values in a critical value chart to assess if the t-value is greater than might be expected by chance. If it is, the null hypothesis can be rejected, and it can be concluded that the two groups are different.

The *Pearson correlation coefficient* (also known as *Pearson's r*, or *bivariate correlation*) is widely used. It summarizes the characteristics of a dataset by describing the direction and strength of the linear relationship between two variables.

The table below gives a general idea of how related and in what direction various effect sizes are considered to be (though specific disciplines can have different thresholds).

Pearson correlation coefficient (r) value	Strength	Direction
Greater than .5	Strong	Positive
Between .3 and .5	Moderate	Positive
Between 0 and .3	Weak	Positive
0	None	None
Between 0 and –.3	Weak	Negative
Between –.3 and –.5	Moderate	Negative
Less than –.5	Strong	Negative

As well as being a descriptive statistic, it is also an inferential statistic as it can test a statistical hypothesis – whether there is a significant relationship between two variables.

TWO VARIABLE STATISTICS
Correlation and causation

When describing how two variables are related, we use the term *correlation*. This describes how when one variable changes, so does the other – they *covary*. It is an indicator of the relationship between the variables.

Causation is the term used to describe how the changes in one variable result in changes in another. The two variables are correlated and there is a causal link.

Correlation doesn't necessarily mean causation, but causation does imply correlation.

A *confounding variable* can make it seem like variables are causally related when they are not. This third variable separately affects both the other variables separately.

Confounding variable

There can also be a *directionality problem*. This is when two variables correlate and may have a causal relationship but is it not possible to determine which variable causes the change in the other.

Correlation coefficient

To measure the strength of correlation between variables, we use the *correlation coefficient*. This is a number between −1 and 1 that indicates the strength and direction of the relationship between variables.

It is a descriptive statistic because it summarizes the sample data from a population, without meaning that you can necessarily determine things about the population. To generalize results from a correlation coefficient to the population, we can use an *inferential statistic*. An f-test or t-test can be used to find a test statistic that determines the statistical significance of a finding.

Inferential statistics

REGRESSION ANALYSIS

We can also make determinations about correlation based on visual patterns in a scatterplot. If there is a *linear pattern* in the data, you can fit a straight line between the datapoints in a line of best fit. Alternatively, there may be a *curvilinear pattern* (a line with a curve or a U-shape). If there is a no correlation, the data may be spread randomly across the graph with no obvious line indicating a relationship.

Linear and curvilinear data patterns

Regression models (linear regression using a straight line, nonlinear if curved) use these lines to estimate how a dependent variable changes as the independent variable changes.

Linear regression

To estimate how strong the relationship between two variables is you can use a *linear regression formula*. For instance, if you wanted to find out the strength of the relationship between average yearly temperature at the poles and sea level rises – what you are looking for is the value of the

Linear regression formula

dependent variable at a particular value of the independent variable (the amount of sea level rise at a certain average temperature).

The formula for a simple linear regression is:

$$Y = \beta_0 + \beta_1 X + e$$

- Y is the predicted value of the dependent variable for any given value of the independent variable: X
- B_0: the intercept, the predicted value of Y when X equals 0
- B_1: the regression coefficient – how much we expect Y will change as X increases
- X is the independent variable (the variable we think may be influencing Y)
- e is the error (how much variation there is in the estimate of the regression coefficient)

Linear regression finds the line of best fit through a set of data by looking for the regression coefficient (B1) that means the total error (e) of the model is as low as possible.

Linear regression calculations can be done manually, but it is quicker and easier to use a statistical program to calculate this analysis. These models can then be used to predict the value of the depended variable at specific values of the independent variable.

DESCRIPTIVE STATISTICS

Descriptive statistics are used to describe data, while *inferential statistics* are used to make inferences based on data. Descriptive statistics can report characteristics of the data:

- Distribution looks at the frequency of each value.
- The central tendency looks at the averages of the values.
- Variability looks at how spread out the values in the data are.

Descriptive statistics precisely describe the data that has been collected, therefore there is not uncertainty.

Multiple regression and data transformation

If there are two or more independent variables, *multiple linear regression* can be used. This shows how strong the relationship is between two or more independent variables and one dependent variable and the value of the dependent variable at a certain value of the independent variables.

CONFIDENCE INTERVALS AND HYPOTHESES

When making an estimate in statistics there is uncertainty around the estimate because the number is based on a sample of a population. A *confidence interval* is the range of values you expect this estimate to fall between.

Confidence intervals are a way of describing the probability of an estimate being correct if a test were run multiple times. Confidence intervals are associated with a confidence level. This tells you in percentage terms the probability of the interval containing the estimate if you repeat the test.

For instance, a confidence interval with a 95% confidence level is a way of saying that if the test was run 100 times, the estimate would fall between the upper and lower values of the confidence interval 95 times. Confidence intervals are the mean of an estimate plus and minus the variation.

The reason that this is only a percentage is because you cannot know the true value of a population parameter without collecting data from the full population. However, with a large sample size and random sampling you can expect your confidence interval to contain this parameter a percentage of the time.

Setting up the hypothesis

The process of formally analyzing statistics using inferential statistics usually involves setting a *hypothesis* (a kind of formal prediction) and then testing it. The goal is to compare populations or look at relationships between variables using the available samples.

These predictions are then tested using statistical tests, which also estimate sampling errors to enable researchers to make valid inferences.

These statistical tests are either *parametric* or *non-parametric*. Parametric tests make a series of assumptions including:

Parametric and non-parametric tests

- the sample comes from a population that follows a normal distribution
- the size of the sample is large enough to accurately represent the population
- the variances of each group (how much they spread) in a comparison are similar

Parametric tests are thought to be more statistically powerful because they are more likely to detect an effect, if one exists.

If the available data doesn't conform to one or more of these assumptions, then non-parametric tests can be used. These are distribution-free tests as they don't assume how the population data is distributed (normally or otherwise).

Hypothesis testing

When setting out a hypothesis, there are two competing claims that need to be established – the *null hypothesis* and *alternative hypothesis* are the two claims that researchers use statistical tests to look at the evidence for and against. The intention is to disprove the null hypothesis.

The null hypothesis is taken to mean there is no effect in the population, whereas the alternative hypothesis indicates that there is an effect in the population.

Null hypothesis

The null hypothesis is often written as H0 and the alternative hypothesis can be written as H1 (or Ha). Usually, the effect is what the independent variable does to the dependent variable.

An example of a null hypothesis and alternative hypothesis might be:

Assume a company reliably sells £10 million total sales' value worth of Product X a month.

Alternative hypothesis: Reducing the price of Product X by 10% will result in a total sales value greater than £10 million a month (due to increased unit sales).
Null hypothesis: Reducing the price will either not increase or possibly decrease the total sales value.

If the sample being studied provides sufficient evidence against the claim that there is no effect (or in the example above, a possible negative effect) then you can reject the null hypothesis. Otherwise, you fail to reject the null hypothesis.

In statistics, 'failing to reject' the null hypothesis is the correct way of referring to this situation – not proving or accepting the null hypothesis.

Computing a test statistic

Expected distribution

To determine how closely the observed data matches the distribution expected you can calculate a *test statistic*. Given the null hypothesis, there will be an *expected distribution*, and the test statistic can tell you how closely the observed data matches the distribution.

It is used to calculate the p-value of the results, a number that helps to determine if the null hypothesis should be rejected.

The *p-value* describes the agreement between the test statistic and the predicted values. A smaller p-value means that the test statistic is less likely to have happened under the null hypothesis.

p-values

Researchers often use p-values to state that a certain pattern is *statistically significant*. This is a way of saying the the size of the p-value is small enough to reject the null hypothesis of the test, because the p-value indicates how likely a particular set of observations are if the null hypothesis is true.

The most commonly used threshold for statistical significance is $p < 0.05$. This means that you would expect to find a test statistic as extreme as the one that was calculated only 5% of the time. Some disciplines or studies require even stricter thresholds of 0.01 or 0.001.

Another way of thinking about p-values is as the relative risk of rejecting the null hypothesis when the null hypothesis is in fact true.

Because of the way statisticians think about hypotheses, the p-value can only be used to determine if the null hypothesis is supported or not supported.

DATA COLLECTION METHODS

When data is expressed in numbers or graphs, and analyzed with statistical methods it is *quantitative*, whereas data expressed in words or other forms is known as *qualitative* data and is analyzed with methods such as interpretation and categorization.

Testing hypotheses, precise measurements and large-scale insights tend to require the collection of quantitative data. Qualitative data is useful for exploring ideas, gaining insights into a context or understanding individual experiences. There are sometimes mixed-method approaches that combine these and collect both kinds of data.

Statistical sampling

In statistics, a *population* refers to the whole group that you are trying to study and draw conclusions about, whereas a sample is the specific group that the data is collected from. The sample is always smaller than the total of the population.

A population can mean people, but it can also mean any group that has elements of something being studied. Objects, companies, countries, species, events, etc. could all be a population in research terms.

Random sampling techniques

Large populations (or those with other characteristics, such as geographical dispersal) mean that is is more suitable to use a sample when researching. Using statistical techniques, this sample data can be used to test hypotheses or make estimates about the population as a whole.

There are two main kinds of sampling methods:

1. *Probability sampling:* Where every member of the population has a chance of being selected in the sample.
2. *Non-probability sampling:* Where there is non-random selection (perhaps selected for convenience or based on the expertise of the researcher).

The ideal sample is randomly selected and representative of the population. *Simple random sampling*, *cluster sampling* (clusters representative of the whole population, randomly chosen) or *stratified sampling* (where sub-groups called strata are created and then randomly selected from to make sure each is represented fairly in the final sample) both reduce the risk of *sampling bias*.

Samples are helpful when gathering data about a large population.

If researchers need to use *non-random selection methods*, due to convenience or other factors, then the statistical inferences that can be drawn (the narrative of the data) will be weaker than with a random sample.

USING DATA AND STATISTICS IN BUSINESS

Statistics can be used to the benefit of business in many ways. Statistical analysis or research can help analyze historical sales performance, make predictions about future decisions, describe the behaviour of markets, help set accurate prices and gauge consumer demand.

Descriptive statistics

Many businesses use *descriptive statistics* to help them understand how their customers behave. These descriptive statistics are used when it is necessary to describe datasets.

For example, a clothing retailer might want to determine these kinds of statistics:

Descriptive statistics

- The mean number of customers per day.
- The median sales amount in $ per customer.
- The total sum of sales made every week.
- The standard deviation of the ages of the customers who come in the store.

These kinds of datapoints will give a better understanding of who their customers are and how they behave.

As another example, a challenger bank in the FinTech space might want to calculate these descriptive statistics:

- The mean number of new customers who open the app each day.
- The percentage of customers who fail to pay back their loan.
- The amount in £ deposited by all customers every week.

This would give the bank insight into how their customers handle their money and broaden their understanding of customer behaviour.

Linear regression models

Models of linear regression

Businesses can use *linear regression* to establish the relationship between one (or more) predictor variables and response variables. This means they can make decisions about things such as spending based on the best return, in statistical terms.

Linear regression is generally performed with statistical analysis tools such as the programming language R or software such as Stata. These will give a result that can be interpreted.

Imagine that a vegan dog treat company wants to assess the total amount spent on radio ads, online ads and their total revenue. Using the available data, this is what their model might look like after computing it in their software:

$$\text{Sales} = 430.25 + 1.57(\text{radio advertising}) + 4.22(\text{online advertising})$$

What this means is that for each additional pound spent on radio ads, their total revenue will increase by £1.57 (if they keep the same level of online ads).

Similarly, for each additional pound spent on online advertising, the total revenue will increase by £4.22 (again, keeping radio ads the same).

This allows the dog treat company to see that they should spend their marketing budget on online ads, and not spend any more on radio ads.

Business insight dashboards and data visualization

Modern companies tend to have most of their data stored digitally, meaning that they can easily upload, combine data sources, manipulate and display it online, with the help of tools like *business insight dashboards*.

Data visualization

These allow a company to track, analyze and report on KPIs, sales data or other metrics that are important to the company. A business insight dashboard usually shows this data in graphs, charts, boxplots and other visualizations that update automatically from existing databases.

These dashboards and analysis tools help employees and management share, understand and collaborate. They can help a business spot trends, identify problems or analyze the success of a marketing activity.

Surveys and customer behaviour

A popular method for gathering data for business use is customer or audience *surveys*. However, the quality of the data from a survey (and how confidently you can make decisions based on those results) depends on well-structured questions, the order of analysis and the way in which respondents are categorized.

Customer surveys

Levels of measurement

When setting up a survey, it is important to decide how the data for the questions will be analyzed. The four levels of measurement will determine how to measure responses and what statistical analysis can be applied.

1 Nominal scale

The *nominal scale* is when data is classified without a quantitative value – an example would be asking what brand of phone you own. It can keep track of the number of respondents who choose each option and which is the most popular.

2 Ordinal scale

Questions with an *ordinal scale* are those that allow the respondent to rank their responses. This has a quantitative value because one rank is lower or higher than another. An example could be 'Rank your favourite pizza toppings from best to worst'. This data can have a mode and median and cross-tabulation analysis can be used.

3 Interval scale

The *interval scale* indicates both the difference between the values and the order, but there is no true zero point. One example of this kind of scale is an IQ test. Mode and median can be calculated, and this data can be analyzed with t-tests and correlation analyses to look at how related dataset are, and ANOVA tests to determine the significance of the results.

4 Ratio scale

A *ratio scale* also shows the order and difference between values, but it can have a true zero point. The absence of an attribute (a zero) still provides useful data. For example, a ratio scale question could be 'Select how much money you spend on chocolate every week'. Mode and median are possible to calculate, and they can be analyzed with ANOVA, t-tests and correlation analyses.

Analyze quantitative data first

Quantitative data first

Qualitative data can give interesting insights or context for a topic, but the information is subjective, meaning it is difficult to analyze statistically. Quantitative data is very useful because being able to convert responses into numeric value means conclusions can be drawn with confidence using statistical analyses.

When analyzing survey data it is usually important to start with the quantitative data as this can help with the understanding of any qualitative data. Imagine you have a survey with two questions, a satisfaction scale and an open review text box. If analysis showed that 70% of customers said they were dissatisfied with the company service, then this quantitative data would suggest that it was most important to analyze the negative reviews.

Consider cross-tabulation for more insight

Analyzing data in one group doesn't always give the most accurate information. For instance, survey respondents may not all be part of a company's target audience, and this could skew the survey results.

By segmenting the responses using cross-tabulation, the responses of the target audience can be more accurately analyzed.

Cross-tabulation compares two sets of data in one chart as it records relationships between variables. It can reveal further insights than the questions alone.

Cross tabulation

For example, if you had survey responses that included location and how much they would recommend the company to others, you would be able to use cross-tabulation to examine the potential level of earned media in a certain city.

How to present survey results

Use a graph or chart

Using a *graph* or *chart* can allow the audience to grasp the overall meaning of the data without having to understand the specific analysis. A graph of sales over time that goes up and to the right is easily comprehended as heading in the right direction, without the need for a lot of explanation.

Graphs and charts

However, the nuance of the specific data means that the type of graph chosen, the axes and scales applied and even the colours can all impact how it is understood. Each of these decisions should be relevant to the data.

Simplify tables

Data presented in a table can be improved with a few simple rules:

How simplification can aid the message

1. Remove colours and gridlines.
2. Remove shading behind data or headers.
3. Remove the borders, bolding and italics.
4. Left align any text and right align all numbers.
5. Line up titles with the data.
6. Resize columns to fit data.
7. Use white space to separate groups and headings.
8. Be consistent with decimal places and round numbers as much as possible.
9. Remove repetitive data.
10. Replace any emphasis at the end.

Overleaf is an example of the same table before and after following these rules.

Category	Product name	Location	Sales	Defects
Toy	*Widget Whacker*	France	89459.01	40.235
Toy	***Rubber Hammer***	**Lithuania**	**97356.00**	**20**
Toy	*Blue Shape*	France	64887.10	33.9
Hand tool	*Heavy Lump*	France	23423.00	45.44
Hand tool	*Large Mound*	England	78889.00	14.4444
Hand tool	*Big Pole*	Lithuania	99877.77	33.332
Electrical	*Round Ball*	Peru	45645.00	21.1
Electrical	*Slimy Bucket*	England	72776.40	23.225
Electrical	*Rough Rock*	Lithuania	56776.20	10.1

Before applying the rules

Category	Product name	Factory location	Sales (000)	Defect rate
Toy	Widget Whacker	France	89.5	40.2
	Rubber Hammer	**Lithuania**	**97.4**	**20.0**
	Blue Shape	France	64.9	33.9
Hand tool	Heavy Lump	France	23.4	45.4
	Large Mound	England	78.9	14.4
	Big Pole	Lithuania	99.9	33.3
Electrical	Round Ball	Peru	45.7	21.1
	Slimy Bucket	England	72.8	23.2
	Rough Rock	Lithuania	56.8	10.1

After applying those rules

Tell a story with data analysis

The main intention of data analysis is to enable an accurate and compelling story to be told about the data. One way of doing this in a presentation is to construct a narrative using layers of information, each building on the last. The foundations of the story are the key datapoints, then the next set of analyses of that data, the important discoveries or findings become the next layer, with the final points being the conclusions you can draw from the research.

Communicating clearly using data can mean finding the compelling narrative that will capture the attention of the audience. This could be about the framing of the data, the order it is presented or the question it answers. Narratives about data, just like any good story, need a hook, momentum and a purpose.

It is also important to think about how it is presented, to aim to simplify the data as much as is possible in the circumstances (always bear in mind the likely data-literacy of the audience) but not to be selective in which data is included, and to decide what the key discoveries from the analysis are to help form your conclusions.

Data presentation expert Edward Tufte says that a good visualization shows 'complex ideas communicated with clarity, precision and efficiency'.

CARLY FIORINA: HEWLETT PACKARD

Carly Fiorina is the former CEO of Hewlett-Packard, and was the first woman to lead a Fortune 50 company. Fiorina began her career as a management consultant at AT&T, and later became an executive at Lucent Technologies. In 1999, she was recruited to HP as its first female CEO.

Her most controversial decision was to lead HP's acquisition of Compaq in 2002. The $25 billion deal was the largest tech merger in history at the time and helped to make HP the world's largest PC maker. Although widely criticized at the time, Fiorina was ultimately vindicated as the deal proved to be a success.

Fiorina also played a key role in HP's entry into the printer market. She oversaw the development of HP's inkjet technology and launched an aggressive marketing campaign that positioned HP as a major player in the printer market. This strategy was highly successful, and HP quickly became the world's largest printer manufacturer.

She was instrumental in HP's expansion into China, establishing HP's first manufacturing facility in the country and helping to build the company's brand in the world's largest market.

Fiorina's time at HP was not without its challenges. She was widely criticized for her handling of the HP-Compaq merger and for her role in the company's layoffs of 30,000 workers. Nevertheless, Fiorina's successes at HP are undeniable. She was a visionary leader who made bold decisions that helped to transform HP into a global technology powerhouse.

CORPORATE FINANCE AND INVESTMENTS

The cost of capital • Capital budgeting • Modern portfolio theory and investments • The capital market line and efficient frontier • Valuing potential investments

THE EFFICIENT FRONTIER AND CAPITAL MARKET LINE

EQUITY AND MARKET VALUATIONS

VALUING POTENTIAL INVESTMENTS

DISCOUNTED FREE CASH FLOW

MEAN-VARIANCE EFFECT

CORPORATE FINANCE AND INVESTMENT

DISCOVERING THE COST OF DEBT

MODERN PORTFOLIO THEORY AND INVESTMENTS

DIVERSIFACTION AND ACCEPTABLE RISKS

NPV, IRR AND PAYBACK PERIOD

THE COST OF CAPITAL

DISCOVERING THE COST OF EQUITY

CAPITAL BUDGETING

CAPITAL STRUCTURE

EFFICIENT MARKET HYPOTHESIS

THE MODIGLIANI-MILLER THEOREM

MONTE CARLO SIMULATION

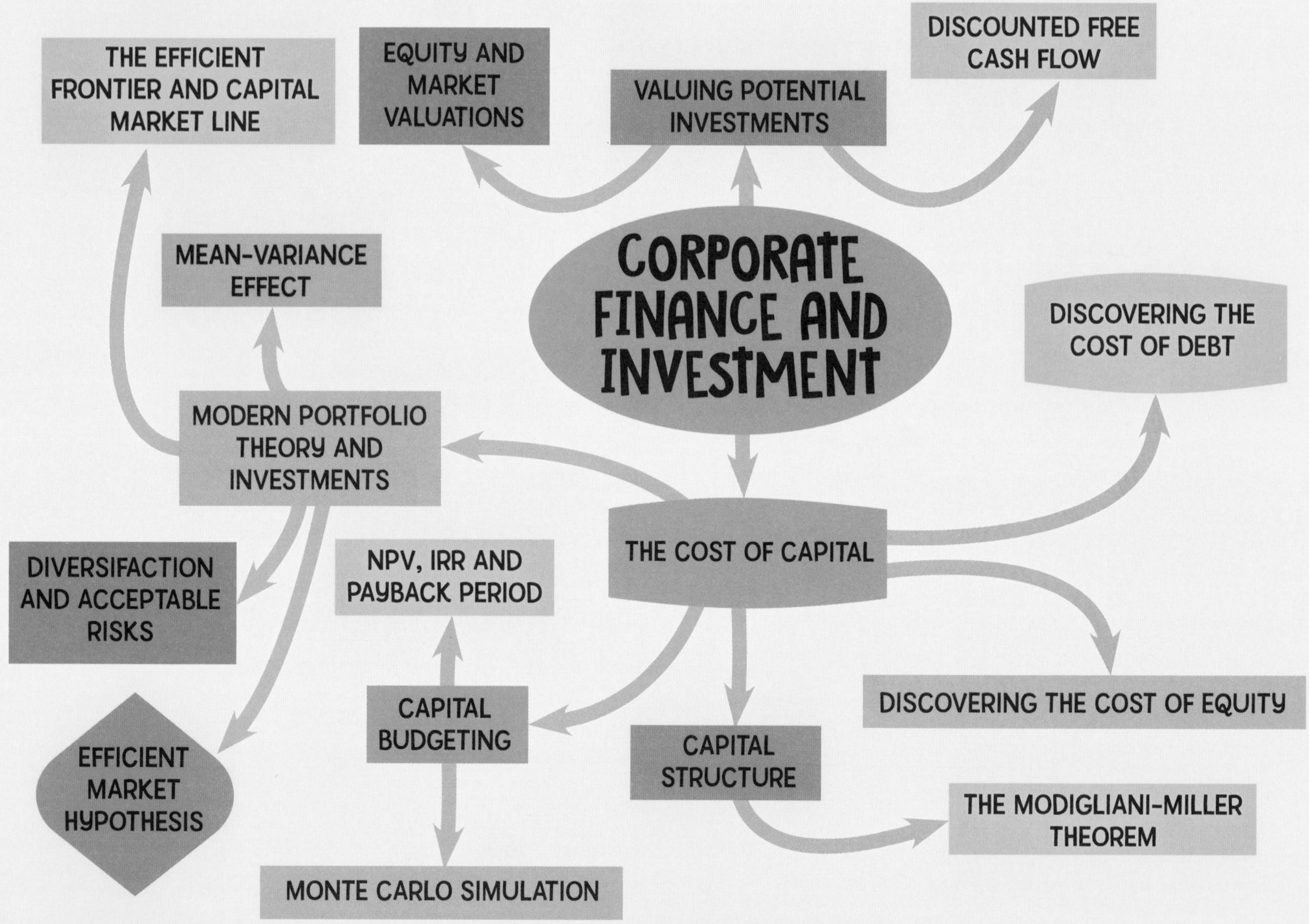

Finance can mean the creation, process of managing or study of money and investments. It covers debits and credits, investing in current projects with future income. Because of how it connects to the future, the time value of money is particularly important, as are interest rates and similar topics.

Public finance includes tax systems, government spending, central bank policies, budgetary policy and other government areas. Personal finance is the financial decisions of an individual (or sometimes household), which could include budgeting, mortgages, insurance, savings and planning for retirement.

Corporate finance is generally concerned with the management of assets and liabilities, revenues, investments and debts of a business.

A company can achieve financing from a range of sources – such as equity investments from shareholders or credit arrangements such as a loan from a bank. Taking on debt as a company is not always a negative, as it can help the company expand and become more profitable.

The city of London, home to many key financial institutions.

THE COST OF CAPITAL

The return that a business needs to make to justify the cost of a capital project (such as building a new factory or buying new equipment) is represented by the idea of *cost of capital*.

The cost of capital includes both debt and equity, which is then weighted in accordance with the existing or intended capital structure. This is referred to as the *weighted average cost of capital* or WACC.

The decision to invest in a new project should always consider whether the return generated will be greater than the cost of the capital used to finance the project.

Discovering the cost of debt

When deciding how to finance a particular project, the cost of capital can help companies decide whether debt financing, equity financing or a combination will have the lowest cost.

Debt history and financing

For startups and early-stage companies, their lack of collateral (existing assets) that can be used for loans means that *equity* is the more likely funding route. An established track record of repaying debts will also mean that older companies have a lower risk premium, so can pay a lower cost for capital.

The cost of debt is the interest rate paid on the debt. But because interest expenses are tax deductible, this debt is calculated on an after-tax basis.

$$\frac{\text{Cost of debt} = \text{Interest expense} \times (1 - T)}{\text{Total debt}}$$

where: Interest expense = Interest paid on the firm's current debt
          T = The company's marginal tax rate

Discovering the cost of equity

Capital asset pricing model

Because the rate of return required by equity investors is not as clearly defined as the interest rates that lenders set, the *cost of equity* is more complicated to determine. However, it can be approximated by using the *capital asset pricing model*.

$$CAPM(\text{Cost of equity}) = R_f + \beta(R_m - R_f)$$

where: R_f = risk-free rate of return
          R_m = market rate of return

To estimate risk, beta (β) is used. If the company is public, then their own stock beta can be used. If it is a private company, then the beta is estimated using the average beta from a group of similar public companies. It assumes that the beta of a private company will be the same as the industry average.

The overall cost of capital for a company is then based on the weighted average of these costs.

As an example, imagine a company with a capital structure consisting of 72% equity and 28% debt; its cost of equity is 10% and the after-tax cost of debt is 7%.

Therefore, the weighted average cost of capital (WACC) for this company would be:

$$(0.72 \times 10\%) + (0.28 \times 7\%) = 9.16$$

Once the WACC has been calculated, it is used to discount future cash flows from possible projects or other investments to estimate their net present value and how much value they might generate.

The ideal mix of debt and equity

Companies try to find the ideal funding mix (of debt and equity) that is based on the cost of capital. Financing projects with debt is generally more tax-efficient because interest expenses are tax-deductible, and the common share dividends are paid with after-tax dollars. But taking on too much debt can mean a company is too highly leveraged, meaning they must pay higher interest rates to compensate for their higher risk of defaulting.

The difference between the cost of capital and the discount rate

In business terms, the cost of capital is effectively a calculation of the break-even point for a project. The *discount rate* is determined by the cost of capital and indicates if the project can give a good enough return to repay costs and provide a reward to shareholders – it is the rate that must be beaten in order to justify an investment.

CAPITAL BUDGETING

The process of *capital budgeting* is about evaluating potential investments or projects for a company, such as a new factory, upgraded equipment or a new arm of the business. The project's potential lifetime cash inflows and outflows are assessed to work out if the potential returns meet a suitable benchmark. The project can then be approved or rejected.

NPV, IRR and payback period

The most common ways of assessing a project are *internal rate of return* (IRR), *net present value* (NPV) and *payback period*.

IRR is the expected return for a project – when the rate is higher than the cost of capital, it makes financial sense to approve a project.

NPV indicates how profitable a project will be compared to the alternatives. This is considered one of the most effective methods of assessing projects.

The payback period shows the length of time it would take to have sufficient cash flows to gain back the original investment.

Calculating IRR

One formula for calculating IRR is:

$$IRR = r_a + \frac{NPV_a}{NPV_a - NPV_b}(r_b - r_a)$$

Formulas for calculating IRR

Where: r_a = *lower discount rate* r_b = *higher discount rate*
NPV_a = *NPV at* r_a NPV_b = *NPV at* r_b

The IRR is defined as the discount rate that can be applied to the cash flows of a project to give an NPV of nil. This discount rate is the forecast return for the project.

THE MODIGLIANI-MILLER THEOREM

The Modigliani-Miller theorem shows that the capital structure of a company is not a factor in its value. The particular combination of debt and equity that a company chooses does not affect its real market value.

Instead, the theorem suggests that market value is decided by the present value of future earnings. In essence, the two forms of capital will balance each other out – if more expensive debt is taken on, then the value of equity goes down, and vice versa.

DISCOUNT CASH FLOW ANALYSIS

Discount cash flow analysis examines the initial cash outflow to fund the project, the combination of cash inflows in the form of sales (or revenue), and future outflows of cash (maintenance or other cost elements). All the cash flows are discounted back to the present date (apart from the initial outflow). This analysis gives the net present value.

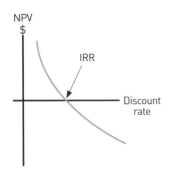

The NPV and IRR shown on a graph.

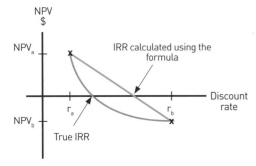

Project cash flows discounted twice using the IRR formula.

When entered on to a graph, the NPV and the IRR can be shown as on the graph at top left, with the discount rates on the X-axis and the NPV on the Y-axis. The point at which the curved line crosses the X-axis is the point where the NPV is zero – or the IRR and this is what needs to be calculated.

Using the IRR formula on page 195, the cash flows of the project are discounted twice (one lower and one higher discount rate). When plotted on the graph, it would look like the graph below.

The true IRR will be on a curve, reflecting the actual inflows and outflows of cash, but the straight line is an approximation of the IRR using the formula.

One of the main advantages of calculating IRR is that it takes account of the time value of money and uses real cash flows rather than profits to assess return. However, it does ignore the relative size of investments, so can be slightly misleading in certain circumstances.

Payback period analysis

Payback period analysis is a straightforward method of capital budgeting analysis; however, it can be inaccurate. It can be useful to give a quick, back-of-the-envelope calculation of an investment.

It calculates how long it will take to recoup the costs of an investment. The payback period is determined by dividing the initial investment by the average yearly cash inflow generated by the project. For example, if it costs $600,000 as an initial cash investment and the project generates $150,000 a year in revenue, it will take four years to recoup that investment.

There are other more involved methods of capital budgeting, such as throughput analysis, which looks at the amount of material passing through the system and tries to focus on alleviating bottlenecks in the system.

Dealing with the risks of investments

When considering capital budgeting or other investments, the risks that must be taken into consideration include:

- corporate risks
- international risks (for instance, currency risks)
- industry-specific risks
- market risks
- standalone risks
- project-specific risks

In each of these areas, sufficient levels of volatility could alter existing plans. For instance, if the currency in the home nation of the investing firm substantially weakens, then completing an overseas project may become more expensive.

There are two main methods that are used to assess risks involved with investment decisions – sensitivity analysis and scenario analysis.

Sensitivity and scenario analyses

Sensitivity analysis looks at how the uncertainty in the output of a model can be connected to different sources of uncertainty in the inputs of that model.

A simple example of sensitivity analysis in a business context might be A/B tests in digital marketing – assessing the effect of including a specific claim in marketing material and comparing sales results from marketing where the only difference is whether or not they include the specific claim. It can be used to decide how to use assets and resources.

Scenario analysis examines potential future events by considering various alternative possible outcomes. Often, this is about predicting the future value of an investment given changes to some existing variables. Scenario analysis usually looks at three possible scenarios:

- *Base-case scenario:* For example, to identify the NPV of a particular investment, using the discount rate and tax rate.
- *Worst-case scenario:* In the earlier example, using the highest possible tax rate or the highest discount rate.
- *Best-case scenario:* Using the same example, using the lowest possible tax rate or the lowest possible discount rate.

The major difference between sensitivity analyses and scenario analyses is that the first looks at the result of changing one variable at a time, while the second assesses the result of changing many possible variables at the same time.

MONTE CARLO SIMULATION

A *Monte Carlo simulation* is a modelling technique used to determine the probability of a range of outcomes when the possibility of random variables is present.

It assigns multiple values to uncertain variables to get multiple results and then averages those results to give an estimate. The output of this is the distribution of frequencies of different outcomes, presented on a bell curve, or a normal distribution. The most probable result will be in the middle of the bell curve.

Because it is presented as a normal distribution, the probability that the actual result in reality will be within one standard deviation of the most probable result is 68% – within two standard deviations it is 95%, and within three standard deviations 99.7%.

It overcomes the limitations of sensitivity and scenario analyses because it looks at the effects of all possible combinations of variables. However, they do assume a perfectly efficient market.

Monte Carlo simulations are used in many fields that have multiple random variables to contend with, particularly business and investments. However, they are also used in other situations, such as estimating the probability of budget overruns on large projects, looking at the probability that an asset price will move in a certain way, predicting telecoms network performance, and measuring potential risks in insurance or the oil industry.

MODERN PORTFOLIO THEORY AND INVESTMENTS
Modern portfolio theory

Modern portfolio theory (MPT) proposes that the risk and return characteristics of a particular investment cannot be viewed in isolation but must be assessed with consideration to how they affect the risk and return or the overall portfolio (entire set) of investments.

This means that a portfolio of multiple assets can be constructed that should give higher returns, without increasing the level of risk. Alternatively, if there is a desired level of return, a portfolio can be constructed with the lowest possible risk that should be capable of having that return.

Mean-variance efficient

Mean-variance analysis is used to determine investment decisions. It establishes the largest reward at a particular level of risk, or alternatively the lowest risk given a desired return. It is one part of the modern portfolio theory.

Showing investment returns over time

The variance shows how spread out the returns of a specific investment are across a particular period (usually daily or weekly). The expected return is expressed as a probability of the estimated return of the investment. In the case of investments with identical expected returns, but lower variance in one, the investment with lower variance is preferred. When variance is the same, the investment with a higher return is preferred.

Diversification and acceptable risks

The MPT is useful when trying to build diversified portfolios. It makes the basic assumption that investors will be risk-averse, given the same potential returns.

Assessing risk tolerance

Because most investments are either low risk and low return or high risk and high return, MPT suggests that investors can get the best results if they choose an optimal combination of the two based on an assessment of their specific risk tolerance.

The expected return of a given portfolio can be calculated as a weighted sum of the returns of the individual assets.

If a portfolio had four equally weighted assets with expected returns of 3%, 6%, 11% and 15%, the portfolio's expected return would be:

$$(3\% \times 25\%) + (6\% \times 25\%) + (11\% \times 25\%) + (15\% \times 25\%) =$$
$$0.75\% + 1.5\% + 2.75\% + 3.75\% = 8.75\%$$

A portfolio's risk is determined by the variances of each asset and the correlations of each pair of assets. As an example, calculating the risk for a portfolio with four assets requires the variances of the four assets, and the six possible correlation values between the four assets. The asset correlations mean that the total portfolio risk is lower than that which would be calculated by a weighted sum.

One criticism of the MPT is that it assesses portfolios on variance rather than downside risk. So, two portfolios could have the same variance and returns, but the variance in one is as a result of many small losses, whereas the variance in the other could be due to infrequent but much larger losses. Most investors would usually prefer the former situation.

The *post-modern portfolio theory* (PMPT) is an alternative approach that looks to minimize downside risk instead of variance.

Efficient market hypothesis

The *efficient market hypothesis* (EMH) suggests that share prices are a reflection of all information. It hypothesizes that on any given exchange, stocks trade at their fair market value.

Supporters of EMH believe that investors will benefit from investing in a low-cost, passive portfolio – that you can't beat the market. Others believe that it is possible to beat the market as stocks can be priced higher or lower than their fair market values.

The theory of EMH is often disputed and those who believe in it will suggest that it is fruitless to try to find stocks that are undervalued or to attempt to predict trends in the market with fundamental or technical analysis.

This is because, theoretically, both technical and fundamental analyses cannot consistently give risk-adjusted excess returns – only inside information could provide this, and this is illegal. Although there is a large body of academic research that supports EMH, there are examples of investors (such as Warren Buffett) who have consistently beaten the market over sustained periods of time – although this is in theory impossible.

Events such as the stock market crash in the late 1980s (when the Dow Jones Industrial Average lost 20% of its value in one day) or asset bubbles such as the internet bubble in the early 2000s indicate that stock prices can deviate significantly from their fair market value.

THE CAPITAL MARKET LINE AND EFFICIENT FRONTIER

The *capital market line* (CML) represents on a graph all the portfolios that combine risk and return in an optimal way. It is a theory that provides the best combinations of a risk-free asset and the market portfolio.

THE EFFICIENT FRONTIER

The set of perfect or optimal portfolios that are expected to give the highest return for a minimal level of return is known as the efficient frontier. This is demonstrated with the expected return placed on the Y-axis and the standard deviation (a measure of the risk) on the X-axis. It shows the risk-return trade-off of a portfolio.

The standard deviation of returns in a particular portfolio assesses investment risk and the consistency in earnings from the investment.

A lower covariance between portfolio investments will mean there is a lower portfolio standard deviation.

Successfully optimizing the return to risk paradigm should put a portfolio on the efficient frontier line, and optimal portfolios that are on the efficient frontier line usually have a higher degree of diversification.

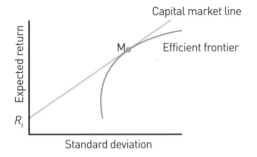

The capital market line.

The *efficient frontier* represents combinations of risky assets.

Drawing a line from the risk-free rate of return and keeping it tangential to the efficient frontier gives the *capital market line*. The point where the two lines touch (the *point of tangency*) is the most efficient portfolio. This slope of the CML is the Sharpe ratio of the market portfolio.

Moving up the CML increases a portfolio's risk, and moving down decreases risk. As a result, the return expectation will also respectively increase or decrease.

The CML is considered better than the efficient frontier because it is a combination of risky assets with risk-free assets.

It is assumed that all investors would choose the same market portfolio, given a specific mix of assets and the relevant associated risk.

The capital market line (CML) formula is as follows:

$$ER_p = R_f + SD_p \times (ER_m - R_f)/SD_m$$

Where: ER_p = expected return of portfolio, R_f = risk free rate, SD_p = standard deviation of portfolio, ER_m = expected return of market SD_m = standard deviation of market

VALUING POTENTIAL INVESTMENTS
Discounted cash flow

Discounted cash flow (DCF) analysis tries to determine the value of an investment today, using projections of the money it will generate in the future.

It can be used to make capital budgeting or decisions on operating expenditures, but it is also used by investors to assess how to invest in companies or securities (stocks, shares or other tradable financial assets).

The present value of the cash flows expected in the future is calculated by using a discount rate. If the DCF is above the current cost of investment, it indicates that there could be positive returns from the opportunity.

When used by companies, it commonly uses the WACC as the discount rate, as this takes into consideration the rate of return that shareholders expect. But the fact that it relies on estimates of future cash flows can mean that it is ultimately inaccurate.

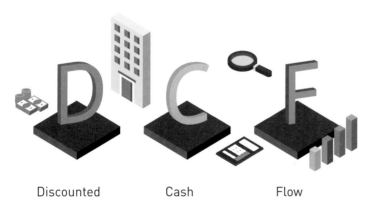

Discounted   Cash   Flow

Equity and market valuations

Assessing the value of a company is most commonly achieved with either *market capitalization* or *equity*. They are slightly different methods of looking at the value of a business.

Often, both are used to achieve an accurate assessment of the worth of a company.

Market capitalization is the number of all the outstanding shares (all the shares held by shareholders) of a company, multiplied by the current price of a single share. Equity is a statement of a company's assets minus its liabilities.

Market capitalization

ELON MUSK: PAYPAL, TESLA & SPACE X

Elon Musk is the founder, CEO, CTO, and chief designer of SpaceX; early investor, CEO, and product architect of Tesla, Inc.; founder of The Boring Company; co-founder of Neuralink; and co-founder and initial co-chairman of OpenAI. A centi-billionaire, Musk is one of the richest people in the world.

Musk was raised in South Africa but moved to America in the 1990s. In 1995 he co-founded the web software company Zip2 that provided maps and business directories to online newspapers. The start-up was acquired by Compaq for $307 million in 1999. Musk co-founded online bank X.com that same year, merging with Confinity in 2000 to form the company PayPal which was subsequently bought by eBay in 2002 for $1.5 billion.

In 2002, he founded SpaceX, an aerospace manufacturer and space transport services company, of which he is CEO, CTO, and lead designer. In 2004, he joined electric vehicle manufacturer Tesla Motors, Inc. (now Tesla, Inc.) as chairman and product architect, becoming its CEO in 2008. In 2006, he helped create SolarCity, a solar energy services company and current Tesla subsidiary. In 2015, he co-founded OpenAI, a nonprofit research company that promotes friendly artificial intelligence. In 2016, he co-founded Neuralink, a neurotechnology company focused on developing brain–computer interfaces, and as well as The Boring Company, a tunnel construction company.

Musk has long been a controversial figure, and regularly makes the news for saying slightly outrageous things, or being outspoken on his Twitter account (he bought the company in 2022) – even talking about taking his company public and affecting the share price. This has landed him in trouble with the SEC and other legal entities.

Chapter Ten
STRATEGY

Strategic analysis • Vertical integration and diversification • International strategy • Other strategic approaches and tools for business analysis • Alliances, mergers and acquisitions • The balanced scorecard • Strategic thinking • Game theory

FOUR ACTIONS FRAMEWORK

BUYER UTILITY MAPS

PORTER'S FIVE FORCES

THE BALANCED SCORECARD

STRATEGY CANVAS

LEADING AND LAGGING INDICATORS

PESTEL ANALYSIS

STRATEGIC ALLIANCES MERGERS AND ACQUSITIONS

STRATEGIC APPROACHES AND TOOLS

VRIO FRAMEWORK

ALLIANCES, MERGERS AND ACQUISITIONS

STRATEGY

STRATEGIC ANALYSIS

RESOURCE BASED VIEW

INTERNATIONAL STRATEGY

COMPETITIVE ADVANTAGE PORTER'S GENERIC STRATEGIES

THE AAA FRAMEWORK

THE CAGE FRAMEWORK

THE VALUE CHAIN

THE OODA LOOP

FOREIGN DIRECT INVESTMENT

ENTRY MODE STRATEGIES

DIVERSIFICATION

VERTICAL INTEGRATION AND DIVERSIFICATION

TURNKEY PROJECTS

When looking to implement strategy in a business setting, it is important to set clear goals that align with the mission statement, establish what the specific performance targets are, and analyze the strengths and weaknesses of both the firm itself and the competition.

STRATEGY ▶ *A strategy is a plan or method with the aim of achieving a goal.*

TACTICS ▶ *The method for putting a strategy into action and achieving the objectives.*

STRATEGIC ANALYSIS

There are a series of useful tools and analytic frameworks designed for use by business to help analyze their situation and help with setting strategy. One of the most basic of these, and commonly used, is a SWOT analysis. This stands for strengths, weaknesses, opportunities and threats.

Both weaknesses and strengths are factors internal to a company. They are the elements or actions of a company that confer disadvantages or advantages over the competition.

Threats and opportunities are external factors – possible areas outside the business that could help improve performance or potential problems from competitors or even the wider economic context that might need to be faced in the future.

Usually, a SWOT analysis is a small part of a broader business analysis, but it can also be used to summarize other findings.

Porter's five forces

Porter's five forces is one of the key tools for analyzing the position of a business, the likely competitive threats, and the other elements at play within an industry. It evaluates external competitive forces.

The five forces are:
1. *Rivalry among existing firms:* This is assessing the level of competition between companies.
2. *Threat of new entrants:* The possibility of new entrants to the industry offering something that can't be easily copied, and therefore reducing profits for established firms.
3. *Threat of substitutes:* The concern that products from a different industry might be able to offer similar utility to consumers (or be used instead).

These sale bargain hunters are subject to several of Porter's five forces!

Porter's five forces.

Conducting a PESTEL analysis

4. *Bargaining power of suppliers:* This looks at how much power suppliers have regarding setting prices for products that are in demand.
5. *Bargaining power of customers:* If customers can switch between products or companies (with little cost to them) then they can collectively demand changes to price or features.

There are certain contexts that can affect some of these forces. Barriers to entry mean that it is less attractive for new players to enter the industry. Existing companies can benefit from established relationships with suppliers, brand reputation, customer loyalty and capacity for economies of scale. All these things can increase the barriers to entry and lower the threat of new entrants.

If there are not many buyers, and lots of sellers in a market, then the threat of the bargaining power of customers increases as well as the threat of substitution.

If there are only a few suppliers in a market, then their bargaining power increases since replacements are not easily available.

PESTEL analysis

The *PESTEL analysis* is a way of studying macroenvironmental external factors that might affect the decisions, choices or performance of a company.

To conduct a PESTEL analysis, six factors need to be assessed for their potential influence on the company:

- *Political:* Government actions policies that might affect the company or their products.
- *Economic:* How the state of the economy might affect the buying power of consumers.
- *Social:* Demographic factors that can alter the market size and the needs of customers.
- *Technological:* The rate of change in relevant technologies and the level of R&D investment.
- *Environmental:* Elements related to the climate and the wider environment.
- *Legal:* Laws or legislation that may affect company performance.

The PESTEL analysis will look to include all the relevant factors in each of the categories above, even when they are seemingly obvious. For instance, labour or environmental laws might be included in the legal section or the potential for a recession in the economic section.

Resource-based view

Another option for assessing the strategic position of a company is a *resource-based view* (RBV). This is the process of making an inventory of the resources owned by a company as well as examining the potential to use those resources for competitive advantage.

The kinds of resources that the RBV model looks at are tangible, intangible and human. The potential of the firm to mobilize these resources is assessed as *organizational capacity*.

Tangible assets are things that can be quantified and can create customer value. *Intangible assets* are things that can't necessarily be seen, such as the reputation of a brand. *Human resources* are the skills and efforts of employees.

The VRIO framework helps determine which resources should be included in an RBV. Each resource is assessed with four questions:

1. Is it *valuable*? – Does it enable a company to
2. Is it *rare*? – Is it only controlled by a few companies?
3. Is it expensive to *imitate*? – Will it mean other companies encounter a cost disadvantage in getting it?
4. Is the company *organized* in a manner that allows them to maximize the utility of the resource?

Competitive advantage and Porter's generic strategies

The competitive advantage of a company is the difference in behaviour or assets that means a company can create more economic value than their competitors. The plan of action used to achieve and sustain a competitive advantage is known as *business-level strategy*.

The three main ways in which a company can gain competitive advantage are outlined in Porter's generic strategies (see diagram overleaf).

The three strategies are usually laid out on a two-by-two matrix with the axes indicating the kind of advantage conferred and the scope of the strategy.

The first of these, which is broad in scope, is *cost*

IS IT...

V ALUABLE?
R ARE?
COSTLY TO I MITATE?
EXPLOITABLE BY THE O RGANISATION?

The VRIO framework.

THE OODA LOOP

The decision-making strategy of observe, orient, decide, act is known as the *OODA loop*. It is designed to filter the available information, place it in context and swiftly make the best decision – looping this process back to the start means that changes can be effectively made as more data is available.

It was developed by the US Air Force Colonel John Boyd in the mid-20th century, initially to enable soldiers to make rapid decisions under time pressure, when not all information may be available, or there is not time to gather all data before acting. Executing an OODA loop quicker than an opponent can disrupt an opponent's decision-making cycle.

Now widely applied in many sectors of business, this strategy can be used at an individual or organizational level, but it is particularly useful when there is strong competition or the ability to react quickly to change might lead to an advantage.

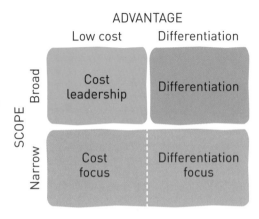

ADVANTAGE

Low cost — Differentiation

SCOPE: Broad / Narrow

	Low cost	Differentiation
Broad	Cost leadership	Differentiation
Narrow	Cost focus	Differentiation focus

Porter's generic strategies.

Office cleaning is a classic example of an activity that is usually better outsourced.

leadership strategy, which involves keeping the costs of operation as low as possible. This might be achieved through economies of scale, so that the per-unit production cost gets lower.

A *differentiation strategy* is about enhancing the perceived value of a product in comparison to rival products. The intention is that customers will then pay more for the product.

The final two sections of the matrix are both *focus strategies*. *Cost focus* applies cost leadership to a niche market, and a *differentiation focus* applies differentiation to a niche market. This focus means that a company understands the unique needs of that specific market and the dynamics involved and then applies a suitable strategy to gain competitive advantage.

If a company chooses to pursue multiple strategies but does not do particularly well at any of them, they may still be profitable but may not outperform the competition.

VERTICAL INTEGRATION AND DIVERSIFICATION

Deciding which industry a company competes in is an example of corporate-level strategy.

Vertical integration refers to the number of activities in a value chain that are performed by a company. This tends to mean running multiple businesses at once. More activities mean that the company is more vertically integrated.

A simple example of vertical integration could be a rowing-machine company setting up a logistics service arm of their business to deal with customer deliveries and installation. This would be a part of the value chain that might previously have been fulfilled by third parties.

Vertical integration is particularly valuable when the threat of opportunism is high (the chance of being exploited by a third party in the value chain because of the need for a specific service) as it decreases this threat. However, it also decreases the flexibility of a company, so is usually only undertaken when the company has VRIO resources in that area and when there is confidence that an investment will be successful.

There is often more value in outsourcing tasks that are commodities but would require a large investment of resources. For instance, very few companies run their own cleaning services for their office as the set-up and ongoing costs would be disproportionate to the benefits. A third party can usually offer this service at a lower cost, as they can work with economies of scale (providing their services to more than one office, buying supplies in bulk, etc.).

There are two main directions of integration: *backwards*, which is activities closer to the supplier end of the value chain and *forwards*, which is activities closer to the customer end of the value chain. Bringing a delivery service in-house is forwards integration, whereas manufacturing your own nuts and bolts for a product would be backwards integration.

Diversification

When a company *diversifies*, it is entering a new market (or creating a new product or service) that is different from its core business.

To be successful and profitable for the company, there need to be *economies of scope* created by these multiple businesses or strands – lowering their average costs by producing a greater number of products. These economies of scope exist when there are activities that are shared or core competencies between the linked business areas.

These core competencies are about efficiently utilizing the skill, knowledge and available technologies across the whole company.

Diversification also means that the revenue from one business or product can be used to invest in

THE VALUE CHAIN

The *value chain* is the sequence of relevant activities that are strategically necessary to bring a product or service to market. Everything from the design and manufacture of the component parts of the product to the packaging and the home delivery of the final product are part of the value chain.

The activities that are about creating a product or service, selling it, delivering it and post-purchase servicing are all *primary activities*. *Support activities* are things that facilitate these primary activities, such as how the company is structured, what technology is used, procurement and recruitment processes.

Mapping out the primary and support activities across an entire company allows for an analysis of the value chain.

PRIMARY ACTIVITIES:

| Inbound logistics | Operations | Outbound logistic | Marketing and sales | Service | PROFIT |

SUPPORT ACTIVITIES:

Procurement

Technology development

PRIMARY ACTIVITIES:

| Inbound logistics | Operations | Outbound logistic | Marketing and sales | Service | PROFIT |

SUPPORT ACTIVITIES:

Procurement

Technology development

Company infrastructure

Human resource management

other areas, meaning that there is an internal capital market – the company can loan money to itself.

With successful diversification, there is corporate synergy, which is when the total of all the parts of the business performs better than they would by themselves.

Categories of diversification

The four main categories of diversification are:

Type	Level of diversification	Description
Limited	Low	70–100% revenue from one business
Related-constrained	Moderate	Products and services are highly linked
Related-linked	Moderate	Few or occasional links between businesses
Unrelated	High	No linkages between businesses

ALLIANCES, MERGERS AND ACQUISITIONS
Strategic alliances

Entering a *strategic alliance means* developing, making or selling a product offering together with another, independent company. These strategic alliances can create a situation that is useful for tacit collusion where two companies indicate that they are prepared to co-operate to reduce competition.

There are three distinct categories of strategic alliances:

1. *Non-equity alliances:* Companies work together to make a contractual agreement, but they don't have equity in each other's companies. These are usually one of three types of agreement:

   – *Licensing:* One company permits the other to use its brand reputation or intellectual property (IP) to help market and sell a product.
   – *Supply:* One company agrees to supply the other.
   – *Distribution:* One company agrees to distribute the other's products.
2. *Equity alliances:* A company takes an equity holding in the other, alongside establishing contracts.
3. *Joint ventures:* Collaborating companies create a legally independent company, in which they both invest (as well as share profits).

Mergers and acquisitions

Mergers and acquisitions are both terms for the process of combining or joining two companies together. They each have slightly different approaches to the process.

When an *acquisition* happens, it is usually a larger company buying all or most of another company's assets. There is a *bidding* company (the company doing the acquiring) and a *target company* (the company being acquired).

Acquisitions can happen for all kinds of reasons, some of the most common being increasing market share, gaining access to and control over new technologies or IP, acquiring skilled employees (this is sometimes called an *acqui-hire*), for vertical integration purposes, to diversify geographically or to increase economies of scale.

A *friendly acquisition* is when the management of the target company want the company to be acquired – this is usually the case with startups, and often being acquired is the main strategic focus of a startup company.

Friendly acquisiiton

There are also *hostile takeovers* (or unfriendly acquisitions) where the acquisition is accomplished without the support and co-operation of the management of the target company. To undertake a hostile takeover, the bidding firm will publicly say that it is willing to buy the target company's shares for more than they are currently worth on the open market. The current set of shareholders then sell their shares to the bidding company, meaning it acquires a majority or controlling share. This is known as a *tender offer*.

Hostile takeover

To avoid the possibility of a hostile takeover, there are some shareholder and board-level strategies that can be put in place such as *'poison pills'*, *greenmail* or a *white knight defence*.

When two companies of roughly the same size look to undergo a *merger* and combine their assets, they are effectively operating a friendly takeover – but a merger means neither side has to look like the weaker party. In a merger, the two companies may sometimes even combine their names to further indicate the parity of the arrangement.

In many jurisdictions, and especially in certain industries, there are strict rules and regulations about large companies merging, to prevent the creation of a monopoly situation in an industry.

However, the completion of a merger or an acquisition does not ensure success for the merged company or the bidder. In many cases, there is a net loss of value. Some of the reasons for this loss of value are incompatible corporate cultures, differing technologies, inadequate due diligence resulting in the discovery of hidden liabilities, and employees or departments that overlap meaning there are inefficiencies or loss of expertise when restructuring.

In terms of share, in an acquisition, the target company ceases to exist, the bidding company absorbs the target business and the bidding company's shares continue to be traded. In a merger, both companies' shares cease to be traded, and shares for the new, merged company are issued in their place.

**SOME KEY TRADE AND
INTERNATIONAL ORGANIZATIONS**

World Trade Organization (WTO): An international organization providing a structure for negotiations to reduce barriers to trade and reach agreements in trade disputes between nations.

International Monetary Fund (IMF): an international organization with 190 member countries that aims to keep the international monetary and financial system stable.

European Union (EU): An economic and political union of 27 European nations. They have a regional trade agreement that lowers tariffs and helps to develop and maintain similar economic and technological standards.

North American Free Trade Agreement (NAFTA): A trade agreement that tries to reduce trade barriers between the US, Canada and Mexico.

Asia-Pacific Economic Cooperation (APEC): A forum for 21 countries that border the Pacific Ocean that promotes free trade.

INTERNATIONAL STRATEGY

When companies operate or intend to operate in multiple countries, they are undertaking an *international strategy* to try to gain a competitive advantage.

As the world becomes increasingly economically integrated across borders, and supply chains are ever more multinational, there is an increase in globalization, making international strategy a key component of the business approach of many large companies.

The CAGE distance framework

When looking to operate in another country, the cultural, economic and administrative differences can impact the options available to a business as they determine an entry strategy.

The *CAGE distance framework* is a method for identifying these differences, referred to as *distances*, between a company and the foreign market they are looking to enter. These distances can impact an entry strategy positively or negatively. Increased distance may mean that an entry strategy needs to change or be adapted to suit the specific market. It looks at these four areas:

The CAGE distance frameork

1. *Cultural distance:* Differences in things like religion, social norms or language.
2. *Administrative/political distance:* The political climate and how rules and regulations might differ.
3. *Geographic distance:* The physical distance for logistical purposes, climate differences and communication or transportation links.
4. *Economic distance:* Any price or cost differences between markets (for instance labour or materials).

The AAA framework

To help manage the cultural and economic differences in new international markets, the AAA framework offers three potential strategies to manage these differences: adaptation, aggregation and arbitrage.

- *Adaptation:* Means adapting a business model to suit the specific needs of a foreign market.

- *Aggregation:* This is about finding similarities between regions to allow for efficient scaling up of production and decreasing costs across a standardized organization.
- *Arbitrage:* This is about using the differences between particular markets to achieve a competitive advantage. For instance, through outsourcing specific processes overseas.

Exporting in progress – containers being processed at a major port.

Entry mode strategies

A company looking to operate in a new, foreign market has a series of *entry mode strategies*, or options for how they choose to enter these markets. The key decision is about how much control and oversight they require of a foreign operation – entry strategies that have more control usually come at greater risk.

The basic entry mode strategies are exporting, international licensing, international strategic alliances and foreign direct investment. Each of these has various options or approaches.

1. *Exporting* – where goods made in one country are shipped overseas to be sold in a different country.
   - *Piggyback exporting:* When a company that already exports to a foreign market (known as the carrier) sells its own products as well as those of a different, often smaller firm (known as the rider).
   - *Indirect exporting:* A middleman provides a company that wants to export with a service that includes the expertise and contacts needed to sell in one or more foreign markets.
   - *Direct exporting:* Companies contact other organizations directly in a foreign market to set up the export of goods.

Exporting

2. *International licensing* – a contract with which a company (the licensor) permits a licensee in a foreign market to utilize their intellectual property and/or manufacture their products.
   - *International franchising:* A licensee in a foreign market strikes a comprehensive agreement to use the whole of the licensor's business model (including elements such as patents, trademarks and training schemes).
   - *Contract manufacturing:* A foreign licensee is contracted to manufacture the licensor's products under the existing licensor's brand.
   - *Technology licensing:* A foreign licensee is permitted to use (or sell) technological IP under their local brand in exchange for payment to the licensor.

International licensing

3. *International strategic alliances* – an agreement between two or more organizations from different countries to manufacture, create or sell products together.

- *International co-operative alliances* (ICAs): These need contracts that specify the contribution expected from each party.
- *Turnkey projects:* A company ensures a project is fully operational before handing it over to the company that will own it.
  - *International joint ventures* (IJV): Companies in collaboration from different countries create a legally independent company together.

4. *Foreign direct investment* (FDI): When a company owns some or all of an operation (or company) in a foreign country.

Companies can acquire businesses that already exist or make a *greenfield investment* – establishing a subsidiary from scratch in the foreign country.

These various types of entry strategy all sit on two axes – *control* and *risk*. Some are riskier, but have more control, and vice versa.

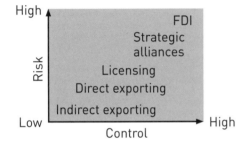

Control and risk in entry strategies.

OTHER STRATEGIC APPROACHES AND TOOLS FOR BUSINESS ANALYSIS
Strategy canvas

A technique from W. Chan Kim and Renée Mauborgne's 2005 book, *Blue Ocean Strategy*, the *strategy canvas* is an easy-to-read line graph that plots factors against the importance or strength of the offering. Competitors or benchmarks for the industry can then be overlaid to help spot opportunities.

The X-axis captures *factors of investment* – areas the company chooses to compete in – and the Y-axis shows the *level of offer* that customers receive from each factor. It can also show what the *strategic profiles* of major competitors are.

The line on the graph for each company – the *value curve* – demonstrates the relative performance of a company across the factors of competition.

The strategy canvas can show the similarities of the strategies of the major competitors, meaning they are competing in the same space, on the same factors. The Blue Ocean Strategy approach then uses this to find the places that a business can compete

An example of a strategy canvas.

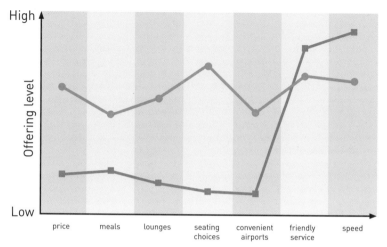

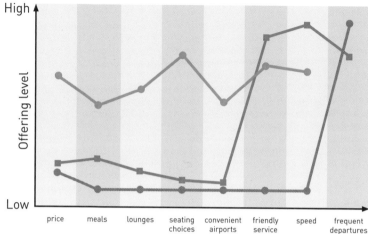

that are not yet a factor considered or invested in by the competition.

In the example above left, the value curve showing the strategy of a long-standing airline company is depicted in red, whereas a new entrant airline's strategy is shown in blue. The new entrant is choosing to aggressively compete on two factors with their offering – friendly service and speed.

In the strategy canvas above right, the set of factors from a different industry or option, in this instance travelling by car, are overlaid in grey. This then shows a factor not considered by the incumbents – frequent departures. The new entrant in blue can then use this as a part of their Blue Ocean Strategy. They are creating their own novel area of business, without competition.

One of the reasons that a strategy canvas can be useful is that it helps companies move the focus from what competitors are doing, towards alternative options. It also tries to look at the part of the market that isn't yet addressed by the industry – customers who aren't being well served by the existing set of strategic factors.

FOUR ACTIONS FRAMEWORK

The *four actions framework* is a set of four questions designed to help translate the insights from a strategy canvas into a strategic plan. It is part of the process of challenging the existing business model in an industry and coming up with a Blue Ocean Strategy that avoids the existing trade-offs between low cost and differentiation.

The four questions are, in relation to the industry concerned:

1. What factors are taken for granted that should be eliminated?
2. Which factors need to be reduced below the current standard?
3. Which of the factors should be improved to above the current standard?
4. Which factors have never been offered by the industry and should be created?

The six stages of buyer experience cycle

An example of a
Buyer Utility Map.

Buyer Utility Maps

The *Buyer Utility Map*, also developed by Kim and Mauborgne for *Blue Ocean Strategy,* outlines the options companies have to deliver exceptional utility to customers, as well as the various experiences customers might have with a product. This mindset helps to identify the range of utility spaces that a product could potentially fill (problems it could solve, etc.) and considers the issue from a demand-side perspective.

There are two sides to a Buyer Utility Map: the Buyer Experience Cycle (BEC) and the Utility levers.

1. *Buyer Experience Cycle* (BEC): This can be divided into a cycle of six stages, usually running in a sequence from purchase to disposal.
2. *Utility levers:* These are the ways in which a company tries to create utility for their customers.

An example of a Buyer Utility Map is above.

THE BALANCED SCORECARD

Aspects of a balanced scorecard

The balanced scorecard (BSC) is a framework used to track and manage an organization's strategy. A balanced scorecard:

- describes strategy
- measures strategy
- tracks the actions being taken to improve results

There are four perspectives that need to be considered when building a BSC: financial, customer, business process, and learning and growth.

1. *Financial perspective:* How this will appear to shareholders?

2. *Customer perspective:* How this will appear to consumers of the company's products?
3. *Business processes:* What things must the company be good at doing?
4. *Learning and growth:* How will the company innovate, maintain culture or skills, and improve?

These questions then frame the objectives, measures, targets and initiatives so that there are not directly competing elements of an overall strategy and that any strategic approach is balanced across all these areas of the organization.

There is also a consideration of the balance between leading and lagging indicators – the *drivers* or *outcomes* of company goals. In the BSC framework, these KPIs indicate if goals are being achieved and if future goals are on track.

The one-page *strategy-map* approach of the BSC gives a visual representation that can be referred to, helps identify key goals and interactions, and unifies all goals into a single strategy. This can allow leaders and teams to see which areas of strategy might need work, as well as giving clear goals for employees. The BSC becomes the authority on strategy.

LEADING AND LAGGING INDICATORS

A *leading indicator* is a measurement that *predicts outcomes,* for example, the percentage of people wearing safety equipment on a work site is a leading safety indicator. A *lagging indicator* is an *output measurement,* for example, the number of accidents on a work site would be a lagging safety indicator.

Each of the four perspectives can have multiple objectives, and therefore multiple measures, targets and/or initiatives. Sometimes, initiatives may overlap more than one perspective.

The measurements and target sections always need to be something that can be quantified – if discussing something subjective, like customer feedback, it would need converting into a *net promoter score,* or a similar numerical metric.

	Objective	Measure	Targets	Initiatives
Financial	Increase margin	Increase in profits (£)	25% margin on revenue	Increase price of basic model and grow sales
Customer	More features on basic model	+n features compared to previous version	At least two new features	Add features most desired by customers
Process	Grow sales	No. of units sold	30% increase in unit sales	Add new features
Learning & growth	Assess most desired missing features	Rank most desired features	Survey 5% of existing customers	Feed most desired features back to product development

INDRA NOOYI: PEPSI

Indra Nooyi is the current chairperson and CEO of PepsiCo, one of the world's largest food and beverage companies. She was ranked #3 on *Fortune's* most powerful women in business list in 2014, #4 in 2015, and #6 in 2016.

Nooyi graduated from the Yale School of Management with an MBA in 1980. After working in various positions in the corporate sector, she joined PepsiCo in 1994 and was eventually appointed as the CEO in 2006.

During her time as the CEO of PepsiCo, Nooyi has been credited with numerous successful strategic decisions that have helped to transform the company into a global powerhouse. Some of her notable achievements include:

- PepsiCo's acquisition of Quaker Oats in 2001, which added popular brands such as Gatorade and Quaker Foods to PepsiCo's portfolio
- Leading the company's successful entry into the healthy snacks market with the launch of brands such as Sabra hummus and Stacy's pita chips
- Overseeing PepsiCo's shift towards more sustainable and health-conscious products, such as bottled water and organic snacks
- Building a more diverse and inclusive workplace, with a focus on empowering women and minorities

Under Nooyi's leadership, PepsiCo has consistently performed well financially, with revenue and profit growth in each of the last ten years. In 2021, the company's net revenue was about $80 billion and its net income was $7.618 billion.

STRATEGIC THINKING AND GAME THEORY

STRATEGIC THINKING
Difference between strategic thinking and strategy

Strategy is generally a plan or a method focused on how to achieve a goal, whereas the aim of *strategic thinking* is to discover new and sometimes creative strategies that 'rewrite the rules of the game'.

Strategic thinking evaluates risks and opportunities in multiple dimensions, usually over a long horizon. This isn't always an advantage or benefit, though it can be particularly useful when focused on the long term, low probability of success, and high payout objectives and opportunities.

Strategic thinking aims to find innovative ways to achieve a defined strategy.

Because thinking is different from planning, the skillset needed to be able to think strategically includes creativity, imagination, ideation, ability to see alternatives, solving problems and being a leader. Some people are more suited to strategic thinking than others.

The tools and techniques that are used to facilitate this kind of thinking include brainstorming, planning for various scenarios, root cause analysis and conducting feasibility studies.

Business School Professor Jeanne Liedtka noted five 'major attributes of strategic thinking in practice' that could be called *key competencies*:

1. *Systems perspective:* This means understanding all the consequences of strategic actions. This involves having a mental model of the whole end-to-end system, their role in it and a knowledge of the competencies involved.
2. *Intent focused:* This refers to the strategic thinker being less easy to distract and more determined than their competition. Liedtka describes strategic intent as 'the focus that allows individuals within an organization to marshal and leverage their energy, to focus attention, to resist distraction, and to concentrate for as long as it takes to achieve a goal.'
3. *Thinking in time:* This is the ability to think about the past, present and future simultaneously, leading to quicker and better decision making. Scenario planning looks to help to achieve this kind of thinking in practice when making strategy.
4. *Hypothesis driven:* This is the explicit incorporation of the scientific method into decision making. It means both creative and critical thinking can be combined most effectively.

5. *Intelligent opportunism:* This is the ability to be responsive to high-quality opportunities. It involves the capacity to see the potential of alternative strategies, even if they might contradict the current strategy.

EXAMPLES OF STRATEGIC THINKING IN BUSINESS
Rewriting the rules – Blue Ocean Strategy

The core concept of Blue Ocean Strategy is one in which a business enters (or creates) a market that has little to no competition. These new markets allow a company to achieve a high competitive advantage as well as low price competition or cost pressures.

It involves pursuing a differentiation plus low-cost strategy that makes the competition irrelevant. Rather than competing for advantage in an environment that is highly competitive (like an ocean 'red' with the blood of competing predators) it looks to find new ground with no competitors.

Novel demand

To do this, businesses need to look beyond existing market boundaries or industry structures to create *novel demand*. This means shifting the focus from supply to demand, from competing to creating innovative value to unlock this new demand. The simultaneous pursuit of differentiation and low cost is what allows businesses to achieve this.

One of the tools used for analyzing markets and creating a Blue Ocean Strategy is a strategy canvas (see pages 212–13). This shows the current state of the known market space, demonstrating which factors an industry competes on and invests in, what customers currently receive and what the basic strategic parameters of competing companies are.

Moving the focus from competitors to alternatives and from existing customers to non-customers (customers not yet captured or served by the industry) shows how a Blue Ocean Strategy can break away from the existing reality (the red ocean).

It demonstrates the four key elements of strategy:

1. the factors of competition
2. the offer level for customers
3. the strategic profiles for competitors
4. cost structures for competitors (and the proposed business)

RED OCEAN STRATEGY	BLUE OCEAN STRATEGY
Compete in **existing** market space	Create **uncontested** market space
Beat the competition	Make the competition **irrelevant**
Exploit **existing** demand	Create and capture **new** demand
Make the value-cost trade-off	**Break** the value-cost trade off
Align the whole system of a firm's activities with its **strategic choice of differentiation or low cost**	Align the whole system of a firm's activities **in pursuit of differentiation or low cost**

Early vs. late mover advantages

The first business to execute a strategy can gain several advantages. They can:

- establish the product they make as the industry standard
- reach consumers first with a strong impression – this can lead to brand recognition and loyalty
- control resources, such as securing a more strategic location, establishing beneficial contracts with key suppliers or hiring the best employees first
- keep customers if there is a high cost to switch to a product from a later entrant

Disadvantages of being a first mover

The company that moves first may have to invest a lot of resources in persuading customers to buy or try a new product. The companies that enter the market afterwards benefit from the 'education' of these consumers, and don't need to spend as much on marketing an entirely new product. They can also avoid mistakes made by first movers. Other benefits include:

- If a first mover is not able to capture consumers with their products, later market entrants can use this to their advantage.
- Later entrants can sometimes reverse-engineer products and improve them or reduce their price to the consumer.
- Later entrants can spot areas that were not improved by the first mover and take advantage of these.

Innovation and dominant design

When a new technology emerges, there is usually a period when there are high levels of competition between companies, often with alternative designs of the same product. Companies will experiment with different features, designs and capabilities while all trying to address the same market needs.

NETFLIX AND BLUE OCEAN STRATEGIES

When Netflix started, they were not trying to compete with Blockbuster, the dominant player in video rental at the time. Instead, they reinvented the market by building a new, online, postal-based DVD rental service without late fees or return deadlines. The Netflix flat-fee model removed these two key pain points for Blockbuster customers.

Netflix subsequently switched to streaming and then became a content creator, producing and financing their own TV shows and films. They have consistently moved to new, uncontested spaces to capture demand, operating a form of Blue Ocean Strategy.

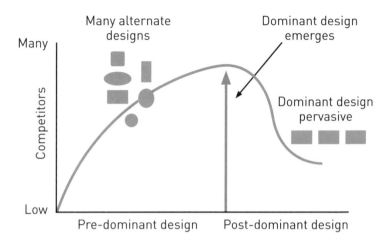

The emergence of a dominant design.

At some point, one design will become the most widely accepted, either in an implicit or explicit way. Once companies and consumers arrive at this consensus point, this is then the dominant design and often results in the mass exit from the market of competitors (or a changeover to the dominant design).

It isn't about looking exactly the same or using precisely the same technology, but it is about defining the expected design norms for meeting the needs of users in that market. The dominant design is not necessarily the best technological solution, and usually has some compromises because it is the design that appeals to a very broad range of users in a market.

The iPhone is a good example of a dominant design emerging. Prior to the first iteration, there were many competing form factors for smartphones, from slide-open cases to touchscreens to keyboard-based phones. Post iPhone, the characteristics of its design choices define the norms in the smartphone industry – touchscreen interface, pocket-sized, integrated camera, virtual keyboards, an app marketplace, etc.

GAME THEORY
Basic definition of game theory

Game theory is a set of tools for analyzing situations where two or more parties need to make decisions that are interdependent – that could affect each other. This means considering the other party's possible decisions when making one's own decisions.

In game theory, the parties involved are called *players*, and the set of possible decisions are referred to as strategies. Game theory models the strategic interaction between two or more players in a situation that has rules and outcomes. It tries to define the optimal decision.

Real-world situations can be modelled using game theory – pricing against competition, product releases, etc. can be laid out and the outcomes modelled.

The 'game' in game theory is the model of an interactive situation between players. The main element of this is that the pay-off (outcome) for one player is contingent on the decisions or strategy of the other player. Identifying the identities, preferences and available strategies (and how they affect the outcome) of other players is all part of setting up the model.

Mathematician John von Neumann and economist Oskar Morgenstern are credited with creating game theory in the 1940s, though it has been extensively developed and adapted since.

Normal form and best responses

A player's *best response* is the strategy that generates the largest pay-off (the most utility, in economic terms) for them given what all the other players are doing.

Normal form games mean that the pay-off and strategies of a game are described in the form of a matrix.

Normal form games can be used to help identify dominated strategies and the *Nash equilibrium* (see overleaf). The matrix shows the strategies adopted by the different players of the game and the possible outcomes.

In the example of the prisoner's dilemma below, assume two criminals have been caught and put in different rooms to be questioned. If both criminals say nothing, they will each get a short jail sentence of one year. If one confesses, they will get out of jail while the other criminal will get a long sentence. If they both confess, they will both get a medium-length jail sentence.

This is represented in the matrix below, with each box showing the outcome represented as 'P1, P2'. So, the bottom left box indicates that P1, who said nothing, gets three years in jail and P2 gets away (because P2 confessed).

Oskar Morgenstern (1902–77) and John van Neumann (1903–57), the originators of game theory.

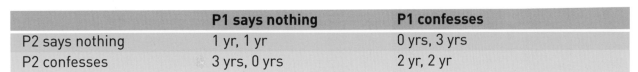

	P1 says nothing	P1 confesses
P2 says nothing	1 yr, 1 yr	0 yrs, 3 yrs
P2 confesses	3 yrs, 0 yrs	2 yr, 2 yr

Once games are represented in this way, it can be easier to see what the best strategy might be, if you have information or assumptions about what decisions the other party is most likely to make.

Extensive form games

Extensive form games are where a game is described in the form of a *decision tree*. They can help when there is a need to represent events that might occur by chance. These games have a branching structure with the players represented on different nodes, and decisions represented by branches.

A simple example

Imagine Company A wants to enter a new market, while Company B is the existing firm in that market. In this example, Company A has two strategies: either enter the market and fight to

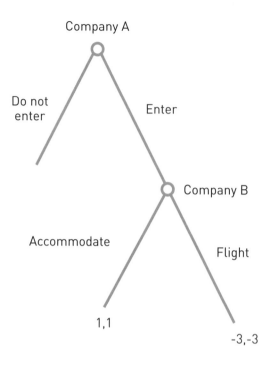

Company A

Do not
enter

Enter

Company B

Accommodate

Flight

1,1

-3,-3

*Extensive form
games.*

survive or do not enter the market (and remain without the profit that could be earned). Equally, Company B also has two possible strategies given a new entrant, either to put up a fight for its position or to accommodate the presence of Company A.

Left is the decision tree for the current situation:

In this example, if company A does not enter the market, then its pay-off would be zero. However, if it chooses to enter the market, the situation will depend on the decisions of company B.

If both companies compete aggressively (for instance in a price war), then both would suffer a loss (marked here as 3 to indicate the relative loss of value). Alternatively, if company B chooses to accommodate the new market entrant, then both would earn equal profits, marked as 2. Company B can presume that company A will enter the market in this example, as company A could gain 1 in value. Given that presumption, it benefits company B to consider their potential loss or gain. In this example, the best option for both is that company A enters the market and company B accommodates them.

Backward induction is one method for solving extensive-form games. The game is broken into smaller sub-games:

1. Identify the opponent's best responses based on their pay-offs at the *terminal nodes* (the last points on the right-hand side). Get rid of the strategies that are worse.
2. Shift those pay-offs back along the chain, creating new terminal nodes. Then select your best response for this step.
3. The remaining chain of strategies is referred to as a *sub-game perfect equilibrium*.

Nash equilibrium

The Nash equilibrium is an outcome reached in a game that means no player can increase their pay-off by changing decisions by themselves. It can be described as a 'no regrets' situation, because once a decision is made, a player will have no regrets concerning decisions, bearing in mind the consequences. There can often be more than one equilibrium in a game.

In the Prisoner's Dilemma example, the most favourable strategy is to not confess. However, because the prisoners don't know the other's strategy (and can't be certain that the other will not confess), both are likely to confess and receive a short prison sentence.

The Nash equilibrium indicates that in a Prisoner's Dilemma situation, both players will make the decision that is the best for them as an individual but worse for the pair collectively.

Strictly dominated and weakly dominant strategies

In game theory, strategies can be strictly or weakly dominated (or not dominated at all) and strategies can also be dominant.

A *dominant strategy* is one that provides a higher pay-off than any other option, regardless of what other players are doing. If a player has a dominant strategy available, they can be expected to choose it.

Dominant strategy

A *weakly dominant strategy* is one that gives a better pay-off in at least one outcome, and equal pay-off in all the other possible outcomes.

A *strictly dominated strategy* gives a lower pay-off than any other strategy, regardless of what other players choose to do. If a player has a strictly dominated strategy, the other players will anticipate it won't be chosen and will make their choices accordingly.

Rationalization is the process of trying to solve a game from the perspective of each player, and one way of doing this is iterated elimination of strictly dominated strategies. From each player's perspective, their strictly dominated strategies are removed. Once this is done for both players, the outcomes that remain are *rationalizable strategies*.

Rationalization

If only one outcome remains, then the game is *dominance solvable*.

As an example, imagine two people, Leo and Andy. They both enjoy hanging out together, but because they have broken their phones they can't communicate before they decide if they should stay at home or go to the pub this evening.

Both prefer going to the pub to staying at home and prefer being with each other over being apart. In addition, they only have the chance of seeing each other at the pub. Here's this game in matrix form (assigning relative values of utility to each option):

	Leo stays home	Leo goes to the pub
Andy stays home	0,0	0,1
Andy goes to the pub	1,0	2,2

In this example, going to the pub is a strictly dominant strategy for both players, because it always gives the best outcome, regardless of what the other player chooses. If the players are both maximizing their individual expected utilities, both will go to the pub.

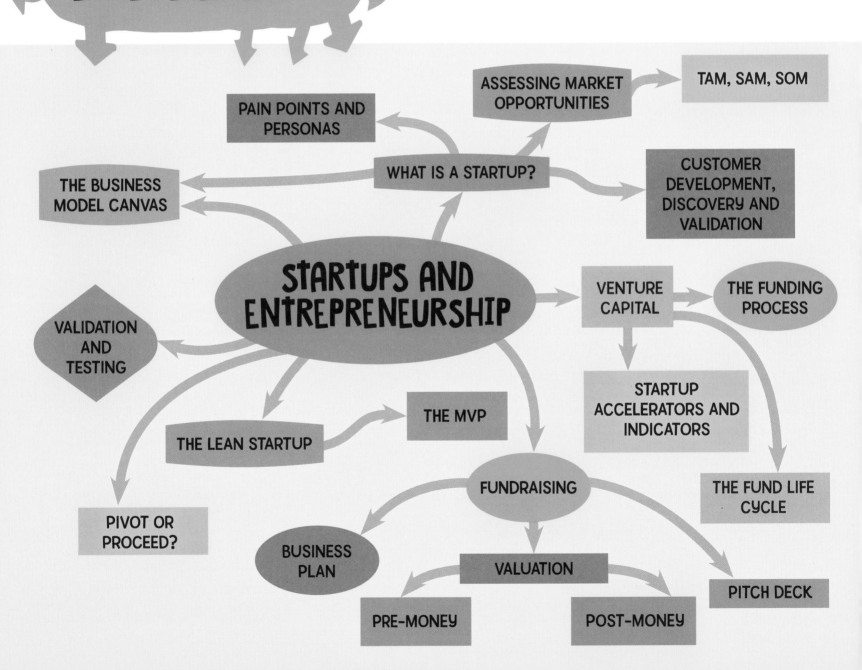

Chapter Eleven
STARTUPS AND ENTREPRENEURSHIP

Startups • Customer development, discovery and validation •
Assessing market opportunities • Pain points and personas •
Validation and testing • Venture capital • The business plan

ASSESSING MARKET OPPORTUNITIES

TAM, SAM, SOM

PAIN POINTS AND PERSONAS

WHAT IS A STARTUP?

CUSTOMER DEVELOPMENT, DISCOVERY AND VALIDATION

THE BUSINESS MODEL CANVAS

STARTUPS AND ENTREPRENEURSHIP

VENTURE CAPITAL

THE FUNDING PROCESS

VALIDATION AND TESTING

STARTUP ACCELERATORS AND INDICATORS

THE MVP

THE LEAN STARTUP

THE FUND LIFE CYCLE

PIVOT OR PROCEED?

FUNDRAISING

BUSINESS PLAN

VALUATION

PITCH DECK

PRE-MONEY

POST-MONEY

STARTUPS

A simple way of defining a *startup* is as a company that is in the initial stages of business.

However, it is usually taken to more specifically mean a young company with a business model that supports innovation and that is quick to grow. The business model of a startup at its very beginning may not be the same as that later in its journey. A key process for early-stage startups is to discover and validate a scalable, repeatable and profitable business model.

Founders of startups often fund the initial stages of the business themselves, via loans, through crowdfunding campaigns or with help from friends and family. Sources of funding to help startups grow or expand also often include *angel investors* and *venture capitalists*.

The predominant characteristics of a successful startup company often include:

- innovative attitude
- disruptive to the product category or industry
- problem-solving culture
- fast-growing
- scalable

Everyone has to start somewhere: a youthful Jeff Bezos in the early days of his Amazon empire.

Many famous companies were startups: for instance, both Apple and Amazon were tiny companies run by the founders that began the company's life in a garage, tested their business models, found their business model and rapidly scaled up to be large, incredibly successful corporations.

Systematically searching for the right business model helps to mitigate the risks to early-stage startups and there are a number of methods available. Three popular approaches are customer development, assessing market opportunities and pain points. These approaches can also be used in combination to help validate and improve a business model.

CUSTOMER DEVELOPMENT, DISCOVERY AND VALIDATION

The *customer development method* has four distinct steps, each helping to refine and test the business model. It was developed by Steven G. Blank.

The first stage is *customer discovery,* where the initial business idea is turned into a testable business model hypothesis. It is an informed estimate of who the customers might be and if the business idea appeals to them or not.

The objective is to identify potential customers, often using personas to describe hypothetical ideal customers for the business. These personas can then be used to find initial customers to talk to, identify the problems they have and to gain insights from users like them about those problems.

As a second step, the process of *customer validation* tests the resulting business model to make sure it can be repeated and scaled. It looks at the assumptions made in the customer discovery phase, where only a small sample of potential customers are part of the process, and tests whether the customer problem, target market and product are correct. This feeds back into customer discovery as necessary.

Evaluating this feedback will help to iterate the product and find solutions that best match customer problems. This process of iteration is what Eric Ries named the *pivot*, where a major change is made to the business model.

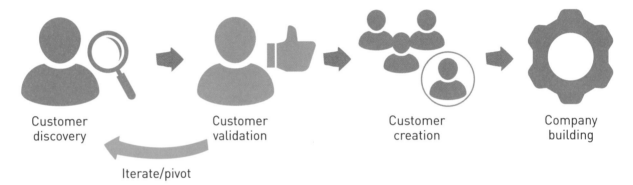

| Customer discovery | Customer validation | Customer creation | Company building |

Iterate/pivot

The customer development model.

Customer creation is the third stage where the market, product position and demand are established.

The final stage, *company building*, is when the business expands to make sure that the business model can be executed at scale. Often, this stage requires significant further investment.

ASSESSING MARKET OPPORTUNITIES

The future potential size or revenue of a business can be referred to as the *market opportunity*. The market is analyzed to determine expected revenues or profits from a product before it is created. It can form a useful part of a business strategy as it helps to assess how desirable a particular business opportunity might be.

The type of market will define the market opportunity, and if the number of customers available is enough to be profitable. For analysis, the market is usually assessed and divided into three overall segments of decreasing size:

1. The *total addressable market* (TAM): This is the total possible demand in the market for a product. It's the theoretical maximum possible revenue a business could generate by selling a product to every single consumer in a specific market.
2. The *serviceable addressable market* (SAM): This is the portion of the market a business is able to address, given any limitations such as geographic location, specialization or business model.
3. The *serviceable obtainable market* (SOM): This is the portion of the SAM that a business is realistically able to capture, given the number of competitors or alternatives. Only a true monopoly could capture all the possible customers in the SAM.

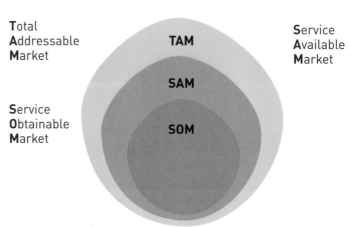

Total **A**ddressable **M**arket

Service **A**vailable **M**arket

Service **O**btainable **M**arket

The TAM SAM SOM model.

Assessing the potential market opportunity involves both primary research (new research by the startup themselves) and *secondary research*, gathered from other, existing sources.

Top-down analyses estimate the total addressable market, then calculate what the final, predicted share of that market might be. *Bottom-up analyses* estimate a smaller component part of a total market, and then extrapolate to see how large it could grow.

A product is usually brought to market by entering an existing market, re-segmenting an existing market, recreating an existing business model in a different geographical area or creating a new market altogether.

PAIN POINTS AND PERSONAS
Pain points

A *pain point* is something that bothers a customer – it is a problem that needs a solution. 'I can't do this X thing' or 'Y is stopping me from doing Z'. They are usually something the customer wants to stop happening.

They can be major problems or tiny inconveniences and the solutions can be simple or complex. Sometimes, a complex solution for a single customer is a much bigger problem than a simple problem shared by thousands.

For instance, a small but common pain point could be 'It takes too much time to return parcels at the post office' whereas a complex problem only a few customers have might be 'I can't correctly predict component failures in a large piece of factory equipment'.

Returning items via the post is a common pain point for many businesses.

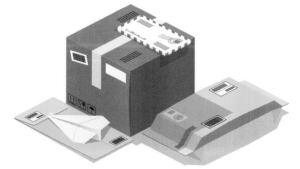

A common issue with positioning attempts is constructing a problem that is self-serving. The first go at positioning often ends up being: 'this specific product is for people who don't have this specific product'. For example, if you were a delivery company, then the problem might look like it should be: 'people don't have a good delivery service', whereas the real problem is more likely to be 'what about their current solution to the problem is irritating enough to change?'

A company that provides delivery solutions may see themselves as 'providing deliveries'. But the customer may not be looking for a delivery solution, as this is not the pain point. The problem isn't necessarily 'I need a delivery solution' but instead, 'I need to send parcels quicker than I currently can' or 'I need a more reliable delivery service'.

Personas

A *persona* is a description of the ideal customer for a business. It includes both specific and general information about the goals, motivations, demographics and character of the user. It can be written as a narrative, with additional fictional details to make it seem more real, or as a more prosaic file of information written as a profile.

There are many templates for personas, but the key idea is that they provide a target for marketing, sales, UX or design goals. For startups in particular, they operate as a proto-user – a name, face and personality to bear in mind when working towards the release of a product and establishing the basic needs and goals of a user.

It is important to properly research the kinds of characteristics that your user personas should contain. This can be a combination of user interviews, primary or secondary market research and information about the product.

Tools for validating the problem

Pass and *fail* tests are used to validate (or make updates to) the hypotheses on a business model canvas.

Problem presentations are conversations often used by startups in which customers give feedback on the assumptions a business has made about their problems. The aim is to talk to around 50 people, to focus on customer problems, current solutions and the solutions that the business proposes.

A *customer discovery scorecard* is a table that is used to score customers' responses on a set of criteria.

An example of a customer discovery scorecard:

Customers	Excitement	Level of need	Would buy this month
X	2	3	3
Y	1	1	2
Z	2	3	1

Every business needs to visualize the customer their products are aimed at.

THE BUSINESS MODEL CANVAS

The *business model canvas* (BMC) is a visual representation of the key components of a business. It is used for developing new business models or documenting ones that already exist. It can be used to develop and communicate a business model and can be helpful in identifying and addressing business model risks.

The chart contains the elements describing a business (or a product) value proposition, infrastructure, customers and finances, helping to illustrate potential trade-offs.

There are nine key components of a business model in a single diagram. The starting point is the value proposition. This shows how the business model will be successful, the benefits and features, as well as concepts for a minimum viable product.

When the BMC is completed, it contains areas that cover customers (for instance, target customers, channels and relationships), infrastructure (for example, resources, activities and key partners) and financial elements.

The BMC is designed to be printed out in large format so that teams can sketch and discuss business model elements jointly using sticky notes or marker pens. It is a collaborative tool that encourages understanding, discussion, creativity and analysis. It is distributed by Strategyzer AG and can be used without any restrictions for modelling any kind of business.

The *lean canvas* is a similar tool but replaces the sections Key Partners, Key Activities, Key Resources and Customer Relationships with Problem, Solution, Key Metrics and Unfair Advantage. It has less of a focus on logistics and operations and more of an emphasis on the customer and ideas.

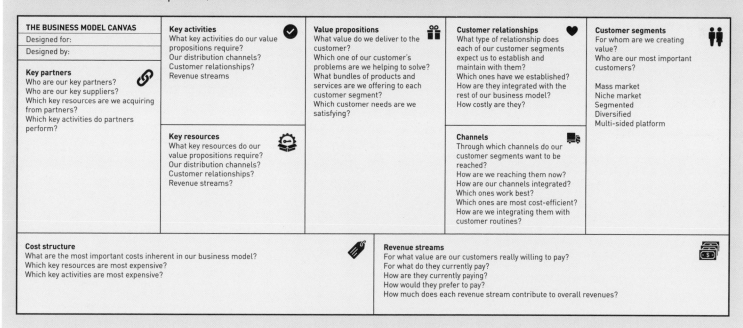

THE BUSINESS MODEL CANVAS
Designed for:
Designed by:

Key partners
Who are our key partners?
Who are our key suppliers?
Which key resources are we acquiring from partners?
Which key activities do partners perform?

Key activities
What key activities do our value propositions require?
Our distribution channels?
Customer relationships?
Revenue streams

Key resources
What key resources do our value propositions require?
Our distribution channels?
Customer relationships?
Revenue streams?

Value propositions
What value do we deliver to the customer?
Which one of our customer's problems are we helping to solve?
What bundles of products and services are we offering to each customer segment?
Which customer needs are we satisfying?

Customer relationships
What type of relationship does each of our customer segments expect us to establish and maintain with them?
Which ones have we established?
How are they integrated with the rest of our business model?
How costly are they?

Channels
Through which channels do our customer segments want to be reached?
How are we reaching them now?
How are our channels integrated?
Which ones work best?
Which ones are most cost-efficient?
How are we integrating them with customer routines?

Customer segments
For whom are we creating value?
Who are our most important customers?

Mass market
Niche market
Segmented
Diversified
Multi-sided platform

Cost structure
What are the most important costs inherent in our business model?
Which key resources are most expensive?
Which key activities are most expensive?

Revenue streams
For what value are our customers really willing to pay?
For what do they currently pay?
How are they currently paying?
How would they prefer to pay?
How much does each revenue stream contribute to overall revenues?

VALIDATION AND TESTING

To test both the problem as the startup sees it and the understanding of customer need, the first step is to state the hypothesis and draw the business model canvas. Then the business can test the problem, test the solution and pivot or proceed.

1. State your hypothesis.
2. Test the problem.
3. Test the solution and/or test sell the product.
4. Pivot and proceed.

Validating the hypothesis and testing

Once there is a hypothesis for the business, it can be explored with user interviews, feedback and broader market research. These are some of the methods that can be used to test the problem and solution:

Feedback

Gather feedback from friends and family

This is a good place to start, but ideally not with your own friends and family. Have a friend ask their family and friends for feedback. If you use your own friends and family, you can get biased feedback, as they have an existing relationship and they may be reluctant to tell you the truth if they don't like the idea.

Find consumers in your target market

Target market

If you already have a sense of your target market and it is relatively easy to identify a group of those target consumers, try to find an existing network you could tap into to ask questions. If the business idea is aimed at young parents, for instance, perhaps find a local toddler group where you could ask parents to come to a focus group where the problem and solution are tested.

Topics can include positioning, distribution, pricing strategy and promotion as well as the idea's strengths and weaknesses. Again, it is often useful to have someone else run this group for you, to avoid bias. Ideally, it should be a free-flowing conversation, not a rigid structure, in order to get a range of honest opinions.

Listen to passionate users of the product (positively or negatively)

Finding those who feel strongly about the product is extremely useful for identifying how to promote it, just as feedback from those who dislike the product can be useful to help improve or adapt the offering. It is important to try to uncover the motivations for the feelings in either case.

Undertake quantitative market research

The previous methods are all qualitative research (opinions, feelings and ideas), but quantitative research and testing can allow the business to refine who to target and discover where they might be found.

Simple analysis tools such as online surveys can help establish if there is a big enough market for the product, basic demographic data and characteristics.

Use a question in an omnibus survey

If it is a simple product proposition that can be explained in a sentence and is aimed at a mass market, it is possible to purchase a single question in a larger survey from professional market research companies. These surveys usually ask around 1,000 people who are a representative sample of all consumers.

Build relationships with existing consumers

Large companies often create communities of people who are part of their target market and have them provide feedback continuously. Startups can emulate this by tapping into groups of people who are already part of a community and start a conversation with them. These groups can be asked to provide feedback over a period to adapt the product and marketing strategies appropriately.

Involving groups of consumers in the target market early on can also help build a team of early advocates for a product even before launch.

VENTURE CAPITAL

Venture capital (VC) is the term for investment from venture capital funds, usually in the form of money and technical and managerial expertise in exchange for ownership of the company. VC investors are looking to fund startups with long-term, high-growth potential.

These VC funds manage pooled investments in a range of high-growth opportunities and are typically only open to accredited investors. The pooled money does not belong to the VC firm.

THE LEAN STARTUP

The *lean startup* method, from *The Lean Startup* by Eric Reis, suggests that startups focus on developing products that consumers have already shown that they want, so that a market already exists before a product is launched. It is an alternative to developing a product and then looking for demand to emerge subsequently.

This method first identifies a problem that needs solving, then creates a minimum viable product that can be introduced to possible customers for their feedback. The logic is that it can be faster and cheaper than developing a final product and reduces the risk that a startup has not correctly identified product-market fit.

It redefines the startup as 'an organization that is searching for a scalable business model' rather than a business that has a plan that it has decided it will execute.

Test-selling

Another component of testing the solution can be to *test-sell* the product. This helps test the understanding of customer needs and if the solution matches this – it allows a business to see if there is a product-market fit.

Test-selling can happen in many forms, but usually requires a working product or service to gather useful feedback, so it isn't suitable for every situation.

THE MVP

MVP is an abbreviation for *minimum viable product*, which refers to the creation of an initial workable (and saleable) version of a new business concept.

The basic principle is relatively simple. Instead of spending the time creating a detailed business plan and painstakingly creating the perfect final product, it suggests that time should be used to determine what the minimum requirements are to get a product or service into the market, so that a product-market fit can be quickly established, and the product iterated to improve over time.

Eric Ries called it 'that version of a new product which allows a team to collect the maximum amount of validated learning about customers with the least effort'.

Pivot or proceed?

The *pivot point* is the feedback step between customer validation/invalidation and customer discovery. If the customer validation process fails, the business needs to *iterate*, or pivot their model to something that will pass the customer validation stage.

The pivot is about changing the model when the hypothesis doesn't match reality. The idea is that by keeping costs low and iteratively building a product, a pivot is a substantive change to one or more of the components of the business model, but one that can be larger than just an iteration.

An example of an iterative change might be altering the product price from £7.99 to £10.99, but a pivot might be about changing the business model from a single charge to a subscription basis.

Once the model is validated successfully, the business model can proceed.

The point of VC funds is to spur innovation, as well as to make the investors money from highly scalable and successful startup ideas.

The funding process and how VC firms work

The *funding* process for a successful startup normally has four main rounds: pre-seed and seed funding, series A funding, series B funding and series C funding. Further funding after this point is likely to come from an IPO – taking the company public.

Pre-seed and seed funding

This kind of investment happens when a startup is in the very early stages, often not even a year old. An example of *pre-seed funding* would be a portion of investment that the founders need to get going on a prototype and start some basic research. Usually considered to be a relatively small investment, this could be anything from $20,000 to $250,000, depending on the business area.

Seed funding is usually something startups look for at prototype stage, as they need the injection of capital to support market research and R&D. It may be this investment that enables a startup to hire its first employees outside the original founders.

Angel investors are common at pre-seed and seed funding rounds, though there are some VC firms that specialize in early-stage funding, such as those that run *accelerator programmes*. It is the riskiest stage for investors as there is often no track record for the startup concerned and it is predicated entirely on potential.

A seed funding round will only contain a small number of investors, often no more than 10–15, and they will receive equity or preferred stock options in exchange for investment. Seed funding investments are generally larger sums than a pre-seed round, with amounts such as $1–2m not being uncommon.

Series A funding

A startup will look to raise *Series A funding* once they have a proven track record, the ability to quickly scale a product that has been proved in the market, and the continued potential for a serious return for the investors involved.

These funding rounds are usually between $2m and $15m, although in certain rare circumstances investors may consider a startup to have the potential to be a 'unicorn' – this is a startup that is valued at over $1bn.

Series A funding is often mainly provided by VC funds; angel investors tend to have less influence partly due to the larger sums involved. In a typical funding round, a few of the larger VC firms will lead the investment – leading a funding round means being the first to confirm their investment, as well as putting energy and expertise into successfully closing the round.

The valuation of a startup at Series A funding is determined by the proof of concept, the progress the company has made with any seed funding, the market size, risks and the quality of the executive team. It is often not particularly concerned with current net profits.

Series A funding gives startups the ability to scale quickly and increases their *runway* (how long it would take for the existing funding and any reserve capital to run out at their current burn rate).

Series B funding

Startups seeking *Series B funding* are out of the development stage, have proved product-market fit and are looking to build and expand their market share. Often, a startup looking for Series B funding may already have significant turnover and should at this point be making a profit.

Series B rounds are often between $6m and $20m – they are similar to Series A funding in process and which investors might be involved. There are, however, VC firms

STARTUP FUNDING AND ANGEL INVESTORS

Angel investors are usually individuals who provide financial backing for small startups and entrepreneurs, in exchange for some equity in the company. Typically, an angel investor is using their own money, and is a high-net-worth individual. This form of investment can be considered less aggressive or predatory than VC investment. Angel investors can also provide technical or managerial expertise and access to their networks.

Often, investments by angel investors in startups will make up less than 10% of their overall portfolio, as it is commonly a risky proposition.

STARTUP ACCELERATORS AND INCUBATORS

A *startup accelerator* provides startups in their early stages that have a minimum viable product or a validated product with education, resources (usually some funding) and mentorship to help speed up what could otherwise have been several years of growth into a few short months.

They normally take a portion of equity in return for those resources and are very high-pressure environments focused on success and scalability. Current examples of accelerators include Y Combinator, Techstars, Startupbootcamp and MassChallenge.

Incubators are designed to help startups solve technical and design issues as they build a product, to learn about lean processes, and to recruit a successful team. They can offer experience and advice on legal, operational and company structure issues

Incubators normally don't take any equity in the company, or operate in such a pressured environment as accelerators, but they also don't offer capital resources.

that specialize in later-stage funding that may join at the Series B round.

This can be a difficult funding round for many startups as it moves from the arena of potential into the realm of profit. It can be a time of slower growth, as the money involved is not enough to seriously scale yet and the investments that need to be made are in areas such as sales, advertising, technology and business development, which may not immediately make a return to the bottom line. It is also more expensive for investors than Series A while still being risky.

One way of thinking about the various rounds is seed funding is raised on vision and potential, Series A is raised on hope and Series B is raised on real facts and figures.

The valuation of a startup at Series A funding is determined by performance in the relevant sector, forecasts of revenue and profit, and any assets being generated, .such as intellectual property.

Series C funding

Series C funding is undertaken when a startup has proven that they can be a long-term success. It usually requires the shares of the original backers to have increased in value substantially. For investors, they are usually looked

on as a safe bet and the valuation of the startup at this stage forms part of the exit strategy for venture capital firms.

A startup at this stage of the funding process will be seeking to further increase its market share, develop new products and services, and is likely preparing for acquisition by a larger company or to acquire a smaller relevant company.

At this stage, investment banks, hedge funds and private equity firms will begin to invest, and successful startups can sometimes achieve funding rounds up into the hundreds of millions.

Other benefits of venture capital

Taking investment from venture capital firms also gives access to other benefits.

Support services: Some larger VC firms have in-house teams of marketing, legal, tech and recruitment that can be used to offer services to startups that don't yet have these capabilities.

Strategic introductions: Because investors in VC firms are often experienced entrepreneurs themselves, they may have a range of contacts that the startup can be introduced to. These might be potential partnerships, new investors, operational experts or potential hires.

Experience in efficiency: They can help to streamline communication or offer their experience to improve board meetings. They can make sure that a startup is focused on the correct priorities from the top of the organization.

Wider market knowledge: Because venture capital firms are looking across industries and have expertise in various areas, they can offer insight into new markets, potential clients or exit opportunities.

Best practice: VCs can support a startup to put in place good governance across ethics, financial reports and controls, contracts and other procedures.

Benefits of using venture capital

The VC fund life cycle

The typical life cycle of a venture capital fund is about ten years, with the possibility of extensions if a private company still requires liquidity. The stages of the fund life cycle include fundraising, investment, management and exit.

Fundraising

Fundraising is the first stage but can take several years. The general partners of the VC fund (those who run the fund) raise money by issuing an *offering memorandum* outlining their expertise or insight into a market segment to the fund's *limited partners* (the investors who provide the money). The general partners close the fund once they have reached the required amount of money and the fixed lifetime of the fund begins. The year in which this occurs is the fund's '*vintage year*'.

Raising funds

Investment

The *investment stage* normally lasts about three to five years and consists of fixed commitments from limited partners to invest certain sums (this is known as a *capital call*).

The VC fund will invest in a series of companies at this stage but will be under pressure towards the end of the stage to make sure that they can gain liquidity from their investments, if appropriate. This means that from a startup's perspective it is better to receive investment at the start of a VC firm's investment phase, so the investment is available for longer.

Investing in the business

Management

The *management stage* of a VC fund should last about five to seven years. It is a period when the VC firm will manage their investments, usually by sitting on the boards of directors of their investments. They will also make follow-up investments in later funding rounds. These commitments to manage the investments limit the total number of startups a fund can invest in.

Exit

The defined lifetime of a VC fund gives a time limit for the general partners to determine when to sell. However, a fund could enter its *exit stage* if there was an attractive offer from a buyer or if they needed to urgently recoup capital from a bad investment. To make the return they hope for, the investors in a fund are usually looking for the startup companies involved to go public, or for them to be acquired.

Basic fundraising materials

When pitching for any round of funding with either VC funds or angel or private investors there are a series of tools, documents and data that a startup needs in order to be able to convince investors to commit. These are some of the *basic requirements* for any fundraising process.

Pitch deck

A *pitch deck* (sometimes called a *slide deck* or *startup deck*) is a presentation on slides that gives a brief, informative overview of a business. It covers the key points of the business plan, the product or service offering, high-level financial projections and how much funding the business requires. It will refer to the other documents mentioned here.

There are many templates available for this presentation, but the basic rule is that it shouldn't be any longer than 8–16 slides.

Business plan

Although this only needs to be a short *business plan* (more recently, the financial model and the pitch deck have become more important), it is meant to be an 18- to 24-month roadmap of how the business model will be executed. A one-page executive summary is also very useful to have.

The model

The financial model

The *financial model* is one of the most important documents. It needs to include the following as a minimum:

- three years of financial projections
- the amount being raised and clear plans of how the investment will be spent
- the valuation of the company

The pitch

The pitch

Alongside the slides, a script or notes for a spoken presentation, or pitch, are key. The pitch should be no longer that 15–20 minutes long, as in a standard 45–60-minute pitching slot this allows for time to recover from technical mistakes with a product demo and for a Q&A session with investors.

The script of a pitch should not just read the content of the slides – the slides should visually support what is being said, and vice versa.

As well as the presentation to support the pitch deck, a one- or two-sentence *elevator pitch* is extremely useful. This is what can be used when in a networking situation or an informal pitching setting.

One other thing it can be useful to prepare is answers to the 100 most frequently answered questions from investors.

Other optional elements

There are many other components to successfully pitching investors, some of which are industry specific, others of which may be preferences of the startup.

Other elements

Online data access: Using a cloud-based storage service allows a startup to store relevant files for qualified investors, and means they can grant, track and revoke access to the data as desired.

Press releases: Being in the news builds visibility and credibility. The more investors know about a startup in advance, the easier it can be to close a deal.

Content marketing: As with being in the news, appearing in blogs or articles or making podcast appearances can increase visibility to investors and help correctly position a startup.

Product demo: Giving a demonstration or showing a prototype (or at least images of a product prototype) can help to convince investors.

Landing a deal
Valuation pre- and post-money

The valuation of a startup is what determines how much a founder, investor or employee's stake in the company is worth and how much they will receive on exit – when the company is sold or taken public.

The deal

Valuations are discussed in pre- and post-money terms. *Pre-money valuation* means how much the company is worth before a new investment, whereas *post-money valuation* is the valuation plus the amount of the new investment.

In the UK in 2020, PwC Raise determined that more than two-thirds of seed-stage deals had a pre-money valuation of less than £5m. For Series A deals, about half were in the range of £5m to £15m. Series B rounds had almost two-thirds of companies in the range of £50m to £600m pre-money.

How term sheets work

A t*erm sheet* is what sets out the basic terms and conditions of an investment. It is what is used by startups when talking to investors about a fundraising round. It is a non-binding agreement that operates as a template and as the basis for more detailed and legally binding documents that are required once an agreement to invest has been reached based on the term sheet.

JEFF BEZOS: AMAZON

Jeff Bezos is the founder and CEO of Amazon, an e-commerce giant that started as an online bookstore and now sells everything from books and movies to food and furniture. One of the most innovative and customer-centric companies in the world, it has become one of the most successful businesses in history.

After graduating from Princeton University in 1986, Bezos worked for a start-up called Fitel, where he helped develop an early version of the Internet. In 1994, he quit his job and moved to Seattle to start Amazon.

In its early days, Amazon was a small startup taking on the mighty book industry. But Bezos had a vision for Amazon as an 'everything store' that would sell not just books, but also music, movies, and other consumer goods. He built a customer-centric company that was committed to delivering the best possible experience to its customers. Amazon grew rapidly, and by the early 2000s, it was one of the most successful businesses in the world – by 2019, it was believed that Amazon controlled 37% of all online retail sales.

Under Bezos' leadership, Amazon has implemented some innovative strategies such the Amazon Prime membership program, as well as some bold bets on new technologies, such as the Kindle e-reader and the Amazon Alexa home assistant. One of their largest successes, however, has been selling the cloud computing power, and storage facilities that run their own complex website to other customers. This now constitutes a significant component of their business.

The term sheet tends to include the company valuation, the desired investment, the percentage stake involved, board structure and voting rights, liquidation preferences (how the proceeds of a sale will be distributed among shareholders), provisions for anti-dilution and investor commitments (how long an investor must remain vested).

Preferential shares

Preferential shares differ from ordinary shares because they have special rights (or preferences) attached. These usually entitle the shareholder to recover additional value per share in the event of a sale or other liquidation event, including insolvency. Investors commonly request preference shares in return for their investment.

This kind of liquidation preference tends to mean that those with preferential shares receive an amount that is N times the amount invested alongside the value of their shares before all other shareholders receive the remainder of the proceeds according to their shareholdings.

Option pools

Option pools are a set number of shares that are set aside to offer to future employees, or as equity incentives for other employees. They are very commonly included in term sheets and calculated post-money.

An *option* is not itself a share but is the right for an employee given the option to purchase shares in the company at a pre-determined price (the strike price) in the future. This means that as the company grows, and all the shares become more valuable, these options can also grow in value.

Usually, the right to exercise stock options can only happen after a defined period – that way, they incentivize employees to stay with the company. After this period, the options are said to have *vested* and the employee can convert them to shares.

THE BUSINESS PLAN

A *business plan* is a formal document detailing the goals of a business, the strategies for achieving those goals, and the resources required to achieve them. It is a document that describes the vision for a business and what the plan is to achieve it.

It is not a static document; it is a living, breathing thing that should be updated and revisited as the business grows and changes. It is a document that should be shared with the team in order to get everyone on the same page and moving in the same direction.

A business plan is very useful for people starting a business as it is designed to be a road map that will help a business grow and succeed. It can also be of value to those already running a business to determine direction, help raise capital and show potential avenues for growth.

All business plans should include a description of the business, the market, the product or service, the marketing strategy, the financial projections, and the management team.

Example contents for a business plan

Business Plan	
1.0 Executive Summary	7.0 Financial Plan
2.0 Company Description	7.1 Start-up Expenses
3.0 Products and Services	7.2 Projected Income Statements
4.0 Market Analysis	7.3 Projected Cash Flow Statements
5.0 Operations, Strategy and Implementation	7.4 Balance Sheet
5.1 Marketing Plan	7.5 Breakeven Analysis
6.0 Management	8.0 Appendices

Writing a company description

A company description is one of the most important parts of a business plan. It should provide a brief overview of the company, its products or services, its markets, its competitive advantages and its management team.

It should be clear and concise and should not exceed two pages. It should be written in plain language and avoid technical jargon. The company description should be realistic and reflect the company's current situation and future plans.

A good company description should answer the following questions:

- What does the company do? Keep it short and to the point. Explain your company's mission and vision.
- What are the products or services? Focus on what makes the company unique.
- Who are the company's customers and target market? Describe the target market or *customer demographics*.
- What are the company's competitive advantages?
- Who is the company's management team?

Customer demographics

Writing a good company description requires a good understanding of the company and its business. An effective company description is essential for a successful business plan.

Analyzing the business environment

Market analysis

Market analysis – sufficiently researching and examining the overall business environment – is a key section of any business plan. It should outline existing businesses or competitors in the space and other factors that might impact the business. It is about conducting both competitive and market analysis.

Research and analysis tools such as SWOT and PESTEL analyses, TAM assessments or the results of product validation and test-selling can be used to establish the internal and external factors the business needs to be aware of as well as the opportunities available in the market. The construction of personas and pain points help to show who is being helped and how this is unique.

Operations and the strategic plan

A critical component of the business plan is the *operations* and *strategic plan*. It describes any physical facilities, locations, the production process, the workforce and the systems that support the operations of the business.

It should be designed to support the goals and objectives of the business, but flexible enough to accommodate changes in the business environment. A business should expect to review and update the operations plan on a regular basis.

Some of the key elements of an effective operations plan are:

- physical facilities
- production process
- workforce
- systems that support the operations of the business
- implementation and control procedures

Marketing plan

The *marketing plan* is the section that describes how the company will generate sales of its products or services. It should include reference to the target market, the overall marketing strategy and the budget for marketing activities. It may also be appropriate to include examples if design collateral already exists.

The management summary

This section provides an overview of the management team and their qualifications, usually expressed as short biographies. This covers the founders, any initial significant employees, and the board of directors.

When writing the *management summary*, it is important to highlight the experience and expertise of the management team to demonstrate the team's ability to lead the business to success. The summary should also outline the team's roles and responsibilities within the organization.

The management summary should also provide a high-level overview of the plans and initiatives that the management team will implement to drive the business forwards.

Financial plan

The *financial plan* outlines the financial goals and objectives of the business and how they will be achieved. It should contain a *financial summary* that forecasts the profitability and potential of the business as well as any assumptions. It also often states the capital requirements of the business, and where this investment will be spent. A break-even analysis and exit strategy can also be presented if appropriate.

The detailed accounting documents referenced can be presented as whole documents in the appendix.

The financial plan usually needs to include reference to a sales forecast, an income statement, a balance sheet and a cash flow statement.

Compiling the executive summary

The *executive summary* is one of the most important parts of a business plan as it gives readers an overview of the company and its key goals. It is usually written last, once all the other elements are in place, as it needs to summarize information from all the sections on the business plan.

It should be as short and as clear as possible, and it should be written in a way that will capture the reader's attention. It includes a brief description of the company, its products or services, the target market, and any relevant competitive advantages. It should also include a very brief overview of the company's financial situation and the plans for the future.

Chapter Twelve

BASICS OF BUSINESS LAW (USA AND UK)

Types of business formation (USA) • Types of business formation (UK) • Basic employment law (UK) • Intellectual property and copyright law (USA and UK)

BUSINESS LAW
INTELLECTUAL PROPERTY AND COPYRIGHT LAW
COPYRIGHT
TRADE MARKS
PATENTS
TYPES OF BUSINESS FORMATION
SOLE PROPRIETORSHIP
PARTNERSHIP
LIMITED LIABILITY COMPANY (LLC)
C CORP AND S CORP
B CORP
NONPROFIT
COOPERATIVE
EMPLOYEE PROTECTIONS AND BENEFITS
SICKNESS
MINIMUM WAGES
HOLIDAYS
BASIC EMPLOYMENT LAW
TYPES OF WORKER
BASIC LABOUR STANDARDS
SAFETY, HEALTH AND PROTECTIONS
WAGES, HOURS AND BENEFITS

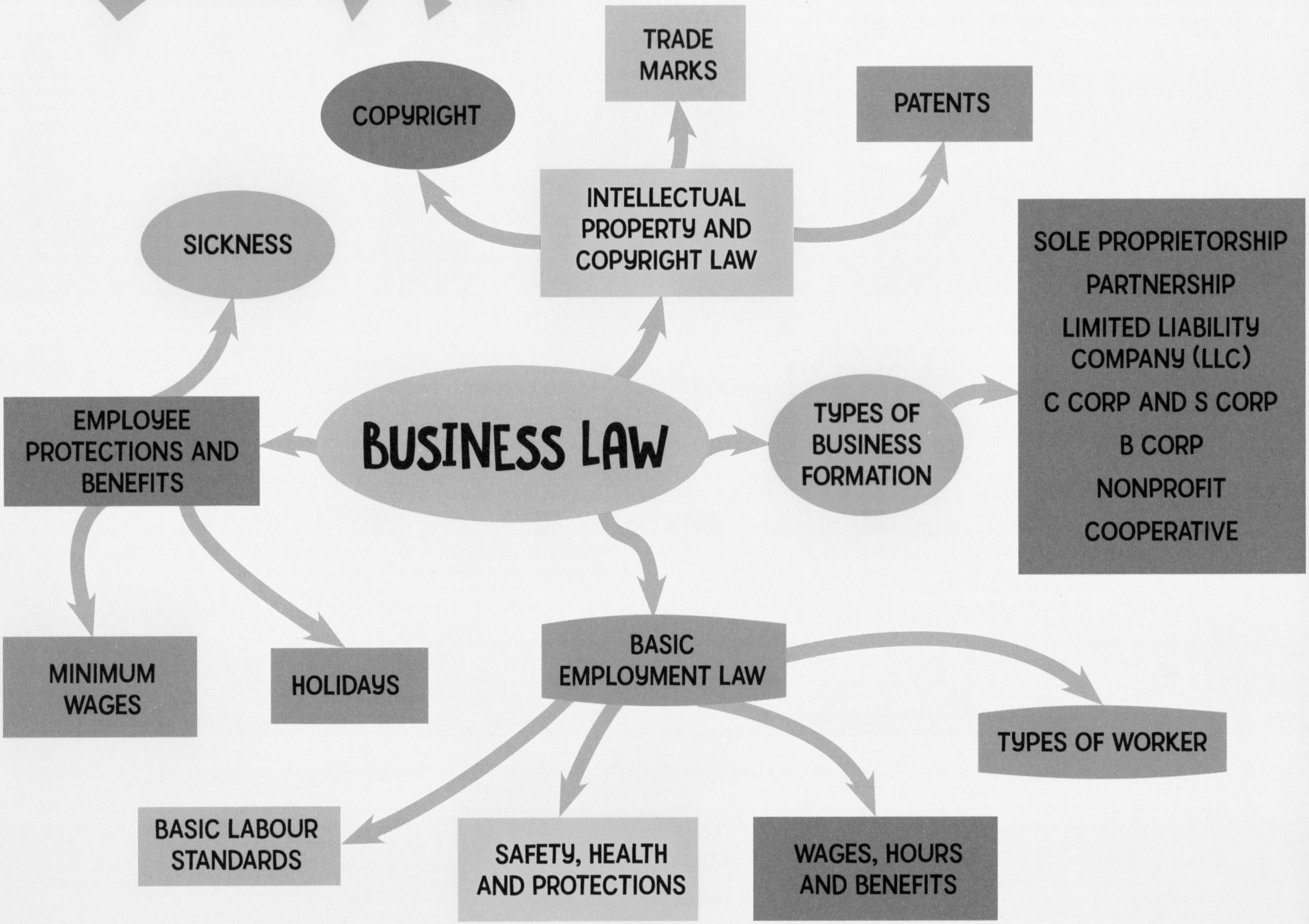

TYPES OF BUSINESS FORMATION (USA)

When deciding what type of business to establish it is important to note the differences between the kinds of business that can be set up, and what advantages or personal liabilities each confers.

Sole proprietorship

Sole proprietorship is the simplest form of business structure suitable for a single owner. It is not a separate entity from the owner – the business assets and liabilities are part of the owner's personal assets and liabilities. This means that the owner can be held personally liable for the debts or obligations of the business.

It is not possible to sell shares in a sole proprietorship, and it can be difficult to raise money. In most states, undertaking business activities without registering as any other structure means you are considered automatically to be a sole proprietorship. Profits are considered part of personal tax returns.

Partnership

The simplest structure for two or more people to own a business is a *partnership*. There are two kinds: *limited partnerships* (LP) and *limited liability partnerships* (LLP).

Limited partnership

A limited partnership only has one general partner with unlimited liability, and all the other partners have limited liability. This means only the non-general partners are protected from liability for the debts of the business, but they also have limited control over the business. Profits are passed through to personal tax returns, and the general partner must also pay self-employment taxes.

A limited liability partnership is similar but offers limited liability to all the owners. Partners are not liable for the debts of the business, or the actions of other partners. They can work well for professional groups like lawyers or accountants.

Limited liability partnership

Limited liability company

A *limited liability company* (LLC) protects the owners from personal liability for the debts of the business. It confers some of the advantages of a corporation and those of a partnership structure. Profits are passed through to personal taxes, without incurring corporate taxes, but members of the LLC must pay self-employment taxes.

Corporations

Corps and S Corps

Corporations (*Co.* or *Inc.*, sometimes referred to as *C Corps*) are legal entities that are completely independent from their owners and shareholders. They can make a profit, pay tax and be held legally liable. They confer the greatest protections to the owners from personal liability although

C Corps

Most corporations base their headquarters in major cities..

they cost the most to set up and maintain (through record keeping and reporting).

Because they are independent entities, corporations must pay tax on their profits. Shareholders must separately pay their personal taxes on any dividends they receive from the company.

Because corporations can sell stock, they can raise capital more easily than other forms of business. They are useful for businesses that need to raise money, and for those that want to go public or ultimately be acquired.

An *S Corp* is a similar structure but does not pay income tax and instead passes tax through to the owners' personal tax returns, and can't have more than 100 shareholders.

B corps

A *B Corp* is a for-profit corporation that is similar in structure and taxation to a C Corp, but differs in terms of the purpose, transparency and accountability standards it must adhere to.

The concept of a B Corp is to be guided by mission and not only profit. They have shareholders who hold them accountable to provide a public benefit as well as a financial profit. There are organizations that certify B Corps and assess their compliance with the relevant criteria.

Nonprofit corporation

Nonprofit corporations

Nonprofit corporations are usually focused on charity, community, education, religious or scientific work. Although their structure may be similar to a C-Corp, the public benefit of their work means that they can receive various state and federal tax exemptions on their profits.

Cooperative

Co-ops

A cooperative or co-op is an organization owned and run by those who use its services (the members). The profits are distributed between the members, who own a form of shares in the company. They usually have a board of directors and officers who undertake managerial responsibilities, but the owner-members have the voting power over the board and the strategic direction of the cooperative. Usually, the voting power of each member is identical, regardless of the shares they might own.

TYPES OF BUSINESS FORMATION (UK)

Just as in the USA, the UK has various types of business structure available. They are similar but have some key differences in name and in obligations.

Sole trader

A *sole trader* is someone who works for themselves – they run their own business. They must register the business with HMRC (His Majesty's Revenue and Customs) and are entitled to keep all the profits as income. This income is taxed, and national insurance must be paid. A sole trader is liable for all debts of the business as it doesn't offer any limited liability.

Sole trader

Partnership

A *partnership* is a business with two or more people who agree to share the profits, losses, risks and responsibilities of the business. They are unincorporated entities as the partners are self-employed and personally responsible for the liabilities of the organization.

Each partner has to pay tax on their own share of the profits. This is a common structure for barristers or other professionals who work independently but can benefit from pooling resources.

Limited liability partnership

A *limited liability partnership* (LLP) is like a partnership, but the partners' liability is limited to the amount invested in the business. LLPs must be registered with Companies House (the UK registry of businesses) and file annual accounts.

There must be two or more members, but a member can be a company or a person. All members pay income tax on their share of the profits and are self-employed.

Partnership

Limited company

Most companies registered with Companies House are limited companies. This is a privately managed business, operating as a separate legal entity but owned by shareholders and run by directors. The company has its own legal responsibilities and obligations and is financially separate from the owners.

They can be *limited by shares* or *limited by guarantee*. Limited by shares means that they are owned by shareholders who have certain rights. Limited by guarantee means that they have guarantors who promise to pay an agreed sum of money to the company if it cannot cover its liabilities. This is the '*guaranteed amount*'. These guarantors do not usually take profit from the company, but they are company members and control its important decisions.

Corporation tax is paid on profits and then distributed to shareholders as dividends. They must file and report accounts annually.

Limited company

Public limited company

A limited company has private owners, and the shares are not transferable – they cannot be sold on the open market. A *public limited company* (PLC) is an organization that has shares that are

PLC, Co,, Inc

available for purchase by investors on the open market. These shares can be easily transferred, and the shareholders can be members of the public.

One disadvantage is that PLCs have a far higher level of regulation to comply with than other forms of business. In the USA, a Co. or Inc. is the equivalent of a PLC.

Employee Ownership Trusts

Employee Ownership Trusts were introduced in 2014 as a model for how a business can move to an employee ownership model. This is where each employee has a stake in the company – although not quite the same as shareholders, the employee is a part owner of the business and receives a share of the annual profits as well as being able to have a say in determining how the company is run.

One major benefit to this is that it aligns the employees' and the business's interests. The best-known example of this type of company in the UK is the John Lewis Partnership.

BASIC EMPLOYMENT LAW (USA)
Employment status
Types of worker

Worker

An employee is a *worker* who works under the supervision of an employer with an express or implied contract. The employer decides what the work comprises and how and when it is accomplished.

Independent contractor

An *independent contractor* is a worker who has a choice over how and when (and sometimes where) the work they are contracted to complete is performed.

Misclassifying employees happens when an employee is incorrectly considered to be an independent contractor (or intern or volunteer) and therefore is denied the relevant benefits they should be due.

To determine this, *the right to control test* is used, which assesses how much an employer dictates a worker's methods. Alongside this, the economic realities test, which measures a worker's economic independence, is used to determine if the worker is an employee or an independent contractor.

Employees can be *full-time*, *part-time*, *temporary* and *seasonal*, with each conferring different levels of benefits.

Wages, hours and benefits

Overtime and federal minimum wage

The basic standards for *wages* and how *overtime* is paid are laid out in the Fair Labor Standards Act and cover the majority of public and private insurance. It requires that employers pay their employees (unless exempt) equal to or more than the *federal minimum wage*, and overtime pay at one and a half times their normal rate. It also restricts the hours that certain employees under 16 can work and restricts the minimum age for certain kinds of dangerous jobs.

There are also *labor standards* contained in the Immigration and Nationality Act, which apply to legal aliens who are allowed to work in the USA and are on particular visa programmes.

Labor standards

The Affordable Care Act (ACA) established a series of guidelines to businesses for providing *health insurance to employees*, and the Family Medical Leave Act means that employees who are eligible can take up to 12 weeks' *unpaid* leave in a 12-month period.

There are also state regulations that businesses that operate within that states must comply with, such as higher levels of minimum wage, or enhanced regulation around hours worked.

Workplace safety, health and protections

The Occupational Safety and Health Administration (OSHA), or their approved state programmes, regulate *safety conditions* and *health requirements* in most private industries. Employers who are covered by the OSH Act must comply with OSHA regulations and standards. OSHA enforces these rules via inspections and investigations as well as offering assistance with compliance and cooperative programmes to help businesses bring their practices up to standard.

Safety conditions and health requirements

Key employee protections

The other key employee protections provided at a federal level include:

- The portions of the Civil Rights Act that *ban unfair or unequal treatment* when hiring, firing or in other areas of employment.
- The Americans with Disabilities Act *outlaws discrimination* against individuals with disabilities and the Pregnancy Discrimination Act provides similar protections for pregnant women. In both instances, reasonable accommodations must be provided unless they would cause undue hardship to the business.

An employee who is pregnant is entitled to a number of key protections in law.

Terminating employment

The typical employee status in the USA is considered *at-will employment*. This means that employees can be fired at any point without warning (and without needing to establish a particular cause). Any contractual obligations around dismissal would need to be provisioned in the specific contract with the employee.

However, collective bargaining by unions and existing public sector contracts means certain industries and jobs do require just cause to fire an employee.

Wrongful termination is the term for a situation where an employee has been fired for a reason that goes against protected employee rights and actions.

BASIC EMPLOYMENT LAW (UK)

There are generally a greater range of employee protections provided under UK law, compared to the US federal system. There are also key differences in the status of employees.

Employment status

Employees

Employee work hours

An employer controls what an *employee* works on and how, when, and often where it gets done. An employee must accept work given to them by their employer. Employees are expected to perform their work themselves (they can't subcontract) and may have to wear a uniform or comply with other business rules.

Self-employed or independent contractor

Terms for contractors

An *independent contractor* or *self-employed* person provides services to a client, normally under a written contract. They determine how, when and where they perform the work, as appropriate, and can hire others to do the work for them.

Worker

A *worker*, in a legal sense, has a contract to perform work, but is not employed on a full- or part-time contract that states their minimum hours. This would normally be for jobs with irregular or as-needed hours, such as delivery drivers.

Recruiting employees

In the UK, the Equality Act 2010 set out laws that prohibit harassment, victimization and discrimination. In an employment context, *discrimination* might be an employer treating an employee poorly due to a protected characteristic.

Affirmative action

However, employers are entitled to take *positive action* (often called *affirmative* action in the USA) where applicants or employees with specific protected characteristics are prioritized because they are underrepresented or socially disadvantaged in comparison to other candidates.

Indirect discrimination is when a policy that may appear neutral at first has a harmful impact on someone with a protected characteristic.

These rules are enforced by the UK courts along with the Equality and Human Rights Commission (EHRC).

Employment contracts

A *contract for employment* is an agreement that lays out the conditions of that employment and the rights and responsibilities of the employee.

A contract may contain both express terms – things that are specifically outlined, such as the location of the workplace – and *implied terms*, such as agreeing to follow the law as an employee.

Implied terms

The *clauses* in a contract are separate stipulations. Common clauses, beyond the basic working requirements, include:

- A restrictive covenant clause, which prevents an employee from doing certain things after they leave employment, often for a limited period. This is designed to protect sensitive business information or customer details.
- A confidentiality clause, which might specify how an employee is allowed to use or share particular kinds of private or sensitive information.

Basic labour standards

The *basic labour standards* in the UK operate as a minimum requirement for wages and working time, and every employer must abide by them. There are also rules around providing *equal pay* – the same compensation for jobs that have similar tasks or demands regardless of gender – although exceptions exist for material factors (a non-gender-related reason for the difference in pay.

Equal pay

Employee protections and benefits

Keeping people safe

The Health and Safety Executive (HSE) is the government agency that enforces health and safety in the workplace. It aims to prevent work-related death, injury and ill health through influencing change, regulating activities and helping workplaces manage risks.

Safety

Any *serious injuries* (or 'near misses') in the workplace must be reported under the Reporting of Injuries, Diseases and Dangerous Occurrences Regulations (RIDDOR). This also applies to members of the public who are injured in a workplace. All businesses must have at least £5 million of liability insurance.

The *maximum working hours* allowed in a week is an average of 48 hours over 17 weeks. Employers cannot opt out of this limit. However, working more than 48 hours a week is possible, but the employee needs to sign an agreement to opt out of the working time limit. There are also certain professions that are exempted from this limit, such as pilots, police or the armed forces. Senior managers and executives who are in control of their own decisions and don't have their working time measured are also considered exempt.

Maximum hours

Minimum wages, sickness and holidays

The *national minimum wage* applies to everyone aged 16 to 25, and the *national living wage* applies to those aged over 25. The *holiday entitlement* for all employees means the employer must provide 28 days of paid holiday, but this can include public holidays.

Parental leave

Statutory parental leave provides at least two weeks off for fathers and 52 weeks off for mothers (there are slightly different arrangements for parents who are adopting), at a reduced wage, though some employers will offer better benefits than this. It is also now possible for parents to share this leave between them.

Sick leave

Long-term sickness of employees is covered by a reduced wage that covers up to 28 weeks of pay in a year.

A business of any size must now offer a *private pension* for all employees over the age of 22 if they are employed at more than £10,000 per annum.

Employment contracts and many of these conditions and legally mandated benefits apply to workers and employees – but not to contractors, who can determine their own terms and propose or agree to different conditions as they see fit.

Terminating employment

Dismissal

When employment ends, the contract is said to have been *terminated*, regardless of the reason. If an employee's contract is ended by the employer, this is often called *dismissal*. If the employee simply resigns from their job (perhaps because they have been hired for a different job), this is called *genuine resignation*, whereas if they do so in agreement with their employer it is a *mutual agreement* to terminate the contract.

Resignation

Fair dismissal can only happen for a certain set of reasons – the parameters for these, and the dismissal process is usually set out in the contract and an employee handbook. They usually include:

- being late or consistently absent
- dishonesty or gross misconduct
- failing to achieve necessary qualifications
- the job stops existing

Unfair dismissal

There are certain kinds of dismissal that are not allowed. *Unfair dismissal* is where there is no reason for the employer to dismiss the employee, they are being discriminatory, or they fail to follow their own dismissal process. *Constructive dismissal* is when an employee is left with no choice but to quit their job because of the actions of their employer (often in the form of employer misconduct).

If there is a disagreement between you and your employer about dismissal you can normally go to an *employment tribunal* to have the grievance addressed. But the first step in this process involves the Advisory, Conciliation and Arbitration Service (Acas), which tries to help the two parties reach an agreement without requiring a full tribunal.

INTELLECTUAL PROPERTY AND COPYRIGHT LAW (USA AND UK)

Intellectual property (IP) is a way of referring to 'creations of the mind'. This could be an invention, a literary work or piece of art, music, designs, symbols, or the names and images used in business practices.

Laws such as those involved with *patents*, *copyrights* and *trademarks* help people to earn money or be recognized in other ways for what they have created or invented. The idea behind protecting intellectual property rights is to balance the interests of those who innovate and the wider public interest of access to ideas, and the capacity to build on previous concepts.

Patents

Trademarks

Internationally, registration of IP rights is administered by the World Intellectual Property Organization (WIPO) in combination with the Berne Convention – an international agreement protecting artistic works under a common framework.

In the UK, IP rights are handled by the Intellectual Property Office (IPO); in the USA, Congress has the power to regulate patents and copyrights via the United States Patent and Trademark Office (USPTO) and other agencies.

In both the USA and the UK, the major kinds of IP regulation, rights and protections are set out below.

Copyright

Copyright is a free automatic right that protects creative expression. It describes the rights that creators have, is protected by federal law, and covers original creative works such as writing, music, paintings, films and photographs but also things like architecture, dance, databases and adverts. The length of time a work is protected for depends on when it was created.

In a legal sense, copyright protects both the economic and moral rights of the creator. *Economic rights* give the creator the right to authorize usage and receive financial rewards when others use their work. It means the creator has the sole authority to translate, reproduce, distribute or adapt a work – or can license others to do so.

Moral rights include things like the right to object to changes to a work that might harm a creator's existing reputation.

A *licence* is an agreement that grants a separate party permission to use an asset without risking infringement. A

A *franchise* is when a creator allows a separate party to replicate their business (and the relevant assets) in return for a royalty.

Fair dealing or *fair use* is an example of an exception to copyright law that allows for limited use of copyright without getting permission

The creator of an original work of art is protected by law in both an economic and a moral sense. The work should not be reproduced without their permission.

from the owner. This is often reserved for criticism, comment or parody – it can't just replicate the content.

Public domain

Public domain works are those where the public has the same rights as the original rights-holder to reproduce, adapt or use the work as they wish.

Trademarks

A *trademark* is an indefinite protection for any sign that represents a company or a brand. Trademarks can be brand names, logos, slogans or other marks or devices that identify a particular product, service or company.

There are different levels of protection available for trademarks at both federal and state level, which can depend on consumer awareness, the type of trademark, the specific products involved or even the area where the trademark is used. There are methods to register trademarks, which can confer additional protection against misuse.

Trademark infringement

Trademark infringement is what happens when another party uses an identical or 'confusingly similar' mark without the necessary permission.

There are also trademark protections available if an unregistered trademark is used to intentionally mislead consumers – the brand or business is passing-off as another.

Patents and trade secrets

Patents are used to protect a business or inventor against the reverse engineering of a product, though they have a limited life span. *Trade secrets* are used when seeking indefinite protection.

Patents provide government-granted ownership of an invention for up to 20 years. To be suitable for a patent, an invention must:

- be novel (new)
- be inventive (more than just simple modification of an existing design)
- be something that can be made or used
- there are also some exclusions – such as mathematical methods or works of art

Trade secrets

Trade secrets are generally sensitive business information and receive some protections in law. They are only considered trade secrets if they confer some advantage to the business, if it is generally kept a secret and is not known by competitors. An example of this might be the specific recipe for a brand of BBQ sauce.

SUGGESTED READING

BUSINESS CASE STUDIES

Case studies are often used throughout an MBA course to help students reinforce and explore concepts, theories or ideas which are presented in the various areas of study. They are considered an intrinsic part of the degree programme at many business schools. The concept of management case studies was adapted from the practice of medical school 'grand rounds'.

In a grand round, a senior doctor brings a group of more junior doctors to see a patient. The students gather information about the patient like vital signs or test results. They question the patient on their medical history and symptoms. Using the information they have gathered, the students can then try to diagnose, ask for more tests, and/or offer various courses of treatment, while being overseen, and questioned by, the senior doctor.

Because companies are made up of a number of people and different perspectives, business case studies are often presented from the point of view of a specific decision maker in the business. The case attempts to put the student reading it into the position of a manager and ask how they would suggest the manager acts.

Some case studies are more of an analytic exercise. The operational processes and history of a company might be presented (not referencing any specific problem), and the student is asked to comment on how the organization operates – for instance outlining the key success factors, important relationships, or the main sources of value.

Many of the case studies used at the top business schools are available online, along with examples of the questions that accompany them. For instance, Harvard Business School, Yale School of Business, The Wharton School, The University of Oxford Saïd Business School all have a range of case studies available to download for free, alongside questions and notes to help explore them.

BUSINESS, ECONOMICS AND STRATEGY

Carnegie, D. (1936). *How to Win Friends and Influence People.* New York. Simon & Schuster.

Chan Kim, W. & Mauborgne, R. (2014). *Blue Ocean Strategy: How to Create Uncontested Market Space and Make Competition Irrelevant.* Boston. Harvard Business Review Press.

Christensen, C. M. (2013) *The Innovator's Dilemma: When New Technologies Cause Great Firms to Fail.* Boston. Harvard Business Review Press.

Collins, J. (2001). *Good to Great: Why Some Companies Make the Leap ... and Others Don't.* London. Penguin.

Ellis, C. D. (2009). *The Partnership: The Making of Goldman Sachs.* London. Penguin.

Feld, B. & Mendelson, J. (2019). *Venture Deals: Be Smarter Than Your Lawyer and Venture Capitalist.* Hoboken, NJ, USA. Wiley.

Ferris, T. (2011). The 4-Hour Workweek: Escape the 9-5, Live Anywhere and Join the New Rich. London. Vermilion.

Fried, J. & Heinemeier Hansson, D. (2010). *Rework: Change the Way You Work Forever.* London. Vemilion.

Godin, S. (2003). *Purple Cow: Transform Your Business by Being Remarkable.* London. Portfolio.

Heat, C. & Heat, D. (2008). *Made to Stick: Why Some Ideas Survive and Others Die.* London. Arrow.

Horowitz, B. (2014). *The Hard Thing About Hard Things: Building a Business When There Are No Easy Answers.* London. HarperBusiness.

Kahneman, D. (2011). *Thinking, Fast and Slow.* London. Penguin.

Knight, P. (2016). *Shoe Dog: A Memoir by the Creator of Nike.* New York. Simon & Schuster.

Lecinski, J. & Venkatesan, R. (2021). *The AI Marketing Canvas: A Five-Stage Road Map to Implementing Artificial Intelligence in Marketing..* Redwood City, CA, USA. Stanford University Press.

Lewis, M. (2004). *Moneyball: The Art of Winning an Unfair Game.* New York. W. W. Norton.

Lidwell, W., Holden, C., & Butler, J. (2007). *Universal Principles of Design.* Beverly, MA, USA. Rockport Publishers Inc.

Mazzucato, M. (2016). *The Value of Everything: Making and Taking in the Global Economy.* New York. PublicAffairs Books.

Provost, F. & Fawcett, T. (2013) *Data Science for Business: What You Need to Know About Data-Mining and Data-Analytic Thinking.* Sebastopol, CA, USA. O'Reilly.

Raworth, K. (2018). *Doughnut Economics: Seven Ways to Think Like a 21st Century Economist*. London. Random House Business.

Ries, E. (2011). *The Lean Startup: How Constant Innovation Creates Radically Successful Business*. London. Penguin.

Rosen, E. (2009). *The Anatomy of Buzz Revisited: Real-life Lessons in Word-of-Mouth Marketing*. London. Currency.

Rumelt, R. (2017). *Good Strategy, Bad Strategy: The Difference and Why it Matters*. London. Profile Books.

Savage, S. (2009). *The Flaw of Averages: Why We Underestimate Risk in the Face of Uncertainty*. Hoboken, NJ, USA. Wiley.

Schultz, H. (2011). *Pour Your Heart Into It: How Starbucks Built a Company One Cup at a Time*. Hoboken, NJ, USA. Wiley.

Shapiro, C. & Varian, H. R. (1998). *Information Rules: A Strategic Guide to the Network Economy*. Boston. Harvard Business Review Press.

Surowiecki, J. (2004). *The Wisdom of Crowds*. New York. Doubleday.

Sutton, R. & Rao, H. (2014). *Scaling Up Excellence: Getting to More Without Settling for Less*. London. Currency.

Taubman, A A. (2007). *Threshold Resistance: The Extraordinary Career of a Luxury Retailing Pioneer*. London. Collins.

Wainer, H. (2009). *Picturing the Uncertain World: How to Understand, Communicate, & Control Uncertainty Through Graphical Display*. Princeton, NJ, USA. Princeton University Press.

Zeihan, P. (2022). *The End of the World is Just the Beginning: Mapping the Collapse of Globalization*. London. HarperBusiness.

ESSAYS, PUBLICATIONS, ARTICLES AND RESOURCES TO EXPLORE

Flyvbjerg, B., & Budzier, A. (2018) '10 Heuristics That Make Leaders of Projects and Programs Successful'. Oxford Global Projects .https://static1.squarespace.com/static/5c312863266c07d084fcd39e/t/5e42855ca5242f007ad04fbe/1581417852385/OGP_Masterbuilder-Heuristics.pdf

Kaplan, R.S. & Norton, D, P. (1992). 'What you measure is what you get.' *Harvard Business Review*.

March, J.G. 2 June 1935. 'An Introduction to the Theory and Measurement of Influence', *American Political Science Review*, vol XLIX. https://stacks.stanford.edu/file/druid:zf609tm0200/zf609tm0200.pdf

March, J. 2 Oct 2014. 'Passion and Discipline: Don Quixote's Lessons for Leadership'. https://www.youtube.com/watch?v=NYmbiv_cbn8&ab_channel=StanfordGraduateSchoolofBusiness

Osterwalder, A., Pigneur, Y. & Tucci, C. L. June 2010. 'Clarifying Business Models: Origins, Present, and Future of the Concept'. Communications of the Association for Information Systems 16(1). https://www.researchgate.net/publication/37426694_Clarifying_Business_Models_Origins_Present_and_Future_of_the_Concept

Rosling, H. (2006). 'The Best Stats You've Ever Seen'. TED. https://www.ted.com/talks/hans_rosling_the_best_stats_you_ve_ever_seen?language=en

Wealthfront Engineering. 15 Aug, 2014. 'Statistics Is Eating the World'. https://eng.wealthfront.com/2014/08/15/statistics-is-eating-world/

Harvard Business School: Working Knowledge Research Hub.

Harvard Business Review: Articles on marketing

Kellogg School of Management: Articles, podcasts and reports.

University of Oxford, Saïd Business School: Research publications.

OTHER IMPORTANT BOOKS YOU MIGHT WANT TO READ

Don Quixote by Miguel Cervantes

War and Peace by Leo Tolstoy

The Prince by Niccolo Machiavelli

1984 by George Orwell

Down and Out in Paris and London by George Orwell

Man's Search for Meaning by Viktor E. Frankl

INDEX

PICTURE CREDITS